STUDIES IN TENNYSON

STUDIES IN TENNYSON

Edited by
Hallam Tennyson

This book is published to commemorate the centenary of Sir Charles Tennyson, the poet's grandson and biographer, born 8 November 1879, died 22 June 1977.

Barnes & Noble Books
Totowa, New Jersey

First published 1981 by
THE MACMILLAN PRESS LTD
London and Basingstoke
Companies and representatives
throughout the world

First published in the USA 1981 by
BARNES & NOBLE BOOKS
81, Adams Drive
Totowa, New Jersey 07512

MACMILLAN ISBN 0 333 27884 4
BARNES & NOBLE ISBN 0 389 20236 3
LCN   79–55520

Printed in Hong Kong

The editor dedicates his share of this book to

James Ancaster
first President of the Tennyson Society: the
devoted friend of Charles Tennyson

Contents

Preface

In 1976 when my father reached ninety-seven in undiminished mental and physical vigour, those close to him became convinced that he would live to see his own centenary. I, therefore, got together an informal group, consisting of Professor Christopher Ricks, Professor Philip Collins and Mr Tom Baker (then Secretary of the Tennyson Society) to decide on how best to celebrate the forthcoming event. We agreed to explore the possibility of a series of lectures to be sponsored by universities and by the Tennyson Society and to be given by some of the leading Tennyson scholars in England and America. The list of these lectures would be drawn up and handed to my father as a surprise present on his ninety-ninth birthday: the lectures would then be delivered during his 100th year and published in book form on his centenary.

When he died—and I am still tempted to add the word 'unexpectedly'!—a few months before he was ninety-eight, the scheme was still little more than a gleam in my eye and I was very uncertain as to whether we should proceed with it. However, Tom Baker, Christopher Ricks and Philip Collins were adamant that the love and respect which my father had inspired in so many made it more than ever necessary that we should celebrate his life. My father's good friends at Macmillan (he had for some time been their oldest author) were equally firm in their resolve to publish the results.

Such is the high critical esteem in which Alfred Tennyson is now held—due in considerable measure to my father's own enthusiastic work—that outstanding lecturers choosing widely different fields of study were not hard to find. In addition it was decided to open the book with a memoir of my father and with a study of his contribution to Victorian scholarship. Compiling and editing the book has been, for me, a labour of love: but I could not have done it without the very special help and encouragement of Professor Ricks, while the generous support of Trinity College and King's College, Cambridge, the Tennyson Society, the Lincoln County Council, the Universities of Hull, Leicester, London, Oxford and British Columbia, who sponsored the lectures, has

been absolutely crucial. I am grateful, too, to my father's old friend, Sir
John Betjeman, the present Poet Laureate, for his moving foreword.

17 December 1978   *Hallam Tennyson*

Foreword

Sir John Betjeman

To know Charles Tennyson was to love him. Yet how can one describe him to those who did not know him? His personality was calm, understanding, modest; he suffered afflictions but he bore them with patience and equanimity. This is the sort of statement usually made about the recently dead: yet in Charles' case there is a difference—the statement is deeply and profoundly true. A study of his immense legacy of papers, such as his son Hallam has undertaken, reveals his uprightness and unshakeable consideration for others. Deceit was quite literally beyond him, and never once during his 97 years did he perform a shabby deed. Loyalty and dependability were the keynotes of his character—even after twenty years of marriage it was usual for him to write two or three times a day to his wife.

All this makes Charles sound like a paragon of Victorian virtue. But that is as far as possible from being the case. Charles was interested in everything—he would go to the Tate Gallery to see an exhibition of Op Art with the same enthusiasm as he went to take his hundredth American guest round Westminster Abbey or to see a Beckett play for the opening of the National Theatre—and he was interested in everybody. In comparison with others he always put himself last, with the result that in his company the others always glowed and felt at their best. Add to this the fact that Charles had inherited a great deal of Alfred's sense of humour, a keen delight in broad farce as well as in dry but unmalicious irony, and you can see why right up to the end he continued to make new friends.

With these characteristics it is not surprising Charles' old age should have been so splendid. Charles had had a busy 'working' life. He was created CMG in 1915 for his work at the Colonial Office and knighted in 1945 for his pioneer efforts in promoting factory design. In between he had been the first secretary and deputy director of the new Federation of British Industries (FBI), leaving the Federation in 1928, at the invitation of Sir Eric Geddes, to become Secretary to the Dunlop Rubber Company. At this time he contributed mightily to the development of the British film industry as Chairman of the FBI's Film Group. Later in the 1930s he was to have an even greater influence on industrial design through the registry of artists which he set up, the Central Institute of Art and Design, and through his twenty-year chairmanship of the Utility Furniture Committee.

It was during the Second World War that Charles, evacuated with Dunlop, away from his wife and family, prepared his definitive life of his grandfather which was published by Macmillan in 1949. When he retired in 1950, already aged seventy, one could have been forgiven for thinking his closing days would be spent in well-earned rest. How wrong can one be! During the twenty-seven years that were left to him Charles published seven books and innumerable essays. He appeared frequently on radio and television. He travelled to Greece, France, Spain and many times to Italy, and made two lecture tours in America.

But, of course, more important than all these activities was the foundation of the Tennyson Society in 1959, on the occasion of the 150th anniversary of Alfred's birth. The Tennyson Society led to the Tennyson Research Centre at Lincoln and here, of course, the generosity of Harold, Lord Tennyson, in making a permanent loan of his manuscripts and memorabilia as well as the whole of Dr George Tennyson's library, was absolutely crucial. To mark this outstanding contribution to Tennyson studies both Lord Tennyson and Sir Charles were presented with the Honorary Freedom of the City of Lincoln.

Owing to the special circumstances of their childhood, Harold and his brother Mark had come to regard their cousin Charles as a second father and Harold's generosity must be thought of, I feel sure, as every bit as much an expression of love and esteem for Charles as a deliberate promotion of the study and appreciation of their common ancestor. Harold knew that his gift would keep Charles endlessly and fascinatingly occupied during his nineties—and how right he was! The Tennyson Research Centre has become the most important Victorian literary quarry in England. It has inspired scholars; it is the inspiration of this book, whose rich variety of contribution and contributors (with Americans, as is proper, well to the fore) perfectly reflects the wide and expanding interest in Tennyson which Charles and the Centre have stimulated.

When working with Charles on choosing *The Hundred Best Sonnets* of the poet's elder brother Charles Tennyson Turner, I came to realise how like Charles was to the great-uncle after whom he had been named.

Not so high church of course and, though absentminded, probably rather more astute and clearheaded. But they shared the same awestruck wonder at the beauty of the Universe and the same total disregard of self.

I remember another incident when Charles and I were working together on a BBC film about Tennyson. On location in Lincolnshire Charles, already well on in his eighties, was the life and soul of the camera-crew, sound recordists and 'grips'. We went to the Isle of Wight for the last shot of the film. Rain came on, the light went and a tractor started up in a nearby field. Then a miracle happened: the sun came out, all the birds started to sing, and aeroplanes and tractors fell silent as if by command. Charles' arms shot up in a typical gesture of humorous triumph and we were able to complete the film.

Charles' life was like that—a thing of beauty, long and carefully prepared for, that ended in a blaze of sunshine.

Abbreviations

All quotations and titles from Tennyson's poems are taken from *The Poems of Tennyson*, edited by Christopher Ricks (London: Longmans, 1969). They will be cited in the text with reference to the first page of the poem in the Ricks edition, followed by line numbers where appropriate, for example R 1772, ll 39–46.

All quotations from *In Memoriam*, however, will be separately cited in the text by reference to sections and stanzas, for example XXI, 4.

All quotations from or references to *Alfred Lord Tennyson: A Memoir* (1897), by his son (Hallam Lord Tennyson), will be cited thus (either in the text or the endnotes): *Mem.*, i, 241.

All quotations from or references to *Alfred Tennyson*, by Charles Tennyson (London: Macmillan, 1949; paperback edn 1968) will be cited thus (either in the text or the endnotes): *Alfred Tennyson*, pp. 61–7.

Other quotations or references will be separately enumerated in the endnotes on each chapter found hereafter.

Part I
Charles Tennyson

1 Charles Tennyson: A Personal Memoir

Hallam Tennyson

In *The Prelude* Wordsworth describes three elements which inspired him in childhood to recognise 'a grandeur in the beatings of the heart'. First came 'the presences of nature' among which his soul was 'fostered alike by beauty and by fear'. Then, after reverence for nature came reverence for man; and this reverence was learned not at the feet of schoolmaster or sage but from the local shepherd suddenly encountered by crag or lonely brook:

> His form hath flashed upon me, glorified
> By the deep radiance of the setting sun:
> Or him have I descried in distant sky,
> A solitary object and sublime[1]

By such experiences Wordsworth found 'the pride of strength, And the vainglory of superior skill . . . interfused with objects which subdued and tempered them'.[2]

These first two elements seem to me to have been present, and abundantly present, in my father's childhood. He loved the downs round Farringford and Aldworth and the level sands round Sheringham, and he loved the men and women he saw in these landscapes: William Knight the Farringford coachman (author of the immortal couplet 'The mare took the fence at a single bound/the earth on its axis went round and round'), Mercy Hammond, daughter of the Aldworth gamekeeper, and the masterful Norfolk fisherman 'Go-Father' Pegg – who was always remorselessly sending his male parent about his business: simple people who taught him the fundamental dignity and pride of the human race. At the other end of the spectrum, to temper any lingering sense of his own importance, were the two personalities who

3

towered over his boyhood like Scawfell and Stybarrow Crag towered over the young Wordsworth. Probably there was not a week in which my father did not recall some memory of his humane and witty stepfather, Augustine Birrell. Certainly there was not a day in which he did not recall his Tennyson grandfather: 'he was a dominant height' my father said in his 95th birthday broadcast 'who made every subsequent event in my life seem rather flat'.[3]

The recollection of these figures in a landscape nourished and sustained my father and removed him from 'little enmities and low desires':[4] they also gave him an extraordinary modesty; they made self-importance and status consciousness from the first totally alien to his character.

There is, however, a third element in childhood which Wordsworth describes and which he sees, significantly, as being essential to the development of our *creative* life. The infant who, 'by intercourse of touch', holds 'mute dialogue with his mother's heart',[5] becomes:

> – an agent of the one great mind,
> Creates, creator and receiver both,
> Working but in alliance with the works
> Which it beholds. – Such verily, is the first
> Poetic spirit of our human life.[6]

In this respect my father was less fortunate. His relationship with his mother was cold and formal in a way which must seem quite extraordinary to anyone who witnessed the intense affection which he was later to lavish on his own children and grandchildren.

Eleanor Locker married Tennyson's second son, Lionel, in March 1878. My father, *their* second son, was born on 8 November 1879. Eleanor was the only child of Frederick Locker, well known in his day for his *London Lyrics*, and Lady Charlotte, who was a granddaughter of Lord Elgin (of marbles fame) and a sister of Lady Augusta Bruce (later Dean Stanley's wife), Queen Victoria's favourite lady-in-waiting. Eleanor was outstandingly beautiful and spoke fluent French and Italian; she had cultivated literary tastes and was one of the early admirers of the Russian novel with a particular love of Turgenev.

Lionel seems to have been a moody and volatile young man; in Julia Margaret Cameron's photographs the large, rather sullen mouth and the heavy-lidded eyes with their hint of egotism and sensuality make it probable that he had inherited far more of the 'black-bloodedness' of the Tennysons than had his sweet-natured brother, Hallam. Margot

Asquith described him as having 'an untidy appearance, a black beard and no manners'.[7] He was reputed to sing German beer-songs in a lusty voice and he was extremely fond of amateur theatricals (his favourite part was that of the cynical Faulkland in *The Rivals*), and blood sports (which Alfred had always detested). Some judicious string-pulling led to a post at the India Office where he seems to have enjoyed his work and in 1885 he and Eleanor were invited to the subcontinent as guests of the Viceroy, Lord Dufferin and Ava. His journal of this visit shows a singularly independent mind. He condemned the British residents for their racial arrogance and cultivated an interest in the exotic practices of the Parsis and Hindus, in the tradition of Richard Burton. Also in the tradition of Burton is the attitude to his wife; the journal is written resolutely in the first person singular and although nautch-girls are frequently referred to, my grandmother rates only one mention ('Eleanor had a headache and went to bed').[8] He caught jungle fever while on a shooting expedition in Assam and died on the Red Sea on the voyage home. He was 32. Spiteful gossip reported that Eleanor had danced through the night on deck while her husband lay in a coma below.[9]

Among Lionel's sparse memorabilia there is one other item of relevance, an essay entitled 'My Baby and My Dog'.[10] The burden of the essay, treated in the jocular style of the day, is that all babies are horrid but that one's own are unspeakably more horrid than others and that fatherhood degrades a man and turns his home into a house of bondage. Not, one feels, a genial paterfamilias!

My father, who was only five when Lionel died, rarely spoke of either of his parents. He once told me that his mother did not have strong maternal feelings and in *Stars and Markets* he makes no more than a few passing references to her: she is described as 'rather a stickler for the proprieties',[11] in unfavourable contrast to his easygoing stepfather. Once he told me that he did not think his parents had been 'well-suited'. This was clearly, and somewhat typically, euphemistic. I am now certain that my father knew only too well that his parents' marriage had been extremely unhappy.

The evidence for both the unhappiness and my father's knowledge of it is slight but, I think, convincing. My father kept only two letters from his mother, in contrast to the extensive correspondence with his stepfather which still survives. One of these letters, written in 1909 at the time of his engagement when he was already a man of 29, was locked in the black strong box which he reserved for his most precious documents; it makes sad reading. Eleanor wrote:

I often—very often—questioned whether I was wise in the course I took. . . . It seemed impossible to speak without disloyalty to the Dead and without giving you pain . . . I should like you to know that I dearly loved your father, and of course for a long time that always made me hope, and my suffering was so acute, and the effort after self-control so great . . . that in after life it was almost impossible to speak. . . . It is heartbreaking to me that we should have lived through your boyhood and young manhood without my having the love from you which I longed for or without you getting from me the sympathy and help that might have been so much to you all these years.

This is not the letter of a woman incapable of maternal feelings but of someone who has repressed such feelings because their associations are too painful.

The second letter from his mother which my father kept was written after the birth of my eldest brother, Penrose, in 1912. It is a formal affair much concerned with describing why she has not sent a wire and why his own wire had taken so long to arrive '*by train*'. It makes a strange contrast with the letter written by his stepfather celebrating the same event, a letter bubbling over with humour and affection. I suspect that, in spite of the hand that was stretched out in 1909, the frozen river of feeling between my father and his mother was never crossed. But Eleanor *was* capable of maternal affection. She did not hold herself aloof from the children of her second marriage. David Garnett describes the passionate love which my half-uncle, Francis Birrell, held for his mother and his desolation at her death in 1915.[12]

What was the secret which had tainted her natural feelings for her Tennyson children? One can only speculate but it seems to me almost certain that Lionel was unfaithful. He carried on a long flirtation with Margot Asquith to whom he sent a stream of love poems. Margot Asquith quotes several examples; they were elegant and amusing. But the year Margot Asquith was writing about was 1883, when she was twenty-one and her mocking thirty-year-old suitor was married to someone else; and even if this particular involvement was light-hearted enough, it discloses an attitude towards sex which was as different from Alfred's as was the attitude of the Prince of Wales from that of Queen Victoria. Was it the tip of an iceberg? If it was, one can understand Eleanor's bitterness: as an only child and the daughter-in-law of the Victorian Laureate the silence imposed on her by convention and loyalty must have been a hideous strain. After all, her father-in-law had

written of Lionel in his lines 'To the Marquis of Dufferin and Ava'
(R 1407, ll 25–8):

> A soul that, watched from earliest youth,
>   And on through many a brightening year,
>   Had never swerved for craft or fear,
> By one side-path, from simple truth . . .

Even to think of staining such an idealised picture must have seemed
almost treasonable.

I am not suggesting that my father's childhood was unhappy as a
result of all this. There were innumerable ·compensations: his adored
grandparents and the moments when he was aware of his kinship to one
of the great Victorians; the awed affection inspired by his grandfather's
large brown hand held out for him and his brother to kiss when the
'Bard' descended the Aldworth staircase at 11 a.m. to go walking on the
Sussex Downs. Then there were those even more sacred mornings when
he and his brother accompanied their grandfather on these walks and a
blurred but vivid memory of the mighty brain bending its powers to
inform and amuse them. Besides, Emily, the Laureate's wife, was
revered and loved almost as much as Alfred himself. She directed the
household from the drawingroom sofa hardly ever raising her voice
above a whisper and smiling with unquenchable sweetness at the
vagaries of her husband or grandchildren.

With my uncle, older than my father by less than a year, the boyhood
relationship was preternaturally close. They were the poet's only
grandchildren until Hallam's eldest son, commemoratively called
Lionel, was born in 1889.[13] My uncle was named not only Alfred but
Browning and Stanley after his two godparents as well. He was a
wayward, brilliant boy with something of his father's egotism and
strong personality. When my father was asked whether Alfred had
bullied him in childhood, he was apt to reply 'of course—but I adored
him'. It was characteristic that my father should have thought that,
while he himself was totally without the creative spark, some element of
the Tennyson genius was inherited by his brother and he chose one of
Alfred's poems for his 'With Great Pleasure' programme on BBC Radio
and closed *Stars and Markets* with these lines from another:

> The Glory dies not: leaves us tired and still;
> We cannot follow, even if we will;
> The Afterglow! Ah! there—beyond the hill.[14]

'We cannot follow'. Perhaps my father was right in thinking that the younger Alfred's creative ability had sunk under the burden of being named after the two greatest poets of the age as well as after a Dean of Westminster who was a byword for moral rectitude and earnest theological reform. My father's names were altogether less presumptuous—Charles (after his great-uncle Charles Tennyson Turner, who died the year he was born), Bruce (the Elgin connection) and Locker (after his maternal grandfather) and for godparents he aspired no higher than a mere *daughter* of Thackeray, the erratic but much-loved Anne (or Annie) Thackeray Ritchie.

It was against this hieratic background that my father grew up 'fostered alike by beauty and by fear'. There was from the first, it seems, a constraint on him in the presence of his elders and a sense that those who surrounded him had talents infinitely superior to his own. The explanation for those who demonstrably were not superior? Simple— they had not had the social and genetic advantages which had fallen to him.

The alien world of the 'prep' school where he was forcibly fed, like a Limousin goose, for an Eton scholarship, was a natural phenomenon; it was not something to be complained about. Indeed, Summerfields appears eighty years later in *Stars and Markets* so discreetly disguised ('an institution . . . in the suburbs of a large town')[15] that one is left with a feeling that he regarded this place of torture with something akin to affection. Doubtless, no sign of misery or complaint crept into his letters which were addressed then, as they were to the end of her life, to 'dear mother' and signed 'your affectionate son'.

He did what his elders required, he was immensely industrious, he got his Eton scholarship. He early responded to the magic of Latin and Greek (my own obtuseness in these subjects was one of the few things in life which caused him irritation; endlessly patient and informative about painting and church architecture, his attempts to inspire his sons with a talent for the classics were uniformly disastrous).

My father was a late developer; he claimed to be one of the few boys who had reached Eton's sixth form while still in 'jackets' (no one under five feet two inches was allowed the privilege of a tailcoat) but he got one of the closed scholarship to King's, Cambridge in the autumn of 1898, and in January 1899 he went to Germany to spend nine months there before the start of the academic year. This period is the first one for which I have found a correspondence of any importance. The letters are still those of a schoolboy; he is surprised to make friends with someone who is 'studying stinks', he himself takes lessons in drawing at $2\frac{1}{2}$d an hour but finds Rubens 'loathly', he is unaware of the difference between fahrenheit and centigrade; in August he makes his first visit to Bayreuth and hears Annie Besant swathed in purple veiling, hold forth on the mystic meaning of *Parsifal.*

His stay in Germany marked the start of my father's passion for art galleries; it also gave him a genuine and lasting admiration for Wagner—he always maintained that *Die Meistersinger* was the greatest dramatic masterpiece of the nineteenth century. Along with Bloomsbury and Bernard Shaw, he tended to regard Verdi's operas as romantic trash, an opinion which he did not seriously revise until he saw his first performance of *Otello*, on television, when he was ninety-two. But in spite of all this he later regretted that he had not spent his time in France or Italy whose art and culture came to mean so much more to him. His knowledge of German literature never developed and not even the ingenious and thorough teaching of Fräulein Gottschald of Dresden was sufficient for him to retain his fluency in German for more than a few years after his return.

Cambridge was a different matter. Here was richness: a burgeoning sense of the beautiful in art and poetry; varied and lifelong friendships; rapid intellectual development (he was placed in the first division of the first class in the classical Tripos) and the discovery of unsuspected sporting abilities (he was among the first to play for the university at golf). He was co-founder and editor of the college magazine *Basileona* and published E. M. Forster's first literary efforts, which were mostly character sketches of persons met on railway journeys or in London streets and showed, surprisingly, no greater degree of literary ability than my father's own contributions. Forster, who was a year senior to my father, remained on friendly terms with him till his death seventy years later, their ninetieth birthdays fell (just!) in the same year and each dutifully attended the other's celebrations. But they were 'Forster' and 'Tennyson' to each other right up to the end, and of the heated intellectual and emotional atmosphere generated by the 'Apostles' under the leadership of Goldsworthy Lowes Dickinson and G. E. Moore with which E. M. Foster was familiar, my father knew nothing. I once asked him, when he had read Michael Holroyd's brilliant biography of Lytton Strachey, who had been my father's contemporary, whether he was surprised at the revelations of homosexuality among the 'Apostles', and he said: 'absolutely flabbergasted'. He did have one close friend in that charmed circle, however: Thoby Stephen, Virginia Woolf's older brother. It was his friendship with Thoby which took him to early gatherings of the Bloomsbury Group at Virginia's and

Vanessa's house in Gordon Square and it is because of this that my
father acquired the reputation of being one of the earliest members of
the set.[16] He himself maintained that he was absolutely terrified of
Virginia, though she was three years younger than he was, and
suggested that the long silences which Virginia describes in *Moments of
Being* as ensuing as soon as one of Thoby's allegedly 'brilliant' friends
entered the room were due to the fact that the tall girl with the large
bright eyes intimidated others besides himself with her habit of asking
sudden, disconcerting questions. Thoby died in 1906 and my father's
tenuous connection with Bloomsbury ceased.

In 1902, faced with the question of a career, my father decided to
study law; he won the Whewell Scholarship in International Law at
Cambridge and was called to the bar in 1905. He fully admits the
importance patronage played in his early efforts to earn a living, for his
stepfather, who had had a moderately successful practice, was now
President of the Board of Education in Campbell Bannerman's
Government. The law gave my father valuable training in logic and
clear thinking, but he was easily rattled in court. Nor did he take the
majesty of the profession too seriously. He tells a delightful story of one
of his first experiences.[17] He knew that his old friend 'Go-Father' Pegg,
the Norfolk fisherman, was engaged in a High Court action over fishing
rights and, partly because he was aggrieved at not being engaged as
counsel and partly to show himself off in his gown and wig, he arranged
to meet 'Go-Father' and his party in the corridor of the court. 'Go-
Father' stared at him, impressed, so my father hoped, by the solemnity
of his bearing. Not a bit of it; what had struck his old friend was my
father's extreme insignificance amidst all the billowing robes and the
'pomposo' officials. After a second's pause 'Go-Father' dug him in the
ribs and in the strongest Norfolk accent greeted him with the remark:
'Why booy, where's yawah belly then?' This is the very first story about
his legal career that my father tells in *Stars and Markets*. At the bar my
father worked for Sir John Simon and Sir Rufus Isaacs, later Lord
Reading, and acted as Marshal on the South Wales Circuit. His
prospects, however, did not seem brilliant owing to his shyness and lack
of confidence.

He had passed well beyond the threshold of manhood with his heart
and his affections still dormant. The world went on somewhere outside
him leaving his ambitions and his sympathies untouched. I remember,
in later life, how he used to wonder at the complacency with which he
had stepped over the figures of drunken working men and women still
lying on the pavements of Holborn and Piccadilly (he always walked to

work in Lincoln's Inn from his stepfather's house in Chelsea). It seemed incredible to him that he could have accepted the disgraceful poverty of Edwardian London as inevitable. A pleasant, neat, handsome, buttoned-up young man at twenty-eight then, with no very strong characteristics or discernible future. And yet by the summer of 1908 my father stood on the edge of golden hours, for sometime that June he had met my mother.

Ivy Gladys Pretious (she always pronounced it 'Precious') came from a very different background. Her father, Walter Pretious, was the son of an Hungarian marine engineer who had built the first steamship to go into service on the Danube. Her mother, born Hannah Swift, claimed to be a collateral descendant of the famous dean, although on her marriage certificate Hannah's father's occupation in Clapham is given as 'butcher'. My mother never really knew her father; after six years of marriage he left Hannah with three children (my mother was the middle one, with a younger and an older brother) and was never heard of again. Hannah seems to have been a convinced 'new woman' (which may have given my mother a quite unfounded suspicion that her parents had not been married; she confessed this suspicion to me only a few weeks before her death); she was close friends with Frederic Harrison the positivist and supporter of good causes and with his help she started a progressive school at Loughton in Essex. After a few years the school went bankrupt and Hannah went to Birmingham where she was appointed secretary to a large charity; she took her two sons with her and left my mother, who was then about fifteen, in the care of the Harrisons. My mother put her hair up, added several years to her age and went to work for a music publisher in Regent Street. Sometime in the late 1890s she was summoned to Birmingham by her mother's charity and questioned in a hostile manner by the committee; she formed a strong conviction (and I was the only person to whom she ever confessed it) that her mother had misappropriated the charity's funds. Some tearful and recriminatory correspondence reached my mother later from South Africa where Hannah seems to have fled with her two sons: but my mother never saw her or her elder brother again (though she was to have a brief and poignant meeting with her younger brother on his way to die in France in the First World War). My mother seems next to have worked for a magazine called *Our Home* where she contributed fluent and practical articles on dressmaking and cooking; then in 1901, again with the help of Frederic Harrison, she started working for Emily Hobhouse whose fight on behalf of the Boer prisoners-of-war involved my mother in the one radical campaign of her career. Through this work she met a number of leading Liberals and in 1903 she was appointed secretary of the Free Trade Union, a national movement of great importance in the early years of the century. This work my mother carried out with charm, incisiveness and skill and by the time she met my father she was living in a flat in Chelsea with a dog and a maid and an income of £900 a year—three times what my father was earning at the bar and in those days a really huge salary for a woman of 28.

My mother's emotional life had been as involved and exciting as my father's had been inhibited and quiescent. Both were, to some extent, orphans and while he had repressed his need to give and receive affection she had allowed hers full rein. When Bertrand Russell met her at the George Trevelyans' in March 1905 he was convinced that she was 'in the gravest danger from a man who is simply a blackguard'.[18] This man was Reginald McKenna, later to serve several liberal governments in important cabinet posts. Bertrand Russell set out to 'rescue' her—it was during the long unhappy years of his failing marriage with Alys but before he had espoused the cause of free love. The 'rescue' operation was so successful that my mother's affections were seriously drawn to Bertrand: Alys became jealous, my mother's letters to Bertrand were suspected of being steamed open and the Trevelyans intervened and counselled that meetings should cease and that the relationship should be restricted to occasional letters of a general nature. The correspondence continued for four years and my mother consulted Bertrand over all important decisions. Like many others, Bertrand had assumed that my mother, because of her background and position, would be radical in her views on sexual and social questions. He was wrong; her unhappy childhood had given her a longing for traditional family life and she did not even support the movement for women's suffrage. In sexual matters things were a little less straightforward; she was clearly both passionate and susceptible but so aware of her exposed position that she had learned, by hard experience, to exercise strict control. One famous MP, the Irishman Tilly Kettle, proposed and was turned down, Lloyd George had to be bundled out of a taxi when his advances became too pressing, and in 1907 McKenna showed renewed interest and was firmly dealt with. More serious was her secret engagement to the son and heir of a Victorian baron. The baron's son, it seems, was already married and may have invoked an 'engagement' to try and persuade my mother to become his mistress; her servant had to be dismissed for spreading malicious rumours, Bertrand weighed in with advice from Sicily where he was on holiday and the gentleman was sent packing. That was in May 1908. A month later she met my father.

Those who only knew my mother in her middle and later years can have no idea of her beauty as a young woman. She was under five feet in height and her hands and feet were no bigger than those of a ten-year-old child. Her figure was exquisite, her skin *café-au-lait* like a Kashmiri Brahmin's, her face heartshaped with large brilliant brown eyes and glossy, dark hair springing from her forehead in natural waves. She had an extraordinarily quick intuitive mind; she made decisions by instinct (usually right ones) and she spoke out with a forthright honesty in a way that was not expected in a young Edwardian woman of unimpressive social origins. In many ways Vita Sackville-West's mother, Victoria, reminded me of my mother both because of her extraordinary charm in youth and because of the tragic change which illness wrought in her character.[19]

From the first my father was captivated, though he was slower to realise the fact than she was. She made it quickly plain that she needed his advice and his company. He was flustered: 'You must not think that I get nothing from our friendship but an occasional pleasant hour—I am a cold-blooded little devil' he wrote on 13 July 1908, 'I have very few women friends and more men friends than is perhaps good for an oyster . . . it is bad to be an oyster and you have done a great deal to wean me from oysterdom'. Then before he left for a walking tour of the Dolomites: 'Compared to you I feel like a little fish who has swum all his life in the sunshine of his own puddle—sunshine is unfortunately not transferable . . . but do say or write to me whatever you think will do you any good'.

The relationship developed quickly. By January 1909 'My dear' had turned to 'My dearest'—the first time my father had used an epithet of such warmth to anybody. From his letters, as the time for their wedding at the end of July drew closer, some of the reasons for the breaking of the ice round my father's heart became clearer. My mother's 'delicacy of manner . . . and spirit' kept 'pure and fresh through such struggles and sorrows', compelled the admiration of someone who realised his life to have been unusually protected. 'You have already brought me to a saner attitude than I should have thought possible. But to your elemental purity I am afraid I shall never attain. That can only come to a person who has grown up in the full glare of life and have survived it as you have.' My mother once told me with a roguish twinkle that she had to teach my father all the 'facts of life' and I cannot help feeling from this letter that even before marriage she had begun to break down the barriers of puritanism and guilt, and had helped my father to realise the sanctity of sexual love. Certainly, the early years of their marriage were extraordinarily happy; it was not uncommon for them to write three times a day to each other when they were separated and their letters breathe a discreet physical passion. In 1919 during a local postal strike my father sent her thirty telegrams in one week.

My mother gave up her work on marriage and my father accepted an appointment as one of the legal advisers to the Colonial Office in order to increase his salary. He also took up journalism more seriously and between 1911 and 1914 wrote 130 articles, 100 of them for the *Spectator* at two shillings and nine pence per column inch. As Professor Martin shows, remarkably few of these articles were on Tennysonian themes; at this stage he had certainly not come to terms with his ancestry, nor did he feel that it gave him any particular insight into the poet's life and work. His reviews contrived to be both generous and well-considered— 'shows signs of wide and patient investigation but as a definitive study it cannot be considered successful'[20] is about the lowest mark he awards. His generosity is often discriminating; he realised the merits of Edward Thomas' 'Icknield Way' in days when Thomas was totally unknown[21] and he defended the 'near-greatness' of Gissings' urban novels to a readership that had patently ignored them.[22] A charming poem recounts a mystical experience while walking in 'Constable's Country'[23] and he analyses the sense of 'perpetual vigilance'[24] in Conrad's use of English. It was his work for the *Spectator* which led to the commission by Chatto & Windus for *Cambridge from Within*.[25]

That marriage released my father's emotional and intellectual energies cannot be doubted and his adoration for my mother, which survived the tragic breakdown of her health and the consequent damage to her personality when she was still a comparatively young woman, was vital proof that he fully realised the immensity of his debt to her. Certainly his growing confidence led to him making an impressive start in his work with the Colonial Office; in extremely tricky negotiations over the joint administration of the New Hebrides my father showed a sensitive understanding of the different psychology of the French and British delegations which proved crucial. By the time the First World War broke out he was too highly placed to be released for active service. This was indeed a blessing; for although my father never considered himself a pacifist—indeed he had the greatest admiration for the traditional military virtues—I cannot conceive that he could ever have shouldered arms. He never held a gun in his life and used to regard my brothers' and cousins' shooting exploits with the kind of incredulous respect he reserved for students of Chinese or nuclear physics.

It is not my purpose to analyse in detail my father's public career; this has been done by others as well as by himself. What I have written about his life so far may help to explain the course that his work was to take. In the war he was engaged on the disposal of captured enemy ships and cargoes, and this led him to an understanding of company law, as well as an insight into foreign commercial development and a realisation that British industry had begun to fall behind. When the Federation of British Industries (now the CBI) was created under Dudley Docker and Sir Roland Nugent, my father was first appointed an Assistant Director and later full-time Secretary. Far from being the ogre of entrenched capitalism as its detractors would have us believe, the FBI was, from the beginning, an extremely progressive body. Its Labour Relations Committee compiled an impressive report which suggested, among a host of other proposals, a national minimum wage, profit sharing and the setting up of joint Industrial Councils. My father ascertained that the TUC's reaction to this scheme was likely to be favourable, but, alas, the Employers' Association was horrified by its revolutionary nature and many of the larger business firms threatened to resign unless the report was withdrawn. Having to convey this news to the Government Minister my father regarded as one of the most miserable episodes in his life. Certainly, if the response of big business had been more far-seeing, the last sixty years in the history of British industry might have been very different.[26]

My mother had done brilliant work as head of the 9000 female staff employed by the Ministry of Munitions, for which she was awarded the OBE, but she had resigned to concentrate on the family — Penrose born in 1912 and Julian born in 1915 (a first child, a daughter, had died from meningitis very soon after birth). Their house in Chelsea became a centre for artists: Frank Dobson, Alan Gwynne Jones and Philip Connard all gave their first one-man shows in the tiny ground-floor of Cheyne Row. Other artist friends were Augustus John, Albert Rutherston (the charming and sensitive brother of William Rothenstein) and Randolph Schwabe (to become Tonks' successor at the Slade); it was clear that painting had outstripped literature and music as my father's chief love. In a letter in 1919 he records visiting the National Gallery and the National Portrait Gallery during his lunch hour and the Tate Gallery on his way home in the evening!

His interest in art was to give my father's industrial work a particular slant. In 1925 he became Chairman of the Film Group of the FBI and his committee, quite literally, saved the British film industry from extinction — for it had been fatally damaged by the war when production had moved to Hollywood. A Film Bill was passed establishing a quota for the number of Hollywood imports to give the British film industry a breathing space. My father's attitude to the cinema was very much his own: he respected it as a popular art form and was totally sympathetic when Penrose left Balliol after only two terms to start at the bottom of the ladder with Gaumont-British, and immensely proud when he graduated to become, at 25, the youngest director in the industry making, in *There Ain't No Justice*, the first original movie based on a straightforward account of working-class life. But I think my father never really responded to the serious aesthetic potential of the cinema; he thought Chaplin, René Clair and the Marx Brothers the only film talents to be touched with genius.

His interest in art was to play an even more important role in industrial design: as Chairman of the FBI's Industrial Art Committee my father did pioneer work in improving the quality of British manufacture. The Central Institute of Art and Design (CIAD) was started, and through this large numbers of artists were registered for work in industry and commissions obtained for them. All this led to my father's Chairmanship of the Utility Furniture Commission and the setting up of the Design Centre. It was specifically for work in this field that he was knighted; as a radical Tory he always got particular pride at having been honoured by the post-war Labour Government at the behest of Sir Stafford Cripps. My parents went in state to Buckingham Palace driven by their taxi-driver friend, Christopher Catlin; unfortunately Christopher's taxi sprang a leak in a heavy downpour and my parents entered the royal precincts sitting under an umbrella in the back of the cab.

In 1943 my father was made Chairman of the FBI's Education Committee — the problems of day-release classes and the development of technological training, in which Britain had already fallen so dangerously behind, never blinded my father to the old ideal that the real aim of education should be to enrich a man's experience of life rather than merely equip him to earn money.

Reflecting on all this varied activity I am convinced that my father was one of that rare breed of people — a genuine committee man. He never saw a committee as an excuse to hide behind a majority decision, but rather as an opportunity to forge a creative compromise with a group of colleagues of differing points of view, backgrounds and temperaments. Moreover, whether as Chairman or Secretary, he was concerned with persuading his committee to act in a responsible and positive manner, was eternally optimistic that common sense must prevail and was totally oblivious of his own importance.

As a father all these qualities were abundantly evident to his offspring. I think he only once took a hairbrush to my backside (for telling a lie that falsely put blame on one of the servants). I was six but I remember clearly my father's embarrassment (he always cleared his throat when he was embarrassed), and his nervous apprehension lest my mother should come in and criticise him for not being severe enough; for once the old adage 'this hurts me more than it hurts you' was actually true. Apart from our failure at Greek and our indifference to golf, my father, though remaining alert and constructively critical, thought his sons had more potential than he had in imagination and sensitivity as well as character. He admired equally the virtues of our cousins, Harold and Mark, who came to spend most of the period from 1928 to 1939 as members of our family; besides, they had added qualities, Harold was good at Greek and both he and Mark developed into excellent golfers. Looking back, indeed, I am struck by the way that my father made me feel from the first that 'the cousins', who were very much my age, were equally important to him and equally deserving of his affection. And he did this in a way so wholly natural and unselfconscious that I accepted it without a trace of jealousy or resentment. With each of us he developed special interests — with Julian bird-watching and country life; with me tennis and Jane Austin; with Harold painting and armour; with Mark the sea; with Penrose poetry and football. And those individual enthusiasms which he could not share he watched with quizzical pride. Two memories must suffice to illustrate our own attitude; first, seventeen-year-old Julian's verses for his father's fifty-third birthday:

Who is it makes directors quail?
However gorged with food and ale,
Under his eyes their faces pale,
They shrivel into something frail,
They draw their horns in like a snail,
And e'en hand in their dinner-pail.
When great C.T. is on the trail,
They know that they are doomed to fail . . .
But they may hide them where they will,
The great C.T. will find them still,
And make them pay full many a time,
These poor directors for their crime.[27]

The other incident was during the first Christmas of the Second

World War. My mother chided us for allowing my father to leave the dinner table to fetch something that was needed from the kitchen; Pen spoke up promptly on behalf of all of us: 'old age hath yet his honour and his toil' (R 564, 1 50).

My father's cheerfulness and unflinching affection were not dependent solely on unclouded good fortune. My mother's health deteriorated soon after I was born; the removal of infected glands from her neck left her with unsightly scars. Then, in 1925, she had an operation for ulcers; serious lesions developed on the site of the operation which were never diagnosed and which slowly and inexorably destroyed her, causing first pain and indigestion and then forcing her onto a diet of rice pudding and vegetable purée. I cannot have been more than seven when I remember for the first time hearing her mistaken for my father's mother—though she was in fact a year younger than he was. Because of her ill health she was deaf by the age of fifty and became increasingly a prey to irritability and bad temper. No doubt my father's goodness was not always easy to live with. He could see nothing but the best motives in others and shrank from standing up for his rights as if it were a sign of ill-breeding and vulgarity. It seemed unfair to my mother that it was she who had to argue with solicitors, scold errant parlour maids, denounce unworthy relatives and generally get on with the dirty business of living. I can see, too, how certain characteristics—my father's clumsiness and his terrible memory for practical things—must have been particularly galling to her with her deft fingers and quicksilver mind. She simply could not believe that someone so intelligent could be such an appalling driver or bridge-player: 'Charley—really! You're not even trying', she would cry. And so with a kind of dazed acceptance of his own ineptitude, my father ground into top gear or wrestled, once more, with an unplayable contract of four-no-trumps.

At the time we despised him a little, I am afraid, for knuckling under so easily. Yet looking back I realise that he not only felt he could never do enough to make up for all that she had done for him but that he knew, in spite of the succession of well-meaning doctors who diagnosed 'premature senility' or 'nervous symptoms due to stress', my mother's illness to be no mere psychosomatic fantasy but a very real and distressing affliction. Certainly, there were moments when her great qualities showed through; she bore the loss of my brothers — Penrose in 1941 and Julian in 1945 — with astounding fortitude. And there were acts of courage and imagination right up to the end which move me greatly when I remember them. She insisted on selling the house in Suffolk in the very last months of her life and moving close to me and my family, although by then she was wasted to under five stone through undernourishment. She knew she was dying, but it was not of herself she was thinking: she was thinking of my father for she wanted him to be near us when she died.

How would my father react to her death? He had not moved from her side during the ten years of his retirement. Every spare minute had been spent trotting along the Brompton Road or Southwold High Street looking for something which might tempt her appetite or keeping her amused with scrabble and two-handed bridge (at both of which she naturally continued the victor). Was it conceivable that at seventy-eight he would feel his old age held any further purpose?

Our first conversation as we drove away after her operation was significant. We had learned that she was not suffering from cancer as we had been led to believe but from a total blockage due to lesions. They had kept her on the operating table for five hours straightening out her colon. I was speechless with fury: it seemed to me beyond belief that the medical profession could have missed for thirty years so elementary a diagnosis. My father was philosophical; everybody had done their best, and if she survived, as it then seemed possible she might, she would at least be granted a few years free of suffering. There was an obvious explanation for the difference in our reactions. I felt guilty; I had found my mother selfish and tiresome, so it was convenient for me to blame the doctors. My father had no guilt; he had nursed her with ungrudging devotion and through all that had happened had never lost sight of the impulsive, vivacious young woman who had turned to him nearly fifty years before at the Trevelyans' dinner table. So, as he had no need to punish himself, he had no need to mourn. Grieve he must and did, but he knew my mother would have wanted him to enjoy his last years to the full and in this, as in so much else, he was ready to obey her wishes.

As soon as my mother died Margot and I thought it important to make plans. My father would come and live with us, and he and she would have a joint holiday in Rome and Florence — where he had never been — as soon as practicable. Little did we foresee all the activity which was about to be unleashed; there were to be many further visits to Italy and several lasting Italian friendships. There were trips to Spain and Paris with Harold and, at eighty-five, a carefully prepared trip on his own to Greece. A flat was rented near Amsterdam one summer with my cousin Rachel; then there were the two trips to America on arduous lecture tours, the second in his ninety-first year when he went on a students' charter flight with my daughter, Rosalind. There were at least two journeys round the British Isles, once driven somewhat erratically by

an old Southwold friend and both times accompanied by my son
Jonathan. There was a torrent of gallery going; in his last years
he visited the great Turner exhibition at the Academy no less than eight
times, the Chinese exhibition and the Treasures of Tutankhamun
(queues and all) hardly less frequently. Each visit triggered off an orgy
of picture postcards which were solemnly stuck into the thirty-two
specially bound volumes of 'stickers' for the delectation of my two
children.

Then, of course, there were the six books all written in the last twenty-
three years and the two dozen monographs; the development of the
Tennyson Society, with the help of Arthur Smith, later the Archdeacon
of Lincoln, and through the great generosity of my cousin Harold, the
setting up of the Tennyson Research Centre; lectures and outings to be
organised; American scholars to be entertained and enlightened as well
as a succession of parties of which, in marked contrast to his early and
middle years, he was inordinately fond.

One striking change wrought by all his Tennysonian activities was
that for the last twenty years of his life my father became very much a
'Lincolnshire man'. Contrary to popular legend there was always a
friendly relationship with the elder branch of the family, the Tennyson
d'Eyncourts. The rift had not lasted long after Alfred's father's death
and my father remembers visits to Bayons in the 1890s; so that when the
d'Eyncourts put their family archive at my father's disposal it was
nothing more dramatic than an expression of a well-established
friendship. Nonetheless, he always marvelled at the good humour with
which his d'Eyncourt cousins accepted his revelations about the poet's
uncle, the founder of the d'Eyncourt family, whose absurd attempts to
break into high society provide some deliciously comic moments in the
early chapters of my father's biography of the poet.[28] An active change
of county allegiance for someone over eighty is striking; but perhaps the
importance and variety of new and really deep friendships which he
found in Lincolnshire is even more remarkable; few people over eighty
can have made so many new friendships. There was Hope Dyson, whose
industry and research made possible *Dear and Honoured Lady* and, the
best of my father's books in my opinion after the biography, *The
Tennysons: Background to Genius*, published on his ninety-fifth birthday. There were Anne and Bill Kochan of Spilsby who must stand, *primi
inter pares*, as the archetype of the not inconsiderable number of people
who came to regard my father as a member of their own family and quite
simply and naturally adopted him. Another 'adopted' relation—from
considerably further afield—was Suddha Biswas, our doctor and

friend. When he went on a long visit to his family in India he urged me to summon him should my father (then ninety-six) become ill. I remonstrated, pointing out that we had an excellent substitute doctor who would take over in his absence. Dr Biswas replied at once: 'I want to be called back as his son—not as his doctor'.

Up till the age of ninety-five my father remained a tireless walker. When engaged on sight-seeing or hunting out some suspected architectural treasure he would enter private property without the slightest trace of embarrassment. He always maintained that there was no law of trespass in the English judicial system (true, until the recent anti-squatters act) and, if threatened by some irate bailiff or landowner, he promptly offered payment of sixpence to offset any damage he might have caused. On all such expeditions he was accompanied by 'Mr T.' (so named from the words 'Mr. Tennyson' crudely incised on the handle), an oaken crook carved for him by a Scottish shepherd in 1899 when he had gone to tutor a laird's son in the Kyles of Bute. Dorothy Milnes remembers how my father could never bear to be carried to the proper bus stop beyond the National Gallery but always leaped off in the midst of the traffic of Trafalgar Square, even while the bus was still moving, in order to avoid having to walk back. Then he would stand on the kerb, waving 'Mr T.', and waiting for her to catch up. My cousin, Harold, writes that my father 'walked with a rapid, steady plod which reminded one of Bunyan's "Christian". But, unlike "Christian" he had been to the wicket gate many times but always turned back for further exercise!'

The miracle of my father's old age had many ingredients all of which were the result of the character and circumstances that I have attempted to describe and, in that sense, he achieved the old age that he deserved. If he had not been the easiest person in the world to live with, we could not have absorbed him without a moment's strain into our family. If he had not had an undiminished capacity to inspire affection, Dorothy Milnes would not have appeared in 1974 to make his very last years especially busy and fulfilled. The great central quality which made all this possible was his lack of egotism. In his youth his modesty had been a negative influence stifling his confidence and his abilities. Now it became a shining and positive virtue, for in spite of his knowledge and experience, he was still convinced, as he had been all his life, that every person he met, from our Sicilian cleaning lady to an earnest bibliophile from Minnesota, was potentially as important and interesting as he was himself. The result was that people who came shyly to sit at his feet, expecting to be awed and impressed, went away with the feeling that somehow it was they who had impressed him. New friendships were thus created as fast as old ones, cut off by the sickle of time, fell away. 'The cold little devil' had come a long way.

Along with his modesty went an extraordinary acceptance of things as they were; he never minded what he ate, where he was, or what he wore as long as he had a good book or someone to talk to. His indifference to clothes was indeed proverbial. He was a handsome old man just as, with his fair hair, regular features and steady gaze he had been a goodlooking youth, but he never thought his appearance worth bothering about. That he usually looked neat was due, I think, to the simple fact that his lean sinewy figure was easily fitted into a readymade suit. But after he was eighty it became his settled principle that it would not be worth his while to buy new garments of any kind since he would not live to wear them out. My wife and Dorothy Milnes have described how in his nineties they used to wave his tattered underclothes at him to shame him into a visit to Marks and Spencer's.

Of his acceptance of his surroundings there are many examples; one I remember particularly occurred during our annual holiday together when he was ninety-five. We were visiting the ancient British sites in Wales and the south of England in the company of Jonathan and his archaeologist friend. Unfortunately, my car broke down in Caerleon and the only transport available for us to hire was a terrible old van without any back seats and which rattled so loudly that you could scarcely hear yourself speak even at a low speed. My father sat with his eyeline somewhat below the windscreen and after a while said, with all the emphasis of a considered judgement: 'You know this car is really remarkably comfortable'. To which Jonny shouted from behind, where he was sitting on his rucksack: 'Would you like to come and try it back here, grandpa?'

His adaptability made it possible for him to come to terms with the postwar world in a way that I would never have expected to be possible. In my own childhood, great as were my affection and respect, I had always thought of him as an Edwardian; he was, after all, already 41 when I was born. But to my children—and the age difference with them was well over seventy years—he seemed ageless, almost contemporary, even. He entered into their lives with a new enthusiasm and simplicity. For us he had been a 'weekend' father, but with my children he was at home all the time; they literally grew up around him. He saw Rosalind's and Jonathan's utterly different approach to life and accepted it. Indeed, he found much to admire in their world; he felt the new young more socially alert than the young of previous generations. He respected their concern for the environment and he was delighted at the new-found freedom between the sexes. He even calmly accepted a future in which family life, as he had known and loved it, would be radically changed by the discovery of safe contraception.[29]

In art and literature the development of his tastes was no less marked. He grew to have a passion for the work of Henry Moore, regarding him as possibly the greatest sculptor since Michelangelo; he was immensely proud of having once helped him through the CIAD. He insisted on visiting every important modern exhibition and came to terms with Hockney, Lichtenstein and Op Art. The music of Britten meant much to him and *Noye's Fludde* and *Curlew River* moved him more directly than any music he had ever heard. In literature he remained rather more conservative, though he thought Eliot a great poet.

His constantly developing zest for life expressed itself in many ways, none perhaps more remarkable than the simple delight in the acquisition of a new personal vocabulary—food became 'nosh' (an indirect way of expressing its unimportance on his scale of values), my daughter Rosalind was 'that fine fowl' (a corruption of the nickname 'bird' developed in her childhood when she was a promising singer), a visit to a gallery or an architectural sight was 'a jaunt', the human head had always been a 'napper', anything boring or pretentious was 'pomposo', the birds he fed daily at the bird table outside his window were 'Uccelli' (in memory of Elena, our Italian au-pair girl), the National Gallery was 'the Nish', a cold day was 'parky' and a hot one 'a real stumer'. Parallel to this was the variety of nicknames used by those close to him; he was known variously as 'Man', 'Mong', 'Ming', 'Mang', 'Grampy', 'Grumpy', 'Granpa' or 'Gramp'. Each clung tenaciously to their own versions as a way of expressing what they thought to be their own special relationship.

I do not wish, with all this, to imply that my father's old age was 'one perpetual progress smooth and bright'[30] nor to sound sentimental about his many remarkable qualities. In the first place his closing years were clouded by some very considerable sorrows. First there was the tragic misunderstanding with his elder granddaughter; it was a great joy when this fifteen-year-old breach was healed.

Next there were the difficulties of his grandson, Simon. It was my father's faith and loving care that, more than anything else, helped Simon to realise his potential and to develop in both character and abilities.

Finally there was the break-up of my twenty-six-year old marriage. He was devoted to Margot and stayed on with her at 23 The Park. And it was at this point that Dorothy Milnes who had known him since 1962, when she was Assistant Warden at the Missenden Abbey Adult Education Centre where he was a regular lecturer, came to the rescue. Dorothy has reported that, in the early days after I had left home, my father used to sit reading old letters or his biographies of Penrose and Julian with tears pouring down his face; indeed she felt, at the time, that he would never recover from the shock. He did and remained on the closest terms with both Margot and myself, and his presence continued to bring all the family together on many important occasions.

As to my father's qualities: they were, of course, even in his extraordinary old age, not free from certain accompanying defects. Professor Martin notes that his definitive biography of his grandfather does not attempt any interpretation of the poet's mind which he feels my father ought to have been uniquely equipped to undertake. My father, who loathed the idea of sitting in judgement on anyone, would have regarded such an act as presumptuous, a sign of the besetting sin of 'hubris'. But this positive virtue was, in part perhaps, the result of the emotional handicap which I see as having impeded his creative gifts and which I have traced back to his lack of 'mute dialogue with his mother's heart'. He had never really faced the truth about his parents' marriage and all his life he tended to ignore signs of distress in those around him unless they were forced inescapably upon his notice. He had learned to suffer in silence and assumed that others preferred to do the same, and although totally oblivious to his own needs and, in consequence, the most obliging and considerate of men, he lacked intuition about the unspoken needs of others. In old age, of course, the results of this weakness were apt to be comic and endearing—as when he engaged Dorothy Milnes in a loud conversation about Swinburne while being undressed behind screens by a nurse after a serious fall. He sometimes liked to explain this characteristic of his as due to the detachment of advancing years. But I think basically it was a variant of the limitation from which he had suffered all his life, soothed by age into something touching and tranquil: but a limitation nonetheless.

It seemed strange to many that my father could achieve so much contentment without the support of any precise religious faith. He respected all the great religions and regarded them as parables of the impenetrable mystery of life. He had love and respect for Christ but little interest in Christian dogma or ritual. Yet I think of my father as essentially religious. To me it is significant that his favourite poems, apart from Homer's epics (which he read every year in the original until he was over ninety) were, in chronological order, *The Prelude, In*

Memoriam, The Song of Myself and *Four Quartets*. These poems differ greatly in style and content, yet they have two things in common; they all treat of the soul's relationship with the infinite and they are all marked by a strong mystical element and describe experiences in which the poets felt themselves transported out of time. Something of the same quality marked my father's favourite painters whom I would list as Raphael, Rembrandt, Turner and the Impressionists up to and including Cézanne. Here again in the landscapes, or the figures in the landscapes, it was the sense of mystery, the sense of the existence of another world waiting to be apprehended beneath the surface realism, which appealed to my father.

An increasing wholeness made my father's life and character achieve great serenity in those last two shining decades. A more remarkable achievement to my mind than the many activities in which he had so successfully engaged. His early self-depreciation in the face of his own inheritance and the outstanding qualities which he saw displayed in those around him, turned later into a deep humility before the insoluble mysteries of life and death. This humility was not imposed by selfconscious or external constraints: it sprang naturally from internal factors. In the end it irradiated his entire personality so that the ego was almost wholly eclipsed and his psyche became a transparent envelope open to the endless intimations of beauty by which, if we have eyes to see it, we are everywhere surrounded. 'Oh yet we trust that somehow good,/ Will be the final goal of ill . . .' (LIV, 1–2). To his grandfather those lines in *In Memoriam* represented a cry of agony, a desperate resistance against the forces of darkness and doubt. To my father they were lines of real hope, expressing an optimism which grew throughout his immensely long life firmer and more complete.

In the last analysis I am struck by the central importance of my father's humility. So many others born into gifted and eminent families are afflicted by either arrogance or, its reverse, a neurotic sense of their own unworthiness. My father avoided these pitfalls. His humility was of a detached rather than a subjective character. He came to estimate his gifts carefully and fairly and even if he did not rate them very highly, he was not, after his early manhood, stultified by any undue sense of self-depreciation. His humility made him unusually aware of the dangers of *hubris*: he never judged his fellows and even when he was forced to weigh the evidence in their disfavour he gave them, as a matter of principle, the benefit of the doubt. I only remember him once in his entire life regarding someone as totally beyond rescue; and this was an early acquaintance whom I never met. 'Fixed opinions are like standing water,' said William Blake, 'they breed reptiles of the mind.' My father's lack of fixed opinions does not mean that he was fluid or easily swayed. His openness to every new experience allowed him to develop in tastes and attitudes long past the age when most of us become entrenched in a carapace of prejudice. But, since he was clear-headed and unsentimental, his mind developed a toughness and tensile strength even while retaining its tenderness and sensitivity.

Clustered round this nucleus of his humility there were two other attributes: first lack of pretension and secondly self-discipline. If he did not understand something—a picture, a poem—he immediately said so: there was no pretence, no fear of appearing old-fashioned or academically inferior. He put the matter aside for later consideration, always observing that his incapacity to respond might be the result of his own lack of perception. This perhaps was the reason he responded so warmly to Americans, because their scholastic tradition is so much more free of point-scoring and academic pretension than is ours in Britain.

As for his self-discipline, this had become instinctive and was bred in him by his boyhood intercourse with the great. He felt he owed it to his inheritance not to fall below the highest standards of which he was capable. It was his self-discipline that allowed him to develop his abilities to their best advantage. Scholar, writer, businessman, teacher, talker, golfer, lawyer, art-lover—he fulfilled all these roles successfully. But in one role he was more than successful, he was outstanding: he became a great human being. Through some mystery of circumstance and chemistry his whole personality had grown as the years passed to become greater than the sum of its parts.

It is, of course, notoriously difficult to bring goodness to life in fiction or biography. In *Middlemarch* George Eliot uses the device of comedy to make in Dorothea one of the few really successful creations of goodness in the whole of imaginative literature. Being without malice or self-interest Dorothea is frequently in absurd collision with a world where these attributes are part of the normal machinery of living. In his last twenty years my father gave us many splendid examples of this comic phenomenon.

There was the time when my cousin Harold congratulated me on the condition of our London garden: I demurred and said quite truthfully that my father, then aged 88, should take a lot of credit. 'Oh, no,' said my father without a trace of irony, 'I only do the heavy work'. Then in the last election in which he voted (October 1974), the local conservatives provided transport for him to get to the polls. In view of his great age and distinction they offered him a rosette as he got out of the car; 'Thank you' he said without a moment's hesitation. 'But I'm going to vote liberal.' Finally if asked what were his favourite television series he would answer 'Basil Brush' and Kenneth Clark's 'Civilisation'—in that order. These are merely random instances of a daily phenomenon. My father was totally unaware of his impact on others: not because he was self-centred but for the exactly opposite reason. He had, as Henry James wrote of Emerson, 'a beautiful mild modest authority and a ripe unconsciousness of evil'.

1977 was a particularly good year. Admittedly he was appreciably more frail and his memory had become a little erratic. But what activity! It was as if he was systematically settling his accounts. He saw everybody who was important to him, visited my cousin Mark in Yorkshire and the Speddings, the inheritors of a 150-year old friendship, in Cumbria. At the beginning of June he visited Blenheim for the first time and stood at the gate looking back, 'I'm just memorising it', he said. Everything he did in those months seemed to have a special meaning for him. On 10 June he heard, secretly, of Jonathan's outstanding achievement in his Cambridge Tripos exactly seventy-five years after his own success from the same college. A week later, on 16 June at 4.30 am, he had his first heart attack and on 18 June, his second. At the hospital he was two hours in the examination room. I stepped into the lift behind his trolley. When I bent over to speak to him, his face lit up with a surprised and dazzling smile: 'Ah—you're still here!!' It had never occurred to him that anyone would have wanted to wait so long on his account.

In the afternoon he talked with strange lucidity. I was compiling a programme on Gerard Manley Hopkins at the time. Suddenly he said: 'His technical tricks are a little obvious. "Felix the Farrier" makes me uneasy. Rhyming "sandal" with "Randall"—one can see it coming a mile ahead . . .'

On 22 June we finished the Hopkins programme by 4 o'clock and I went straight up to the hospital. The charge nurse advised that the machinery be switched off as my father was now being kept alive artificially. We had ended the Hopkins programme with the sonnet which begins:

Not, I'll not, carrion comfort, Despair, not feast on thee.[31]

I do not think I shall ever forget that line.

2 Charles Tennyson: Writer and Scholar

Robert Bernard Martin

The belief that biography is irrelevant to the study of a writer's work has long been obsolete, and nowhere does it seem more wrong than in the works of that most personal of writers, Sir Charles Tennyson. Not that he deliberately gave much of himself away, or that he was in any sense confessional—I can think of few men who were less so—but his personality was so vivid that it inevitably suffused everything he wrote. What I have to write therefore will be as concerned with the man as with his works, but to me they seem indivisible.

This fact he recognised himself. His delightful autobiography, *Stars and Markets*, begins with a very plain statement of the problem: 'I suppose the most important influence in my life . . . has been the fact that I am a grandson of the great poet of the great Victorian era'. The relationship in part dictated his splendid series of Tennysonian studies, but it may also have acted as a brake on other interests that might have found their way to the printed page.

When his eldest son Penrose went to Eton, he wrote home to say that 'It is better here to have been born with the name of Tennyson than to be the son of a Duke.' Sir Charles said that as long as he could remember, the first remark of strangers was 'Are you related to the poet?' With the humorous reticence that characterised his writing, he continues: 'Whether or not this influence has been psychologically good for me—a point which I do not propose to discuss—I have certainly found it of considerable material benefit, securing me over and over again consideration and sympathy which would probably not otherwise have been forthcoming, and giving me advantages which I should not otherwise have enjoyed'.[1]

It is typical of the man that he should write only of the help that his name was to him, not of how it could also stand in his way. For a statement of that problem, we have to turn to what he had to say of his brother Alfred: 'He alone of our generation inherited some share of our grandfather's poetic gift and force of personality, and, had he not been burdened with the poet's name as well as those of his godfathers, Browning and Dean Stanley, might have won for himself an honoured position in literature.'[2] To an aspiring poet the name of Alfred Tennyson is probably as great a handicap as that of William Shakespeare would be to a young playwright. But the name of Charles Tennyson also took some living up to, and I cannot help feeling that Sir Charles, however unconsciously, was writing of himself as well as his brother when he speculated on what had brought his writing to an abrupt end: 'Was it the shadow of his name?' asked Sir Charles. 'I shall never know, nor shall I ever know how much suffering the decision, or realization, that he would write no more poetry, caused him.'[3]

But his Tennyson heritage was not the only family literary influence on the young Charles Tennyson, for he was also the stepson of the essayist Augustine Birrell, one of that extinct breed known simply as literary men (although Birrell was, of course, a great deal more than that). Some of his stepfather's influence seems to have rubbed off on the first identifiable publications of the young Charles, in *Basileona*, the King's College undergraduate magazine of which he was co-founder while at Cambridge. According to the excellent bibliography by Lionel Madden of the writings of Sir Charles,[4] he made eight contributions of his own over a period of two years, including a monologue, a dialogue, three short stories, a poem, a series of parodies, and a humorous essay on the barbarity of shaving called 'What are you doing to your chin?' It would be idle to pretend that any of these is a neglected masterpiece, but that might also be said of the contributions to the same periodical by his friend E. M. Forster. After all, it is a rare undergraduate who knows, as Alfred Tennyson had done, precisely what his future will be, and the attempt to seek out a suitable branch of writing is apparent in Charles Tennyson's conscientious exploration of a number of different forms. But these undergraduate pieces do show two aspects that were to be characteristic of his later writing: a wry, almost deadpan humour, and a kind of objectivity in dealing with persons. I deliberately say persons rather than personalities, for it was typical of him to look hard at the exterior of others, rather than to try to worm out their inner secrets. He was not a writer who tried to inhabit the mind and skin of those of whom he wrote; rather he tended to see persons three-dimensionally, set in relief against the background from which they emerge. He had an intense respect for the privacy of his friends, and he extended that consideration to his subjects, whether members of his own family such as his grandfather, his brother, and his sons, or the imaginary characters he created at King's. It is a form of observation, however, that can be a limitation to a writer of fiction, and he may have recognised this in deciding to give up the sort of writing he had been trying as an undergraduate.

Not surprisingly, in the years after Cambridge and during his early days at the Bar, he wrote little, and he published nothing between 1902 and 1908. Then the old urge for literature returned with a powerful impulse, but he was still unsure of himself as a writer. At the time he was sharing rooms with J. E. G. Montmorency, literary editor of the *Contemporary Review*, who asked him to contribute to that magazine, and he was also promised work reviewing for the *Spectator*. Between then and the outbreak of the First World War, a matter of five or six years, he wrote more than 130 reviews. Not all of them were long, but the total is impressive when it is remembered that they were written when he was first a busy young barrister, then later employed at the Colonial Office. Even more surprising is the diversity of subjects on which he felt competent to speak his mind. Some of them are to be expected; cricket, golf, and walking are natural topics for a man of his love of sport, and so is legal theory for a barrister, and Latin and Greek for a man who had taken a first in classics at Cambridge. But with equal facility he wrote about the Icknield Way, naval wars, eighteenth-century France, the plays of Yeats, the place of the Jews in history, and the growth of women's rights. To one single issue of the *Spectator* he contributed three reviews, of which the topics could hardly be more diverse: 'Smollett's England', 'Up-Country in New Zealand', and 'The art of public speaking'. For another he wrote both a review of Maurice Baring's *The Russian People* and a charming poem of his own, 'To Sleep'.[5] Since these were either published anonymously or identified only by initials, there was no indication that all this activity was the product of the leisure of a man with a fulltime career elsewhere.

All the reviews were written with care, critical intelligence, and a commitment not to be expected from someone so occupied with other things. Frequently his quiet humour comes bubbling out as when he writes about the utility of compulsory study of his beloved Greek; sadly he has to admit that 'he who takes the higher ground of the value of an early exercise in the ideals and expression of the spiritual founders of our society, finds it hard to demonstrate any considerable access of spirituality in the average Public School boy'.[6]

Today, reading these reviews together, as no reader had a chance to do when they appeared, one can easily see a clear pattern emerging from the diversity, and that is his absolute love of literature, which gives sparkle to everything he has to say of it. For the *Spectator* he regularly reviewed the Loeb Classics as they appeared, and he was also writing increasingly about English literature, particularly that of the Victorians, the works of Dickens, Meredith and Gissing, as well as that of late eighteenth-century authors like Cowper, and Edwardians such as Conrad. In 1912, reviewing John Bailey's *Poets and Poetry*, he inadvertently characterised his own criticism:

'One does not think of him, as of Professor Saintsbury, approaching his subject, like a Japanese wrestler, with strange cries and uncouth gesticulations, or as of Mr Chesterton, standing both opponents and supporters on their heads with genial impartiality. With Mr Bailey criticism is a sober business. . . . He very seldom thrills you with a sudden illumination, but on the other hand he never outrages by a fault of taste or ignorance. He is no phrase-maker, and his style, though always sound and clear, is apt to be a little impersonal, but his sure taste and sympathy often illumine a chance sentence.[7]

It was, of course, during these years that he first began writing about the subject that was to secure his name in literary studies, the poetry of Alfred Tennyson. It may be worth mentioning here that at the time it must have been difficult for him to do so, since he lived under the inhibiting shadow of his uncle, Hallam Lord Tennyson, son of the poet, who thought of himself as guardian of his father's reputation. Hallam Tennyson's attitude was not the result of fear of revelations to the world of unspoken horrors about Tennyson, but came of absolute love and the assurance that his father was too sacred to be discussed with anything but adulation. Anyone who has ever looked at the manuscripts of the sections contributed by others to Hallam Tennyson's *Memoir* of his father or to its companion volume, *Tennyson and His Friends*, knows how ruthlessly—he would have said steadfastly—he rewrote other men's words, changing their style and their opinions, on occasion correcting even his father's grammar and rhetoric to make it conform to that of the icon he thought Tennyson was. In spite of a public career that included the Governor-Generalship of Australia, Hallam Tennyson had always tended to be reclusive, and Charles Tennyson writes graphically of the sad Jamesian decade after the First World War when his uncle lived among the dark, unchanged corridors of Farringford with the vegetation gradually engulfing it, as he mourned the loss of his first wife and two of his three sons. He was the guardian of the past, and the chief element of the past was Alfred Tennyson.

During his uncle's lifetime Charles Tennyson made two major contributions to Tennyson scholarship, but both were connected with the family rather than the poet. For the 1911 volume, *Tennyson and His Friends*, he wrote the section on 'Tennyson and His Brothers Frederick and Charles', which in spite of its title is almost entirely about the two elder brothers, who had both led lives of comparative failure. 'Both had great talents,' wrote Charles Tennyson, 'but neither the tender felicity of Charles nor Frederick's heart of cloud and fire ever came to full development. They represent two extremes of the Tennyson temperament, the mean and perfection of which is found in Alfred.'[8] This excellent essay, although it incorporates a good deal of new material, actually says little about Alfred Tennyson. This, however, must reflect Hallam Tennyson's wishes rather than those of his nephew. Charles Tennyson was very fond of his uncle, and even had it been possible, he would never have published anything to disturb the older man.

Two years later came a more characteristic piece of his scholarship, the edition of *The Shorter Poems of Frederick Tennyson*. Characteristic because it demonstrated his wish, unlike that of his uncle, that everything important about the Tennysons should be made known, so that they might be admired for what they were, not what someone else thought they should have been.

In the light of his later work, two reviews of 1913 and 1914 are even more interesting, for they show where his real enthusiasm lay and point the direction of his future studies. The first of these, 'Tennyson and the Critics', is a review of the edition of the *Poems of Tennyson, 1830–1870*, by his grandfather's old friend, Sir Herbert Warren. In part it is a defence of Tennyson's waning reputation, but to those who know Sir Charles's later writings it makes startling reading, for in 1913 his attitude towards Tennyson's late poems was very different from what it was to become. He felt that too much importance had been attached to the intellectual inertness of the *Idylls of the King*, the plays, and the philosophical poems, but he nonetheless shared the general opinion of them current at the time. Many of his strictures sound more like the objections of Harold Nicolson to Tennyson than his own criticism in later life. In speaking of the natural reaction against Tennyson immediately after his death, he admits: 'Something must be attributed to a weakness in the quality of Tennyson's genius. . . . It was when he began to feel himself the voice of the nation that the weakness showed itself.' In later life Sir Charles profoundly admired the *Idylls of the King*, but at this time he said that 'one cannot read them without being aware of a certain self-consciousness in their patriotism and their morality. . . . Only one, the "Passing", achieves greatness . . .'. Although he was to change these opinions, he was constant all his life to his conclusion of the long review when he considers the propriety of publishing poems that Tennyson had discarded: 'A man who is not great enough to bear a full revelation is not worthy to be protected against it . . .'.[9]

His review the following year, 1914, of R. Brimley Johnson's *Tennyson and His Poetry* shows that he had not yet begun to revise his opinions: 'few readers will agree with his claim that "the later and longer poems are technically more perfect, more beautiful, and more stimulating" than the poet's early work'.[10]

There is one other work of this period that should be mentioned because it had a pivotal place in the literary career of Charles Tennyson, the book he was commissioned to write about his old university for Chatto and Windus. *Cambridge from Within* appeared in 1913, a lighthearted set of essays from the point of view of a recent undergraduate that manage but poorly to conceal his own love of the place where he had been so happy. Over and over he makes the reader aware of how much it meant to him to go to the university that had been his grandfather's first major excursion away from Lincolnshire. And some of his grandfather's prejudices show through amusingly. It has often been told how the Apostles wrote of Cambridge's sister university without capitalising the initial letter. With the same joking lack of respect for the elder institution, Charles Tennyson referred to the great amounts of money that chefs of the Cambridge colleges were reputed to have amassed. At Trinity, for instance, the chef 'is said to drive a carriage and pair and have sons at Oxford'.[11]

With the advent of the First World War Charles Tennyson virtually stopped all publishing until 1930: 'I had long ago come to the conclusion that I was deficient in creative ability'.[12] He had found difficulty in padding out *Cambridge from Within* to book length, and he felt no impulse to begin another book. I think that his description of his brother's concealed pain at giving up writing must reflect many of his own feelings at the realisation that he was never going to be a great creative artist. In the face of that knowledge, book reviews and literary essays seemed parasitical and secondhand. With what was surely deep perturbation he put down his pen and threw himself into a career with the Federation of British Industries. Had he never written again, it is fair to say that this essay would not have been written.

Dr Madden's bibliography lists exactly 140 pieces that Charles

Tennyson published before 1930, and of these only the four that I have already mentioned are concerned in any way with Alfred Tennyson. From 1930, when he was fifty-one years old, until his death in 1977 there were seventy more items added to his bibliography, including many books, and articles that were practically all more substantial than the reviews that he had written before the First World War. Even more interesting than the bulk of this late flowering is the fact that all but ten of these items, if my figures are correct, were concerned primarily with either Alfred Tennyson and his family or the Tennyson Society. Of the ten, one is the touching biography of his own son Penrose, one is a group of biographical essays on three friends and his two dead sons; on these it would be intrusive to make a comment. Three of the publications are concerned with cricket, and on these I feel a national incompetence to make a judgement. But what is overwhelmingly apparent is the concentration on Tennyson and his poetry. In part this reflects the changing status of Tennysonian and Victorian studies, but what might not be patent is that it is largely because of Charles Tennyson that this whole revaluation of his grandfather has taken place.

Hallam Lord Tennyson had died in 1928, leaving some of his father's unpublished manuscripts to Charles Tennyson. Although he never said so, Hallam Tennyson undoubtedly realised at least subconsciously that his own preservation of his father's reputation in amber could not continue forever, and that his nephew was the ideal person to begin any change that was to be made. Certainly, Charles Tennyson's inheritance of the manuscripts and his release from the unspoken but totally clear restrictions of his uncle brought about a torrent of work on Tennyson and his poetry. All the love of his grandfather's works that had been implicit in the early reviews was now made overt, and the result was the pouring of light onto the life and poems of Tennyson, opening them up for inspection, as Charles Tennyson opened up Farringford itself, flooding light into its dark corners.

Alfred Tennyson had said repetitively that he hated having successive revisions and discarded parts of his poems made public ('chips from the workshop' he called them), and Hallam Tennyson had done his best to keep anything out of print that his father had not authorised for publication. Charles Tennyson recognised that the time was long past when his grandfather's reputation could be harmed by the printing of his juvenilia and discarded works. Many of them deserved public knowledge on their own merits, and even more of them were important for what they said of Tennyson's development and his methods of writing; their publication could do nothing but good for Tennyson studies. The modern era of Tennyson scholarship may be said to have begun in 1930 with Charles Tennyson's publication of his grandfather's precocious comedy, *The Devil and the Lady*, written at the age of fourteen. The following year Charles Tennyson edited *Unpublished Early Poems by Alfred Tennyson*, and within two or three years this volume was followed by studies of early manuscripts of the *Idylls of the King*, *The Princess*, and the J. M. Heath *Commonplace Book*, containing copies of poems that had circulated in Cambridge when Tennyson was an undergraduate and shortly afterwards.

But from the time of his uncle's death Charles Tennyson had been fascinated by the realisation that only part of the poet's life had been told in the official biography by Hallam Tennyson. At the same time he was editing the previously unpublished early poems, he was beginning to write about the circumstances of his grandfather's life, about Dr George Tennyson, Farringford, and the events leading up to Edward Bulwer's attack on Tennyson in *The New Timon*.

Hallam Tennyson's conservatism in concealing a great deal of the information about his father had had the fortunate result of maintaining the Tennyson papers virtually intact, papers of the sort that have gradually disappeared in the families of other writers. No one had examined the Tennyson papers, and it is hard indeed even to imagine the temerity it would have taken to approach Hallam Tennyson with a request to see them. But the secretiveness about the family papers implied the possibility of their disappearance in another fashion, by their being simply forgotten or lost, slowly mouldering away as they were never looked at. Charles Tennyson was probably the first person to have seen all the Farringford papers after the publication of Hallam Tennyson's *Memoir* of his father in 1897. Of the original 40,000 letters that Hallam Tenyson had when he began his book, about a quarter had survived the rigorous sorting of Henry Sidgwick and Francis Palgrave, who ruthlessly threw away any that they thought either uninteresting or unfit for publication. Besides the remaining letters there were family journals and diaries, mountains of clippings and contemporary reviews of Tennyson's poetry, proof-sheets and trial copies corrected by Tennyson himself, Tennyson's library ranged on the gloomy shelves of Farringford and stored away in boxes in the stables, and all the successive stages of the *Memoir* from its initial pinned-in vellum volumes through several successive private printings up to the book that finally appeared. Today, neatly housed on the shelves of the Tennyson Centre and sorted into boxes, the sheer quantity is enough to strike terror into the heart of the Tennyson student seeing these materials for the first time. Sir Charles has described how as each precious cache came into view he was constantly alternating between excited joy and stunned trepidation, until finally he was no longer even sure whether he wanted to find still more.

In the preface to his biography of his grandfather Sir Charles makes his own decision to write it sound like a matter of some wrestling with his conscience, but in his heart he must have known from the beginning that a new biography was the only way to deal with the material, and that there was only one person who should write it. There had been several biographical studies since the appearance of the *Memoir*, but there were only two to consider seriously, and neither of those had been written with access to the materials that he had inherited. T. R. Lounsbury's biography was left half-written and totally uncorrected at his death, and though it attempted to take into account what new material lay in the public domain, its chief virtue was the way it related Tennyson to his age. Harold Nicolson's brilliantly written study had relied for its scant facts on the *Memoir*, filled in by his own luxuriant and somewhat malicious imagination, to create a picture of a great but deeply neurotic poet who slowly subsided into an unthinking public institution.

What was needed, as Sir Charles realised, was a biography that spoke with authority because it was grounded on documents and facts, rather than being derivative from the spirit of the age as Lounsbury's was, or created out of reckless prejudice as was Nicolson's. Only from fact could an accurate picture be drawn of the man who had produced some of the greatest poetry in the language, and to that greatness his grandson felt an allegiance that transcended even Tennyson's own frequently ex-pressed opinion that all his readers needed to know about him was in his poetry. Sir Charles saw that a clear-headed and accurate account of the life was necessary for the future of Tennyson studies, and he also knew that if writing about Tennyson was choked off, interest in his works might die with it.

The fact that Sir Charles was the grandson of the poet made it easier to ask assistance of distant relatives and of those older people who had known Tennyson. Charles Tennyson was hardly over fifty himself when he first thought of writing the biography, but he had plenty of memories of his own long stays with his grandfather before his death when he himself was a boy. As a child he had known Aldworth almost as a second home, and he remembered the look and feel of his grandfather's great brown hand that he kissed in greeting each morning. (I have often wished I had thought to ask Sir Charles whether all small boys kissed the hands of their grandfathers in the 1880s, whether it was his own spontaneous tribute to Tennyson's greatness, or whether it was a peculiar family custom of the Tennysons.) Such minutiae of Victorian life were in Sir Charles's bones, so that he never had consciously to think of them. Most importantly he had grown up with an intimate knowledge of family traditions and stories that no one else could have had.

After he had begun the research for the biography, he was offered the use of something that he had known nothing of, the voluminous archives belonging to his cousins, the Tennyson d'Eyncourt family, now so generously deposited in the Lincolnshire Archives Office. In this enormous collection, surely one of the most complete records of a Victorian family extant, Charles Tennyson gradually came across the startling information about the quarrels between the Somersby Tennysons and the Tennyson d'Eyncourts, the pathetic story of the decline of the poet's father Dr George Tennyson from drugs, drink, and disease, the record of the leaping but disappointed ambition of the poet's uncle Charles Tennyson d'Eyncourt. Once more Sir Charles described to me his mixture of dismay and excitement at the sight of so much additional material. What it contained had scarcely been touched on in Hallam Tennyson's biography, and so far as Sir Charles could determine, his uncle had known almost nothing about it.

Besides all this, there was the vast amount of published material about Tennyson that had appeared since the *Memoir*. Sir Charles worked on the biography for some twenty years between his uncle's death and its eventual publication in 1949. By then all the great Victorians were dead, and their biographies, memoirs, diaries, and letters were being published. Tennyson has often been described as being, together with Gladstone and the Queen, the most famous of all persons living in England during the latter part of the last century; naturally, he met most of the great men of the day, of whom a large number had recorded their impressions of him.

In his autobiography Sir Charles tells how he used to go for the odd half-hour to the London Library from his office in St James's Street, to wander through the biographical stacks, pulling out books that might contain contemporary accounts of his grandfather. I have often followed in his footsteps at those shelves, and in some of the volumes I have found brief notes written in a familiar hand in defiance of the regulations. Of all these notations, my favourite is that in a copy of H. D. Rawnsley's rather inaccurate *Memories of the Tennysons*. On page 130 Rawnsley said of Tennyson: 'It was on April 2nd, 1896, that I was with him at

Farringford. Alfred and Charley, eldest sons of Lionel Tennyson, were
at school with me in the New Forest.' In the margin is the pencilled note:
'I think 1889 or 1888'. It is signed simply, 'Charley'. It tells us a good bit
about Charles Tennyson, I think, both his desire for accuracy and his
sense of responsibility about the correction. And, I need not add, his
impish sense of humour.

I cannot claim to have been in any sense a Tennysonian in 1949, when
Alfred Tennyson, by his grandson Charles Tennyson, first appeared, but
I can well remember the sense of excitement in the reviews of the book,
and I can remember feeling for the first time some understanding of
what had created the phenomenon known as Alfred Tennyson. Wisely,
Sir Charles did not try to replace the work of his uncle, only to
supplement it, to fill in many of the places that Hallam Tennyson had
skimped in the *Memoir*, which Sir Charles described as 'rather a
presentation of material than an attempt at an objective biography'.
What he might have added was that he was unobtrusively correcting
some of the many errors in his uncle's work.'You will discover,' he once
said in a wry warning, 'that Hallam was to be admired for his generosity
but not for his accuracy.' Sir Charles's own generosity to the errors of
others, never feeling the need to rap them over the knuckles, might be an
object lesson to more contentious scholars.

He used to speak with guarded respect of the racy brilliance of Harold
Nicolson's book about Tennyson, but he was constantly surprised that
anyone should take it seriously as a biography. I suspect, however, that
it was influential in his own biography in two major ways: Nicolson's
scorn of the later poetry probably helped Sir Charles in part to learn its
virtues, and Nicolson's cavalier disregard of fact surely only strength-
ened Sir Charles's native caution about speculation. His typically
modest statement of his intentions was that he would confine himself 'to
facts and obvious inferences, without any attempt to make good the
gaps in the evidence by the exercise of the imagination'.

Here is the root of my major reservation about the most authoritative
biography of Tennyson we have. The diffidence that had kept him from
trying to inhabit the minds of his characters when he was writing fiction
was now reinforced by a dislike of irresponsible guesswork about
Tennyson's motives, and as readers we may feel that he too often shied
away from going behind the facade of words in the poetry, in
Tennyson's own letters or in the accounts of others. Irresponsibility is
something of which Sir Charles would never have been guilty, and he
was equipped by his inheritance and early life to understand the
workings of his grandfather's mind better than others could have done.

I for one am sorry that he deprived us of his own uniquely authoritative speculations about the psychological sources of Tennyson's personality.

Nearly thirty years after publishing the biography, Sir Charles's own chief reservation about it, which he often expressed, was regret that he had not included more detailed annotation of his sources, which he knew would have been of great help to all scholars who succeeded him. I suspect that he had originally begun to write a biography for the general reader, then later wished that it had been of a more academic sort. Yet how characteristic it was of him to have left all his working notebooks to the Tennyson Centre, so that seriously interested persons could trace the origin of his factual information.

As any work of this quality and magnitude must do, the biography immediately brought offers of material that had not previously been forthcoming, and it equally inevitably brought floods of questions from scholars who wanted to know even more than he had told them. Fortunately, he had retired shortly before the publication of the book, and he now took up what amounted to a new career. For the guidance of future writers, he kept records of the material that he had seen or heard of after the appearance of his biography. The questions presented a more difficult problem, since their answers often depended upon seeing the family papers, which were deposited in a London bank vault after the sale of Farringford. The owner of the papers, the present Lord Tennyson, was generous in letting others see part of them, but it was obviously impossible to allow free access. It was a problem to which there was no immediate easy answer.

Like all good scholars, Sir Charles was constantly inspired to work of his own by trying to help others. In the decade after the biography, he published seven books, besides a number of articles. Of these the most important was his *Six Tennyson Essays*, one of the most balanced, sane books ever written on his grandfather's poetry. The chapters on Tennyson's politics and religion thread a careful way through the sometimes confused views of the poet on these subjects, and the chapter on his humour is important in considering an aspect of his poetry that is too often neglected, although perhaps not every reader can agree that Shakespeare and Tennyson are the most humorous of all the great English poets since Chaucer. The love of the classics Sir Charles had felt since his schooldays made him particularly responsive to rhythm and prosody, probably more than to imagery, but Latin and Greek had done nothing to make his views on English versification rigid, as his chapter on that aspect of Tennyson shows. For example, in a comment on a famous passage in 'The Holy Grail', he has the modest flexibility of a man who knows that informed and loving taste can sometimes find truth where rules are of no help. Of the lines, 'There rose a hill that none but man could climb, Scarred with ten thousand wintry water-courses . . .', he simply says, 'This is enormously improved by the substitution of "a hundred" for "ten thousand", though it is hard to say why.'[13]

It sometimes seemed that the older Sir Charles grew, the more he wrote and the freer and more relaxed his writing became. It is impossible to mention most of the works of his late years, but two major ones must be noticed, both written with the co-operation of his good friend Hope Dyson. The first of these was *Dear and Honoured Lady*, the whole surviving correspondence between Queen Victoria and her Poet Laureate, with long narrative links inserted to show the growing affection between these two delightfully awkward persons. The second was *The Tennysons: Background to Genius*, which appeared when Sir Charles was ninety-five years old. In it for the first time he consolidated all the information he had been patiently gathering for seventy years about that incredible group of eccentrics who were the immediate family into which Alfred Tennyson was born. Some of it had been published in part before, but it was assembled into a fresh and wholly absorbing book.

I must skip the other distinguished publications of Sir Charles's later years in order to mention briefly what has been so often described before, the foundation in 1965 of the Tennyson Research Centre, which he and Lord Tennyson finally evolved as the answer to the difficult problem of how best to let others use the contents of the Tennyson archives. It is probably the richest, and it is certainly the most imaginatively conceived repository of materials about any of the great Victorian writers, and it is unique in being the brainchild of the grandson and greatgrandson of the poet himself.

One final service to the freedom of scholarship in which Sir Charles took a leading part was that benevolent conspiracy with Lord Tennyson, the Master and Fellows of Trinity College, and Professor Ricks to make available for almost unrestricted use the great collection of manuscripts that had been given in earlier years by the family to Alfred Tennyson's old college and put under a strict ban as far as quotation or publication were concerned. If one were in any doubt about the importance of Sir Charles' contribution to Victorian studies, there is the evidence not only of the honorary degrees and fellowships, the citations, the bibliography of 210 items (on which this essay is only a sketchy commentary) but also the grateful and affectionate dedications and acknowledgements of nearly every important work on the poetry of Alfred Tennyson that has appeared over the past thirty years. One might adapt the words of Falstaff to describe Sir Charles Tennyson, for truly it may be said of him that he was not only scholarly in himself but the cause that scholarship is in other men.

Part II
Alfred Tennyson

1 The Present Value of Tennyson

W. W. Robson

I think many of those who care about literature share my misgivings
about the present-day vogue for enormously detailed biographies of
writers. It is not only because they minister to a taste for gossip, which
for many readers is more attractive than all those tiresome lines of verse.
Too often they diminish the author's work by restoring it to its context
of origin, the outgrowing of which is what makes it poetry. They force
on the reader particularities which the author, with good reason, may
have wanted to leave out. They sometimes make it impossible for us to
experience the text. They turn poems into documents. I agree with
Alfred Tennyson in yearning for the days 'Before the Love of Letters,
overdone/Had swampt the sacred poets with themselves' (R 1321,
ll 13–14). The ideal condition for a reader is that of a child listening to a
story, who cares everything about what is in the story, and nothing
about who wrote it.

But in the adult world things cannot be as simple as that. Often we
cannot help having an image of the author behind the page. Sometimes
this is part of our pleasure. Some authors, we feel, are our friends. But
sometimes the image of the author influences what we read to the
detriment of the work. For that image can be grossly misleading, the
product of myths and unreliable anecdotes and baseless prejudices.
That is why Sir Charles Tennyson's life of the poet Tennyson is so
valuable, because it is so frank, because it lets in air and light. We like
and respect him all the more because we understand his personal
problems. He is clearer to us as a human being. But what gives Sir
Charles's memoir its special virtue is that on every page it is guided by
the recognition that the only reason why we should want to know about
Tennyson is because we care for his poetry.

I want to write about how Tennyson's poetry looks today. But at once we are confronted by the problem of critical judgement. This is an age when subjectivism is rampant everywhere—in moral philosophy, in political theory, in religious thought. Nowhere is it so notoriously powerful as in the arts. It is often taken for granted that 'beauty is in the beholder', that if you think, or profess to think, that a pile of rubbish is more beautiful than Chartres Cathedral, you cannot be wrong, because there are no rights and wrongs in the matter. This general question about value is, of course, much too large for me to go into here. This is a moment for testimony, not discussion. All I will say is that I regard subjectivism as wrong, and that I think its influence in every sphere of life has been poisonous.

But, as Spinoza says, it is better to try to understand one's enemy than to hate him. And where the arts are concerned the attraction of subjectivism is very understandable. In poetry, for example, the art with which we are concerned here, variations of taste and fluctuations of opinion are obvious. Quite apart from the contemporary chaos, one age ridicules the idols of another. Yesterday's fashions look absurd. Poets' reputations go up and down. Opinions vary from person to person. More than that, our own opinions change from one time of our lives to another. When I was a boy I loved the poems of Tennyson which I read in Arthur Mee's encyclopaedias, such as 'The Lady of Shalott' (R 354) and the lyric in 'The Brook' (R 1025) and 'Flower in the crannied wall' (R 1193). I would have been amazed to discover that there was someone who did not consider Tennyson a very great poet. When I was an undergraduate, however, I took it for granted that Tennyson was a very outmoded and dated author, one who did not speak to my condition at all. And once again I assumed that all thinking people agreed with me. (Today I have reverted to my first opinion.) I dare say many readers could report similar fluctuations. But then how can there be anything objective about this, anything on a par with the basic statement that Tennyson was born in 1809 and died in 1892? Is it not just a matter of personal taste? And do we not all know that *de gustibus non est disputandum*?

I cannot hope in a short space to convert those readers who hold that view. I will only ask them to suspend it for a moment and try and look at the matter as the literary objectivist sees it. First of all, the objectivist tries to avoid the word 'value', which carries an irremovable suggestion of subjectivity. He prefers to talk about goodness, or beauty, or truthfulness. And if he has to use an even more general term, he prefers to talk about 'quality' or 'virtue' or 'excellence', which suggests things that exist out there, irrespective of what you or I personally happen to think about them. But how then does the objectivist cope with the notorious variations of taste to which I have referred, the ups and downs of the literary stock-market? His first step is to get people to admit that there can be many kinds of excellence—some kinds are more admired by some people than by others, and some kinds are more popular at some periods than at others. This is apt to be forgotten in times of literary revolution, like our present century. Literary revolutions occur when some hitherto neglected or underrated kinds of excellence are re-cognised again in new writers. At such times the authors of the past who exhibit it, or are thought to exhibit it, are hailed as the forerunners of the moderns. They become the 'heroes' of the history of literature and art. The authors who do not exhibit this excellence, who may have been previously admired for other excellences, are abused, or dropped from the canon, perhaps for a time, perhaps indefinitely. Now it is certainly possible to write the history of art and literature in this way; and it may be psychologically necessary for a new age to remodel the past to suit its own needs. All the same, to follow the crowd in these revolutions is not only to commit the sin of injustice, it is to miss a great deal of pleasure. There are unfashionable kinds of excellence as well as fashionable ones. And to be out of step with our ancestors is not always a good thing. It is parochial, and—what may be a more cogent objection for some people—it is undemocratic; as Chesterton said, tradition is the de-mocracy of the dead, a refusal to commit everything to the judgement of the minority of people who merely happen to be walking about.

Nowhere is this parochial tendency more obvious than in the habit there once was of treating the mid-Victorian age as a very odd period. All those taboos on the physical side of sex, for example—how ludicrous! Now I do not deny that there were ways in which—as the late-Victorian H. G. Wells put it—mid-Victorian literature was 'clipped and limited'. But those who took that line did not always remember that later ages have their inhibitions and shallownesses too, and that in some respects the great mid-Victorian writers can be seen as more 'normal', more in harmony with what has always been recognised as great in Western literature, than our own age. Let me take one or two examples especially pertinent to Tennyson. The first is what the poet Thomas Gray—not a Victorian—called 'the sacred source of sympathetic tears'. Can it be denied that in our uncomfortableness about this it is we, and not the mid-Victorians, who are out of step? All the great heroes of epic and romance wept copiously, and were thought more, not less, manly for doing so, Shakespeare is full of pathos. But how often is a writer today praised for his command of pathos? We can still laugh with Dickens, as the Victorians did; but are we prepared to admit that we weep with him as the Victorians did? Let me refer to a poem which everyone knows, taken from *The Princess* (R 741, Part iv, ll 21–39).

> Tears, idle tears, I know not what they mean,
> Tears from the depth of some divine despair
> Rise in the heart, and gather to the eyes
> In looking on the happy Autumn-fields,
> And thinking of the days that are no more.
>
> Fresh as the first beam glittering on a sail,
> That brings our friends up from the underworld,
> Sad as the last which reddens over one
> That sinks with all we love below the verge;
> So sad, so fresh, the days that are no more.
>
> Ah, sad and strange as in dark summer dawns
> The earliest pipe of half-awakened birds
> To dying ears, when unto dying eyes
> The casement slowly grows a glimmering square;
> So sad, so strange, the days that are no more.
>
> Dear as remembered kisses after death,
> And sweet as those by hopeless fancy feigned
> On lips that are for others; deep as love,
> Deep as first love, and wild with all regret;
> O Death in life, the days that are no more.

This poem has been greatly admired and loved. But I have read modern accounts of it which are strongly hostile. Others respect its sincerity of feeling, but obviously react to it much as Tennyson's *The Princess*, that sturdy progressive, reacts to it in its context.

>   If indeed there haunt
> About the mouldered lodges of the Past
> So sweet a voice and vague, fatal to men,
> Well needs be we should cram our ears with wool
> And so pace by . . . (R 741, Part iv, ll 44–8)
> (*She asks the singer for a song*)
> Not such as moans about the retrospect,
> But deals with the other distance and the hues
> Of promise; not a death's-head at the wine. (iv, ll 67–9)

F. R. Leavis, while acknowledging the distinction of 'Tears, idle tears', contrasts it unfavourably with D. H. Lawrence's 'Piano', in which the poet fights against his wish to weep. I am reminded also of the moment in George Eliot's *Middlemarch* when the heroine Dorothea says that organ-music makes her sob, and her uncle Mr Brooke says 'That kind of thing is not healthy, my dear'. I think we find it difficult to deal with such poems today. Either we condemn them, or allot them to a minor category because there is no critical or ironic element in them to counterbalance the pathos. Or, if we admire them, we try to show that the counterbalancing element is there. We are somehow reluctant to take pathos straight, to admit that something in us answers directly to the timeless poignancy of 'Break, break, break' (R 602, ll 9–12):

And the stately ships go on
To their haven under the hill;
But O for the touch of a vanished hand,
And the sound of a voice that is still!

The twentieth century has a horror of sentimentality, though no one seems able to say exactly what sentimentality is. So far as I can see, it means the appeal by an author to a mood which for some reason we do not want to feel at the moment. But sometimes nowadays it seems to mean the expression of any distinctively human emotion whatever. I think this dread of sentimentality has been one of the most crippling limitations on writers at the present time. A writer who is afraid of sentimentality can never write anything emotionally full-blooded, just as a writer who fears melodrama can never write a tragedy.

Another excellence that has been devalued today, a quality in which Tennyson especially excels, is one for which there is now no acceptable positive word. The best I can suggest is 'pomp', in the sense in which Shakespeare means it when he makes Othello speak of the 'pride, pomp and circumstance of glorious war'. It is significant that we cannot use this word without explaining that we do not mean it pejoratively. And its adjective, 'pompous', is exclusively pejorative, another indication of the constrictions of modern literature in the age of irony. Everything has to be, as Auden put it, 'ironic, *sotto voce*, monochrome', and Auden thought that for a sincere poet today this must be so. Farewell to the grand style. Tennyson could write his 'Ode on the death of the Duke of Wellington' (R 1007, ll 1–4):

> Bury the Great Duke
> With an empire's lamentation.
> Let us bury the Great Duke
> To the noise of the mourning of a mighty nation.

But so far as I know no modern poet has succeeded in writing a single memorable line, let alone a good poem, on the deaths of, for instance, Winston Churchill or John F. Kennedy. We have a word for pomp in the wrong place: pomposity. But where is our word for pomp in the right place? It may be said that we do not believe in Great Men as the Victorians did. Similarly, when it is observed that no modern poet since Kipling—Tennyson's disciple—has written a great hymn, it will be said that this is because we do not believe in God any more: ours is not an age of faith. But Tennyson himself, as he was well aware, did not live in an age of faith, and yet he could write a great hymn (R 861, ll 1–4):

> Strong Son of God, immortal Love,
> Whom we, that have not seen thy face,
> By faith, and faith alone, embrace,
> Believing where we cannot prove.

The greatness of *In Memoriam* is that it destroys any simple contrast between 'faith' and 'doubt'; even agnostics can have religious feelings, and Tennyson is the devotional poet of agnosticism.

   Many other kinds of excellence that are not characteristic of present-day writing could be illustrated from Tennyson. Besides rising to these grand occasions he is the poet of private celebration and commemoration, as few moderns are. I think for instance of his capacity for a happy blend of dignity and informality, as in 'The Daisy' (R 1019), or 'To the Rev. F. D. Maurice' (R 1022), or 'To Mary Boyle' (R 1402); and his power to join the touchingly personal to the impersonally grand, as in 'To E. FitzGerald' (R 1317). All sorts of things are scattered about the margins of Tennyson's work, which if they were better known would quite transform the simplified picture of him some people still have. There is a frequent critical habit of splitting up Tennyson into the morbid mystic and the celebrant of Victorian domesticities, the gruff Lincolnshire pipesmoker and the exquisite dreamer, the angry young man and the ancient sage, and then declaring one's bafflement at how to put him together again. The fact is, as Christopher Ricks pointed out, that Tennyson was all those things, and other things too: 'he was many things'.[1]

So far I have been talking about excellences that are excellences *sometimes*, and which may be more valued in one period than in another, may sometimes be out of place. One of the things that once attracted readers to Tennyson, and may now put them off, is his passion for the minute description of nature. Who could deny that this is an excellence? Take, for instance, this line from *Maud* (R 1037, Part i, 1 102): 'A million emeralds break from the ruby-budded lime . . .'. Who could look at a lime-tree again without relishing that? *In Memoriam* alone is full of single lines which have that quality, in which Tennyson put into words with more delicate precision than we could ever find what we may have seen for ourselves. But I suspect that these things were more admired by Victorian critics than they are today, and that many of us find that our own response to them, while it may be admiring, is cool. Tennyson's lines on the sunflower '. . . shining fair,/Ray round with flames her disk of seed' (CI, 5), would help the police to an identification better than Blake's: 'Ah Sunflower, weary of time,/Who countest the steps of the sun . . .'[2] But what Blake gives us is not so much a recognition of what we already know, but something that flashes on us as a new insight, something that takes us beyond a beautiful transient phenomenon to a glimpse of the eternal; not what the sunflower looks like, but what it 'is', what it 'means', in the world of the spirit. I am not, of course, reproaching Tennyson for not writing like Blake. That would be quite contrary to the principles I recommend. Every poet is entitled to his own singularity. What I am trying to do is to specify a quality in Tennyson's verse which is sometimes an excellence but sometimes not. When the May Queen says: 'The building rook'll call from the windy tall elm-tree,/And the tufted plover pipe along the fallow lea . . .' (R 418, ii, 17–18), it detracts from that poem to have to think of her as a keen amateur naturalist. When Burns said his love was like a red, red rose he would have weakened the poem by mentioning the species of rose, as I fear Tennyson might have done. It is one of Tennyson's faults as a poet that he was sometimes betrayed into over-elaboration. In this respect he is Hellenistic, not classical.

Some excellences, then, can be out of place. But the literary objectivist is committed to the view that there are some excellences which are never out of place. No work of art can be called great without them. Poignancy and unambiguous feeling, pomp and stateliness, minute description and felicity of observation—all these are excellences, and all can be found in Tennyson's work. But they are not excellences always or all the time. What we must be concerned with, if we are to substantiate the claim of Tennyson to a place among the great

poets, are those excellences that are always excellences—what might be
called the marks, or to use Newman's word, the 'notes', of great poetry,
and great art in general. These permanent excellences may be many. I
propose to select four of them, and see how far they apply to Tennyson.

The first essential excellence, something that is always a virtue in a
poet, is effectiveness of communication. It might be objected that this
seems an almost tautologous requirement. If, to use an expressive
vulgarism, the poet cannot 'get his stuff across', we can hardly call him a
poet at all. Yet, especially in modern times, the communicative aspect of
poetry has not been much stressed by some poets and critics who write
about poetry. Some have even pooh-poohed it as a rather banal
conception. Leave that sort of thing to the people who write singing
commercials. It was a commonplace in the early Modernist period that
the poet's only duty is to find the unique expression for the unique thing
he wants to say. As Eliot put it, he may be talking to himself, or to no
one. It is a matter of good luck if the reader's point of view happens to
coincide sufficiently with the poet's for him to be able to understand
what the poet is saying. And the poet should not be expected to do
anything about this—at any rate, to do anything deliberate about it.
I. A. Richards said that poets who can be suspected of paying conscious
attention to communication will probably be found to be of a lower
order. There are historical and cultural reasons for the rise of this
doctrine which I cannot go into here. All I will say is that it has not been
universally shared. Some critics have attached paramount importance
to communication. For Tolstoy it was the sole criterion of art. Stern
moralist as he was, he was prepared to allow the title of art even to
works which, as he thought, promoted immorality. Communicative
efficacy was enough. Thus his objection to the French Symbolist poets
was not that they were bad men communicating bad things. His
objection was that they were bad men communicating nothing at all. I
think Tolstoy was fundamentally right. My only criticism of him is
that—influenced as we all are by his own tastes and training—he was
too ready to proclaim the communicative inefficacy of what he did not
like without finding out whether it was so for other readers. Tolstoy was
convinced that the Symbolists were completely unintelligible, and a
critic like Georges Ohnet was quite representative of his kind when he
urged Mallarmé, the most obscure of the Symbolist poets, to give up
that sort of thing and write comprehensibly like the immensely popular
authors of the time. But today Georges Ohnet and those authors are
forgotten and Mallarmé has thousands of readers. One should not be
too ready to say in advance what will or will not communicate.

The case of Tennyson, of course, is precisely the opposite. He has been blamed for not being obscure enough. It would be as rare to find him accused of obscurity as it would be to find him accused of bawdiness. As a matter of fact some of the reflective passages of *In Memoriam* are very difficult, and Tennyson is by no means always as sweetly pellucid as he is commonly held to be. And in his early work, when he was still a coterie poet, he was often ridiculed by reviewers for his obscurity. But no one will deny that Tennyson in many of his poems did eventually strike chords in the bosoms of his mid-Victorian public. It is not only that some of his poems were popular and his volumes sold well, that he represented poetry for the Victorians as Lord Roberts represented soldiering or W. G. Grace cricket. The evidence is in the very fabric of the language, all those familiar quotations that put Tennyson beside Shakespeare and Pope and Kipling as a source of literary ornaments and clichés. It is almost a test of knowledge of the English language to recognise 'Nature red in tooth and claw', and the 'little rift within the lute', and 'kind hearts are more than coronets', and ' 'tis better to have loved and lost than never to have loved at all', and all the rest of them. Tennyson's lines and phrases are quoted and misquoted, his best-known short poems parodied, his aphorisms cited for approval or mockery, as much today as they were in the nineteenth century. I am not saying that these things are Tennyson's best lines, or that the test of a poet is whether he supplies quotations for Victorian calendars. Quotability and memorability are not, it seems, thought specially important virtues nowadays. I have found that admirers of a new poet who were recommending him to me were somewhat put out by my request that they should quote a line or two of his. Certainly to have become a poetic father-figure is not a proof of permanent excellence; but it is a proof of communicative efficacy.

However, what I had in mind in suggesting this as the first criterion for permanent excellence is not so much this sort of communal communication as a capacity which only the individual reader can judge; the power to make us feel that what the poet says 'finds' us at once, immediately and finally. This is something that cannot be talked about, only indicated. We can only say that this or that poem hits the mark, does what it does so perfectly that there is nothing the critic needs to say. The following is an example from 'Come not, when I am dead' (R 699)

Come not, when I am dead,
    To drop thy foolish tears upon my grave,

To trample round my fallen head,
   And vex the unhappy dust thou wouldst not save.
There let the wind sweep and the plover cry;
   But thou, go by.

Child, if it were thine error or thy crime
   I care no longer, being all unblest:
Wed whom thou wilt, but I am sick of Time,
   And I desire to rest.
Pass on, weak heart, and leave me where I lie:
   Go by, go by.

But communicative efficacy will not take us very far as a criterion. It has often been pointed out that bad poems can have it as well as good. There are poems that stick obstinately in my mind that I would not dream of calling good, including some by Tennyson. I loathe, for example. 'The Lord of Burleigh' (R 603, ll 1–4).

In her ear he whispers gaily,
   'If my heart by signs can tell,
Maiden, I have watched thee daily,
   And I think thou lov'st me well.'

I find the whole poem distasteful, and if there is one word that particularly makes me want to retch, it is 'gaily'. So often in inferior Tennyson what we flinch from is not any clumsiness or bathos, but some kind of false, specious glitter. But I cannot deny that 'The Lord of Burleigh' has had many admirers, along with other poems of that kind that I do not particularly care for, such as 'Lady Clara Vere de Vere' (R 636). So communicative efficacy may be a *necessary* condition of good poetry, but it is not a *sufficient* condition.

We come nearer to a sufficient condition—indeed, some have held that we have a complete definition of poetry—in the second criterion of permanent excellence I am going to mention. This is what I will call abundant felicity of expression. Now here again we are in danger of tautology. Croce, as is well known, held that art *was* expression. At any rate no one will deny that it is impossible to talk about literature without it. Any poem, any literary work whatsoever, must be held to be in some degree expressive. Nor can the expression be thought of as something superadded. If you change the expression, you change the poem.

All the same, everyone will surely admit that there are some authors—and I mean good authors, not bad authors—in whom it is possible to imagine the expression bettered. Take the case of Anthony Trollope. There are good reasons for calling Trollope the best Victorian novelist, with his range of character, his comic genius, his wonderful gift for convincing dialogue—surely unsurpassed in the language—his profound tolerance, his moral sense that is all the more convincing because it works without the aid of self-importance and evangelical exhortations. And it could be said that, conservative as he was in temperament and literary habit, he really did more than some more lively authors to tackle unpopular and disturbing subjects and to change public opinion and not merely amplify it. But if we hesitate to call Trollope the best Victorian novelist, it may well be because of his undistinguished style. It is adequate, no doubt, for his purposes, but again and again we feel that Trollope has made no particular effort to find the right word. The result is a sort of greyness and drabness about the writing. No doubt if it had been livelier Trollope's novels would have been different. But it seems to me that they need not have been *radically* different. We could imagine a Trollope who wrote better, while still retaining the qualities for which we value him.

I am suggesting, then, that it is possible to separate, to some degree, what delights us in a writer's power of expression from the general pleasure and interest his work has to offer us. And it is in incidental felicities of expression that Tennyson is peculiarly strong. I could fill pages with the passages that come into my mind at this point. Is there a greater technical master in the language? I can illustrate only one aspect of this felicitousness, something rather neglected in poetry today, the emotional suggestiveness of sound-effect. It is by the use of this that through the elaborate syntactical patterns what I would like to call the essential *cry* of Tennyson comes through; take, for example, the following, from the 'Morte d'Arthur' (R 585):

So all day long the noise of battle rolled
Among the mountains by the winter sea . . . (ll 1–2)

. . . the many-knotted waterflags,
That whistled stiff and dry about the marge . . . (ll 63–4)

'I heard the ripple washing in the reeds,
And the wild water lapping on the crag.' (ll 70–1)

Dry clashed his harness in the icy caves
And barren chasms, and all to left and right

The bare black cliff clanged round him, as he based
His feet on juts of slippery crag that rang
Sharp-smitten with the dint of armed heels . . . (ll 186–90)

. . . and from them rose
A cry that shivered to the tingling stars,
And, as it were one voice, an agony
Of lamentation, like a wind, that shrills
All night in a waste land, where no one comes
Or has come, since the making of the world . . . (ll 198–203)

And on the mere the wailing died away. (l 272)

And from 'Godiva' (R 731, ll 73–6):

. . . and all at once
With twelve great shocks of sound, the shameless noon
Was clashed and hammered from a hundred towers,
One after one . . .

And from *The Princess* (R 741, Part iii, ll 348–53)

The splendour falls on castle walls
And snowy summits old in story:
The long light shakes across the lakes,
And the wild cataract leaps in glory.
Blow, bugle, blow, set the wild echoes flying,
Blow, bugle; answer, echoes, dying, dying, dying.

And from 'The Passing of Arthur' (R 1742, ll 29–37):

Then, ere that last weird battle in the west,
There came on Arthur sleeping, Gawain killed
In Lancelot's war, the ghost of Gawain blown
Along a wandering wind, and past his ear
Went shrilling, 'Hollow, hollow all delight!
Hail, King! to-morrow thou shalt pass away,
Farewell! there is an isle of rest for thee,
And I am blown along a wandering wind,
And hollow, hollow, hollow all delight.'

But it is unnecessary to go on with these examples. Even Tennyson's detractors have always conceded his skill in this kind of effect. Indeed the judicious admirer of Tennyson may well feel that he delighted too much in what Whitman called his 'finest verbalism'. I feel that I share the poet's own delight in this little bit from *Maud* (R 1037, Part i, ll 310–11): '. . . The snowy-banded, dilettante,/Delicate-handed priest intone' where, as a critic has said, Tennyson is turning double and treble somersaults. But I am slightly uneasy about whether this is quite in place in a tragic romance like *Maud*. I have the same sort of reservation even about a wonderful lyric like this from *The Princess* (R 741), which conveys the essential 'message' of the whole work better than the poem as a whole manages to do.

> Come down, O maid, from yonder mountain height:
> What pleasure lives in height (the shepherd sang)
> In height and cold, the splendour of the hills?
> But cease to move so near the Heavens, and cease
> To glide a sunbeam by the blasted Pine,
> To sit a star upon the sparkling spire;
> And come, for Love is of the valley, come,
> For Love is of the valley, come thou down
> And find him; by the happy threshold, he,
> Or hand in hand with Plenty in the maize,
> Or red with spirted purple of the vats,
> Or foxlike in the vine; nor cares to walk
> With Death and Morning on the silver horns,
> Nor wilt thou snare him in the white ravine,
> Nor find him dropt upon the firths of ice,
> That huddling slant in furrow-cloven falls
> To roll the torrent out of dusky doors:
> But follow; let the torrent dance thee down
> To find him in the valley; let the wild
> Lean-headed Eagles yelp alone, and leave
> The monstrous ledges there to slope, and spill
> Their thousand wreaths of dangling water-smoke,
> That like a broken purpose waste in air:
> So waste not thou; but come; for all the vales
> Await thee; azure pillars of the hearth
> Arise to thee; the children call, and I
> Thy shepherd pipe, and sweet is every sound,
> Sweeter thy voice, but every sound is sweet;
> Myriads of rivulets hurrying through the lawn,

> The moan of doves in immemorial elms,
> And murmuring of innumerable bees (vii, ll 177–207)

The poet here is like a dancer who moves from point to point with never an ugly movement. But there is a saying that *ars est celare artem*, and for me the poem does not conceal its art quite enough. For that reason 'And murmuring of innumerable bees' strikes me as less effective than Keats's: 'The murmurous haunt of flies on summer eves'.[3] Perhaps Tennyson was overfond of echoic verse. I say echoic verse rather than onomatopoeia, for onomatopoeia, the mysterious matching of sound to sense, is a more general quality of poetry. I would call 'Music that gentlier on the spirit lies,/Than tired eyelids upon tired eyes' (R 429, ll 50–1), onomatopoeic, for it is the soothing effect of music, not the actual sound, that is imitated. Homer and Virgil, of course, did use echoic verse now and then, but they used it more sparingly than Tennyson. It is the kind of thing that can help to make poetry more attractive to literary beginners, but more experienced readers are less impressed by it.

This overdoing of directly imitative verse is closely related to something that Gerard Manley Hopkins, when he began to 'doubt' Tennyson, called Tennyson's Parnassianism. I hesitate to call this a fault, as Hopkins hesitated when he drew attention to the passage I am going to quote. It comes from 'Enoch Arden' (R 1129). I do not think 'Enoch Arden' is one of Tennyson's best poems, but I am quite awed by the brilliance of the description of the shipwrecked Enoch's desert island (ll 568–95).

> The mountain wooded to the peak, the lawns
> And winding glades high up like ways to Heaven,
> The slender coco's drooping crown of plumes,
> The lightning flash of insect and of bird,
> The lustre of the long convolvuluses
> That coiled around the stately stems, and ran
> Even to the limit of the land, the glows
> And glories of the broad belt of the world,
> All these he saw; but what he fain had seen
> He could not see, the kindly human face,
> Nor ever hear a kindly voice, but heard
> The myriad shriek of wheeling ocean-fowl,
> The league-long roller thundering on the reef,
> The moving whisper of huge trees that branched

And blossomed in the zenith, or the sweep
Of some precipitous rivulet to the wave,
As down the shore he ranged, or all day long
Sat often in the seaward-gazing gorge,
A shipwrecked sailor, waiting for a sail;
No sail from day to day, but every day
The sunrise broken into scarlet shafts
Among the palms and ferns and precipices;
The blaze upon the waters to the east;
The blaze upon his island overhead;
The blaze upon the waters to the west;
Then the great stars that globed themselves in Heaven,
The hollower-bellowing ocean, and again
The scarlet shafts of sunrise—but no sail.

It *is* magnificent, is it not? But I see what Hopkins meant by calling it Parnassian. Tennyson is writing too much within himself. He is giving us 'Tennysonian' poetry, though of the very best quality.

Abundant felicity of expression, then, is one mark of the great poet; but it should not, I think, be the one on which advocates of the present value of Tennyson should lay most stress. Indeed to lay stress on it might be to concede too much to the view that at one time I was inclined to hold, that Tennyson is only at his best in lines and passages, not in complete poems. The decoration is splendid, but there is a kind of hollow at the centre. This was Matthew Arnold's view, though we must remember that Arnold was a rival poet and a bit tinged with artist's jealousy. Here, I have come, of course, to another sempiternal excellence, and one which Tennyson has often been accused of lacking. Again there is no agreed term today for what I have in mind. Matthew Arnold used the term 'architectonic power', but this may too much suggest Victorian classicism. Perhaps Clive Bell's 'significant form' is better; or perhaps one might speak of 'self-evident internal coherence'. Put more simply, it is a question of how well the poet's clothes fit him. Now there seem to me some poems of Tennyson that do suffer from structural weakness. In 'The Palace of Art' (R 400), for example, the allegory does not really come alive, and 'A Dream of Fair Women' (R 440), exists in the memory only as a series of cameos. But there are many of Tennyson's shorter poems in which no one has found any structural fault. It would be difficult to imagine how 'Mariana' or 'The Lady of Shalott', 'The Lotos-Eaters' or 'Ulysses', could be improved in this respect. But this perfect fittingness has often been denied to

Tennyson's four most ambitious poetic creations, *The Princess, In Memoriam, Maud,* and the *Idylls of the King.* Was Tennyson capable of poetic creation on a large scale? This may not be an essential characteristic of the great poet, but it has been very marked in the poets whom posterity has agreed to number among the greatest. And I think the feeling that Tennyson did lack this capacity is often behind the modern view that the Victorians were wrong to think him a great poet. So this question should be looked into.

The Princess does not give grounds for saying yes to it. Tennyson might be thought implicitly to have conceded the point by subtitling it 'a medley'. It contains both some of Tennyson's most delightful and some of his most irritating work. For me, despite some beautiful passages, especially at the end, *The Princess* remains interesting Victoriana rather than engrossing reading for its own sake. The exception that proves the rule is the blank verse lyrics it contains, such as 'Tears, idle tears' and 'Now sleeps the crimson petal, now the white', and the rhymed songs that were inserted into it later. And I am afraid that for me the *Idylls of the King* falls into the same category as *The Princess*. It is a remarkable document rather than a remarkable poem. As an epic it seems factitious. It should be said in Tennyson's defence that no English writing has succeeded in making a whole epic out of the Arthurian material. From *Sir Gawain and the Green Knight* onwards the best things that have been done with it have always been particular episodes or adventures. The Arthurian material still awaits its Virgil. Tennyson came nearer to being that than any other writer. But for me the *Idylls of the King* lives only in episodes and fragments, though a few of them contain some of Tennyson's finest poetry. They are not convincing evidence of his architectonic powers.

So we are left with *In Memoriam* and *Maud*. I will speak of *Maud* first, though it was published later. It is the most problematic of Tennyson's poems. The reader who tries to sum up his impressions of it finds himself pulled in different directions. It seems an extraordinary farrago. First of all it can be read for the story, which is not very clearly told and rather melodramatic, about a young man who has been ruined by the old 'Lord of the Hall', falls in love with the lord's beautiful daughter, kills her brother in a duel and escapes to France, has a mental breakdown and is finally cured by responding to the call of his country at war and (as I interpret the end of the poem) is killed in battle. Here Tennyson is offering entertainment in competition with popular novelists and dramatists of the time. But *Maud* can also be read as a denunciation of the manners and morals of the day, like the earlier 'Locksley Hall' (R 688).

And here Tennyson seems to be speaking through his unbalanced mouthpiece as the sage-poet and moralist in an angry mood. Finally, to the reader who has read Sir Charles Tennyson's biography, and R.W. Rader's fascinating study of the poem, *Maud* looks like an autobiographical document. Behind it must lie Tennyson's relationship with his strange father, the 'black blood' of the Tennysons, the fear of madness and mental disorientation which clouded Tennyson's life down to the 1850s and sent him after those endless 'water-cures'. It is all very remote from the pillar of the Victorian household he was to become. Behind *Maud* also is the rage against his relatives the d'Eyncourts, and his rejection, because of his poverty, by the girl he loved, Rosa Baring, at the prompting of her well-to-do family. And his relations with other women, Sophy Rawnsley and Emily Sellwood, are also shadowed in this way. And there is the whole complex of his love for Hallam, and his feeling, in the troubled years after Hallam's death, that he had lost the pivot of his life. What with the stagey plot, the denunciations of the age, and the constant pressure of personal material, it is no wonder that many readers both in the poet's own time and in ours have found the poem perplexing and chaotic. For some it is saved only, if at all, by its wonderful craftsmanship and exquisite lyric passages. And these it certainly has. Whatever we may think of *Maud* (R 1037) as a whole, it is surely impossible not to be moved by one part of it.

O! that 'twere possible
    After long grief and pain,
To find the arms of my true love
    Round me once again! (ii, 141–4)

A shadow flits before me,
    Not thou, but like to thee:
Ah Christ! that it were possible
    For one short hour to see
The souls we loved, that they might tell us
    What and where they be. (ii, 151–6)

Then I rise, the eavedrops fall
    And the yellow vapours choke
    The great city sounding wide;
The day comes, a dull red ball,
    Wrapt in drifts of lurid smoke
    On the misty river-tide.

Through the hubbub of the market
  I steal, a wasted frame . . . (ii, 202–9)

But the broad light glares and beats,
  And the sunk eye flits and fleets,
And will not let me be.
  I loathe the squares and streets,
  And the faces that one meets,
  Hearts with no love for me:
Always I long to creep
To some still cavern deep,
And to weep, and weep and weep
  My whole soul out to thee. (ii, 229–38)

If it is possible to say that any one passage takes us to the heart of the poem, it is surely this. But I believe that *Maud* is more than a few exquisite lyrics. There is a clue to the maze, and if we miss it we shall miss something essential that Tennyson has to give us. It is the presence of this clue that explains why, as Rader says, 'of all his poems *Maud* was peculiarly dear to Tennyson'.

Throughout his long later life, it was the poem he loved best to read aloud and the one he read most often and most powerfully. It was, above all, the one he most wished others to feel and understand. Shortly after the poem was published, for instance, a perplexed and annoyed Mrs. Carlyle watched Tennyson going about at Lady Ashburton's 'asking everybody if they had liked his *Maud*—and reading *Maud* aloud, and endlessly talking Maud, Maud, Maud'. Earlier, in Chelsea, he had forced her to approve the poem by reading it to her three times in insistent succession; so that now, used as she was to his crotchets, she thought his actions odd indeed. 'He was strangely excited about Maud,' she said, 'as sensitive to criticisms as if they were imputations on her honour.' . . . Rossetti describes a reading in which the poet shed tears and felt obviously strong emotion, and we hear of another occasion on which he read the poem 'with such intensity of feeling that he seized and kept quite unconsciously twisting in his powerful hands a large brocaded cushion which was lying at his side.' 'There was a peculiar freshness and passion in his reading of *Maud*,' his son writes, 'giving the impression that he had just written the poem, and that the emotion which created it was fresh in him. This had an extraordinary influence

on the listener, who felt that the reader had been *present* at the scenes
he described, and that he still felt their bliss or agony.'[4]

What then is this clue to *Maud*? I believe that the American writer
Henry Van Dyke realised what it was, when he heard the old Tennyson,
shortly before his death, read the poem. Van Dyke found himself

> amazed at the intensity with which the poet had felt, and the tenacity
> with which he pursued, the moral meaning of the poem. It was love,
> but not love in itself alone, as an emotion, an inward experience, a
> selfish possession, that he was revealing. It was love as a vital force,
> love as a part of life, love as an influence—nay, the influence which
> rescues the soul from the prison, or the madhouse, of self, and leads it
> into the larger, saner existence. This was the theme of *Maud*. And the
> poet's voice brought it out, and rang the changes on it, so that it was
> unmistakable and unforgettable.[5]

I think it is what Van Dyke calls the 'theme' of *Maud* that makes an
emotional unity out of the poem and makes it a convincing example, if a
strange one, of Tennyson's power to create order out of turbulence.
In Memoriam does not seem to me to have an equivalent principle of
unity. There is a better case than with *Maud* for regarding it as a
collection of separate poems, held together by the uniform metre which
Tennyson made his own and by recurrent similarities of thought and
mood. However it may have been for the Victorians, the intellectual
framework of the poem's debate is not now a living one for us. And
despite the efforts of A. C. Bradley and others I cannot see in the form of
the poem a manifest inevitability of structure. Yet I believe it to be the
greatest of Tennyson's poems, and for a reason which brings to me to
the last of those marks or notes of the great poet that I want to mention.
Once again our modern critical vocabulary fails to supply an adequate
term. What I have in mind is what the ancient writer known as Longinus
called 'the echo of a great soul'. Unlike the eighteenth century, or the
Victorians, we find such words, or words like 'sublime' or 'noble'
slightly embarrassing. Perhaps I can best convey what I am trying to
remind you of by using some words of C. S. Lewis from another context.

> It is sobering and cathartic to remember, now and then, our collective
> smallness, our apparent isolation, the apparent indifference of
> nature, the slow biological, geological and astronomical processes
> which may, in the long run, make many of our hopes (possibly some

of our fears) ridiculous. If *memento mori* is sauce for the individual, I do not know why the species should be spared the taste of it. . . . Those who brood much on the remote past or future, or stare long at the night sky, are less likely than others to be ardent or orthodox partisans.[6]

It is in the capacity to transcend the pettiness and egocentricity of most human concerns (including some of his own) that Tennyson seems to me among the supreme poets. He lives in a larger world than any other poet. Sometimes, it is true, the sheer immensity of the universe revealed by science is felt as a terrible alienation of man, as in *Maud* (R 1037, Part i, ll 634–8) when the narrator speaks of modern scientific knowledge of the stars as:

> A sad astrology, the boundless plan
> That makes you tyrants in your iron skies,
> Innumerable, pitiless, passionless eyes,
> Cold fires, yet with power to burn and brand
> His nothingness into man.

But sometimes, as in Tennyson's translation of a famous passage of Homer, this very largeness is what gives consolation and perspective.

> As when in heaven the stars about the moon
> Look beautiful, when all the winds are laid,
> And every height comes out, and jutting peak
> And valley, and the immeasurable heavens
> Break open to their highest . . . (R 1156, ll 11–15).

Nothing is more profoundly Tennysonian than the finale of *The Princess* (R 741, Conclusion, ll 106–15), when the poet soars away from Victorian preoccupations to a timeless serenity.

> But we went back to the Abbey, and sat on,
> So much the gathering darkness charmed: we sat
> But spoke not, rapt in nameless reverie,
> Perchance upon the future man: the walls
> Blackened about us, bats wheeled, and owls whooped,
> And gradually the powers of the night,
> That range above the region of the wind,
> Deepening the courts of twilight broke them up

Through all the silent spaces of the worlds,
Beyond all thought into the Heaven of Heavens.

In Memoriam has many aspects, and I have left myself time only to
mention this one, this largeness of vision.

There where the long street roars, hath been
The stillness of the central sea. (CXXIII, 3–4)

Listening to the roar, and the stillness, I find myself reminded of a
remark of A. J. P. Taylor's, that in politics and public affairs the
nineteenth century thought of itself as very chaotic, but in fact was very
stable. Perhaps something like this could be said about Tennyson, in
those parts of his work where he is truly classical.

And perhaps I may be allowed a final comment on that last word.
Eliot in his essay on Kipling says Kipling and Dryden were both
'classical poets'. 'They arrive at poetry through eloquence. For both,
wisdom has the primacy over inspiration. . . . Both are more concerned
with the world about them than with their own joys and sorrows, and
concerned with their own feelings in their likeness to those of other men
than in their particularity.'[7] (A romantic poet is presumably the
opposite.) When I read these lines I wonder whether Tennyson was a
classical or a romantic poet. Some of the poems and passages which may
appeal most to modern readers reflect the struggles and frustrations of a
divided nature and a sick soul. Here he seems a romantic poet. In other
poems he strives hard to achieve the balance and serenity for which his
soul yearned. But they strike a note which, while it may be sincere, is not
authentic, if I can use Lionel Trilling's distinction. They say what he
wanted to feel rather than what he really felt. It is my claim for *In
Memoriam*, and the reason why I believe it to be the greatest of
Tennyson's poems, that in it he unites the romantic and the classical. A
personal voice, while never ceasing to be a personal voice, becomes at
the great moments of the poem the voice of all humanity. That is, I
believe, the present—and the permanent—value of Tennyson.

2 Tennyson Inheriting the Earth

Christopher Ricks

I

Tennyson was angered by those who told him that what he had so well expressed had oft been thought and indeed oft expressed. Their tone implied that he had been detected.

> As is always the case with great writers, resemblances to something he had written were often found in books which he had never read, and in languages which he did not know, and he complained with much reason that there were critics who imagined that the same idea could never occur independently to two men looking on the same aspects of Nature. 'Tennyson suspected of plagiarism!' I once heard Browning say, when this subject was mentioned: 'Why, you might as well suspect the Rothschilds of picking pockets' (*Mem.*, ii, 204).

So, even to well-wishers, Tennyson was gruff.

> To the Rev. Arthur E. Moule
>
> > Jan 6th/80
>
> Dear Sir
>   I thank you for your book &
> your quotation from the Chinese
> Poet.
>   No man can write a single passage
> to which a parallel one may not be
> found somewhere in the literature
> of the world.
>
> > Yours very faithfully
> > A. Tennyson

He was galled by this two-sided foolishness: a foolishness about his poetry (poetry which it was preposterous to yoke locally, in sentiment and wording, to all these *outré* analogues), and a foolishness about the nature of poetry (a glory of which is its unreflecting apprehension of the community and commonalty of man). When, at the end of his life, he agreed to furnish for his poems some notes, he prefaced them with a note:

My paraphrases of certain Latin and Greek lines seem too obvious to be mentioned. Many of the parallelisms here given are accidental. The same idea must often occur independently to two men looking on the same aspects of Nature. There is a wholesome page in Eckermann's 'Conversations with Goethe', where one or the other (I have not the book by me) remarks that the prosaic mind finds plagiarism in passages that only prove 'the common brotherhood of man'.[1]

'I have not the book by me . . . .' Yet, though he was exasperated by any suggestion that his poems were ubiquitously, deeply and minutely in debt to foreign writers (whether from languages he knew, or with another fatuity, from those he did not know), such exasperation was necessarily different in kind from that which he felt when it was English poets whom he was told he was awash with. For to have translated must at least mitigate any tattle of plagiarism. If Tennyson did in fact call John Churton Collins a 'louse on the locks of literature' (I say 'if' because there is reason to believe that Edmund Gosse was prone to exaggeration, and that what Tennyson really called Churton Collins was a jackass—see also Chapter 3, especially note 10 for further discussion of this point), this may have been because Churton Collins's nit-picking made it seem that literature, Tennyson's and others', always had in its locks many a louse from the locks of its forebears. My note in *Notes and Queries* (March 1963) gives the opinions for this suspicion. Tennyson spattered with exclamation-marks and with growls the margins of Churton Collins's *Cornhill* articles about parallel passages, articles which became a deferentially hurtful book *Illustrations of Tennyson* (1891).

Since Tennyson was often under attack here, most notoriously from the absurd Bulwer-Lytton who in *The New Timon* (1846) had disdained Tennyson's 'borrowed notes' and his 'purloined conceits', it would not be wise to ask why he was so defensive. (*Cet animal est très méchant; quand on l'attaque, il . . . devient défensif.*) Yet for someone who had become so securely in possession of genius, talent, fame, respect, and reward, the mature Tennyson does manifest—in the intensity with which he responded to what he saw as the insinuation that he had unlocked other men's word-hoards—one aspect of that insecurity which is so evident in spite of his no-less-evident strength and staunchness of character. Early in his life the hideous anguish of his father, and then his hopes deferred and his heart made sick; these, with the black blood of the Tennysons, may be alive in Tennyson's morbid (he knew it was morbid) propensity to feel as if he were tattooed with every dispraise of his work while brushing off the outnumbering praises. Not that a reader of Tennyson, the man and the poet, should feel secure of biographical-critical affiliation even in this case; and Tennyson's passion about parallel passages is even less amenable to biographical interposing.

Such a passion, though, is likely to be related to an intense privacy in Tennyson's poetic practice. It was a privacy which took many forms because it guarded many different things from many different threats; a privacy, both personal and generalisable, which Tennyson publicly defended both inside and outside his poetry; a privacy which animated Tennyson's principles and practice as a poet, amongst other places in the tacit assurance which he finds within his own way of using the words of previous English poets. Tennyson, though the very words of previous English poets are of interest, value, and support to him, does not most characteristically *allude*. Or rather, the world of those readers who are to take Tennyson's allusions is in one respect (again most characteristically, not invariably) a smaller circle than what might be called the usual world of educated common readers such as one associates with Augustan allusion (or than the equally large world of now-insufficiently educated common readers which T. S. Eliot assists—something between a hindrance and a help—with the notes to *The Waste Land*).

Tennyson addressed a huge audience in *In Memoriam*, and it is a poem which often avails itself of the words of previous poets, but some of its strongest and deepest poetical reminiscences (Tennyson 'when he should have been broken-hearted had many reminiscences') are of words which only a tiny circle within the large circle of its original readers could ever have recognised and participated in. There is here one kind of privacy, the privacy of intimates. *In Memoriam* is and was magnificently accessible, because it has such anonymous amplitude of sense and of experience, open to such readers as know nothing of any particular words which had been uttered by that unnamed 'A.H.H.' whom it commemorates. But Tennyson was freed to achieve such width of accessibility by his incorporating within it, as a solid and substantial privacy, an intimate world of private allusion.

The most important of these confidential allusions are, naturally, those to the words of Arthur Hallam, whether in prose or in verse. Here it may be enough to recall[2] how delicately, with what freedom of gratitude and with what freedom from self-congratulation, Tennyson turned one of Hallam's compliments (XVIII, 1–4).

> 'Tis well; 'tis something; we may stand
>> Where he in English earth is laid,
>> And from his ashes may be made
> The violet of his native land.

With quiet grace and with a deeper timbre (this is no affectionate hyperbole), Tennyson is returning the compliment which Hallam had paid him: in his essay on Tennyson's poems, Hallam had quoted Persius, *Nunc non e tumulo fortunataque favilla/nascentur violae*, remarking: 'When this Poet dies, will not the Graces and the Loves mourn over him?' 'And from his ashes may be made . . .': Tennyson truly makes something, his allusion to Hallam's allusion murmuring something special for some few special readers and for the poet himself. For all readers, there is a public allusion which is to mingle with the confidential one; Tennyson acknowledged the presence of *Hamlet*:

> Lay her i' the earth,
> And from her fair and unpolluted flesh
> May violets spring.

And from Hallam's ashes, from his words (as Hallam had from Persius's) may be made this violet of his native land—'native land' being words not in Latin but in Hallam's and Tennyson's and Shakespeare's native tongue, words which return to, yet change, the words 'English earth'.

Tennyson's love of Hallam was itself part of a community of feeling. Section I (3–4) of *In Memoriam* solemnly declares 'That men may rise on stepping-stones/Of their dead selves to higher things'. The phrase 'their dead selves' recalls Tennyson's earlier self, and those of his other Cambridge friends, which may yet live as part of a moral evolution: the phrase had formed part of a poem by one of Tennyson's Cambridge friends in 1829 about another.

One strange thing about *In Memoriam*'s relation to time is that the modern reader is better able to appreciate the existence of these private allusions than almost all of the poem's original readers. The words of Arthur Hallam, and of smaller men, are known to us, and can be marshalled for us, precisely because Tennyson's words have given these other men's words a lasting importance. So that though no modern reader can feel the poignancy of personal reminiscence (unavailable even then except to intimates of Hallam), a modern reader may at least be able to imagine the existence of such feelings—within the poem of 1850—as very few readers then could have done.

One last instance of these intimate allusions may act as a stepping-stone to the other crucial way in which Tennyson's words call up the words of other poems—poems, rather than poets, since I come now to Tennyson's lifelong habit (remarked upon by Sir Charles Tennyson) of self-borrowing, of using again what he had originally created within quite another poem or passage. Tennyson rises on the stepping-stones of his past self, a self that is not dead. Tennyson combines these two aspects of allusive privacy—of sharing an intimate reference with a few special readers, and of sharing (with one's own earlier self alone, perhaps) a reference to the earlier origins of his own words—in the poem with which he chose to end his *Poems* (1832), 'To J.S.' (Edward, the brother of Tennyson's friend James Spedding, had died in August 1832). For the opening of 'To J.S.', Tennyson adapted the opening (all he had written) of part two of a poem which he had already sent to James Spedding. Spedding had quoted this in a letter to Edward, and so the adaptation acts as a kindly private allusion.

> The wind, that beats the mountain, blows
>   More softly round the open wold,
> And gently comes the world to those
>   That are cast in gentle mould.

The lines themselves have now been gently cast in another mould. Is Tennyson alluding here? The word allusion is inappropriate in so far as we think of an availability which is that of education or culture; and yet the word is appropriate if we think of an intimate, well-nigh private availability. For James Spedding had already seen, cast in their original mould, all these lines about the 'open wold' which now open 'To J.S.', and the only respectful and touching way in which the poet could acknowledge this (this fact which, malignly construed, would suggest that Tennyson was not moved by Edward's death to a new grief, to firsthand first-felt art) was by making this very fact alive within the meaning of the lines; that is, by incorporating within them an allusion—for J.S., at least (a person who is made public yet left private by being invoked by initials only, as 'A.H.H.' was later to be)—to their own changed movement and mould. Perhaps an allusion is like a congregation—it needs only one other than the priest. Perhaps even a single celebrant can allude, if he calls up that past self who first formed the lines which are now reformed in an inspiration of self-borrowing, the borrowing not only *from* a past self but *of* a past self.

I have written elsewhere about Tennyson's self-borrowing,[3] but I need now to do one further act of self-borrowing of my own: to reassert, first, that it was on the subject of time that Tennyson wrote those lines of his which are most likely to stand against time; second, that again and again Tennyson's self-borrowings explicitly concern time, so that the practice of self-borrowing manifests both an awareness of, and a means of countering, time; and, third, that Tennyson—often torn and tormented—stabilised his mind and found some rallying point in this particular evidence of the continuity of his own creativity.

Moreover, Tennyson quarried his past self and his past poems even when he was too young to have had much of a past. But then this self-borrower is the poet who said 'The first poetry that moved me was my own at five years old' (*Mem.*, ii, 93); who heard his own young voice call up an ancient voice: 'Before I could read, I was in the habit on a stormy day of spreading my arms to the wind, and crying out "I hear a voice that's speaking in the wind"' (*Mem.*, i, 11); and who, in a youthful poem, 'Ode to Memory' (R 210, ll 92–4), characterised memory in just this spirit:

> Artist-like,
> Ever retiring thou dost gaze
> On the prime labour of thine early days.

Tennyson's earliest surviving letter, written at the age of twelve, not only alludes but then alludes to another's alluding:

This passage,

> Restless thoughts, that like a deadly swarm
> Of hornets arm'd, no sooner found alone,
> But rush upon me thronging, and present
> Times past, what once I was, and what am now,

puts me in mind of that in Dante, which Lord Byron has prefixed to his 'Corsair'. 'Nessun maggior dolore, Che ricordarsi del tempo felice, Nella miseria.' (*Mem.*, i, 7–8)

Tennyson was later to recollect this sentiment of Dante's, in 'Locksley Hall' (R 688, ll 75–6): 'this is truth the poet sings,/That a sorrow's crown of sorrow is remembering happier things'. But what matters to my present purposes is the self-referential nature of Tennyson's instance or rather instances, the way in which the lines from Milton's *Samson Agonistes* now themselves 'present/Times past'; the way in which 'thronging' then describes a restless activity of mind ('puts me in mind of . . .'), as not only Milton but in quick succession Dante and Byron throng in (rather as, in 'Timbuctoo' [R 170, l 29] Tennyson's glimpse 'with ghastly faces thronged' is thronged with Milton: 'With dreadful Faces throng'd'); the way in which Byron's epigraph-allusion to Dante is itself an act of remembering, of being put in mind of times past. A restless hungry feeling for the life of past literature is in this young letter, and makes it a much more striking earnest of Tennyson's genius than is his poetical collocation elsewhere of three poets (two of them Milton and Dante again) in 'The Palace of Art' (R 400, ll 133–6):

> For there was Milton like a seraph strong,
>   Beside him Shakespeare bland and mild;
> And there the world-worn Dante grasped his song,
>   And somewhat grimly smiled.

There is a truer sense of tragedy in that early letter, and there is a counterbalancing sense of comedy in an early poem which Tennyson never published. 'I dare not write an Ode' (R 156), a poem which runs through all the reasons why the Muse or the reviewers will scorn him if he attempts an ode, a sonnet, an essay, an epic, or a sketchbook of sentiments, and finally comes to rest (ll 31–6):

> But ah! my hopes are all as dead as mutton,
>   As vain as Cath[oli]ck Em[anci]p[atio]n,
> E'en now my conscience pulls me by the button
>   And bids me cease to prate of imitation.
> What countless ills a minor bard environ—
> *'You're imitating Whistlecraft and Byron'*.

For even while writhing under the accusation of imitating, Tennyson is at it.

> Ah! what is man? what perils still environ
>   The happiest mortals even after dinner!
> A day of gold from out an age of iron . . . (*Don Juan*)

But then why should Tennyson not avail himself of Byron, since Byron had availed himself of Butler? 'Ay me! what perils do environ/ The Man that meddles with cold Iron!' (*Hudibras*). For if it was Butler, not Byron, who first brought out how charmingly the word *environ* may environ the word *iron*, it is Tennyson who then brings out that Byron's own name is in the environs.

But let me return to self-borrowing, which can act as a private or even secret act of allusion. It therefore has something in common with any allusion which calls upon secrecy itself, as when Tennyson created his line 'The secret bridal-chambers of the heart' ('The Gardener's Daughter', R 507, 1 244) from memories among which was a phrase from Arthur Hallam, 'my heart's chambers'. The privacy or secrecy here is the opposite of Milton's open audacity with the word 'secret' within the opening of *Paradise Lost*:

> Sing Heav'nly Muse, that on the secret top
> Of *Oreb*, or of *Sinai*, didst inspire
> That Shepherd, who first taught the chosen Seed . . .

—an audacity which made Bentley wish to change 'secret' to 'sacred'. Or, to stay more strictly with allusion, Tennyson's line from Hallam is the opposite (since Hallam's poems were a private possession, unlike Milton's) of Wordsworth's allusion, when, having unmistakably woven together his verbal reminiscences of *Paradise Lost*, 'On the Morning of Christ's Nativity', and *Comus*, Wordsworth at once continues 'And sure there is a secret Power that reigns/ Here . . . .'.[4] Yes indeed, but the secret power is also the unsecret power of Milton. Tennyson's heart-chambering of Hallam is more straightforwardly secret, and is part of the paradox of this poet, a paradox which was caught in a fine sentence of Richard Holt Hutton's: '*In Memoriam* is full of such magnifying-glasses for secret feelings, and doubts, and fears, and hopes, and trusts'.[5]

Self-borrowings and allusions have in common that they will often effect most when they manage to be unnarcissistically self-referential, when what is primary, their subject-matter, is secondarily at one with some impulse which underlies the making of allusions at all; it is characteristic of art to find energy and delight in an enactment of that which it is saying. When Tennyson's self-borrowings about time confront the challenge of time with their own nature, time is certainly not reduced to being merely part of the allusion's solipsistic workings; the parallelism is genuine, and it is respectful both of what is inside the

poem and of what is outside all poems. Self-borrowing was for
Tennyson a way of qualifying his own past without disowning it, and so
it is a pleasant coincidence that the lines from Tennyson ('Edwin
Morris', R 708, ll 25–7) which Churton Collins tactlessly or slyly chose
for the title-page of his *Illustrations of Tennyson*, unctuously putting
them into the present tense—

> And well his words became him: was he not
> A full-celled honeycomb of eloquence
> Stored from all flowers?

—are lines (the second and third) which Tennyson had borrowed from
an earlier poem of his and was here being critical of. Yet those words did
become him, words now placed dramatically as a criticism of the gifted
but self-gratifying poet Edwin Morris. Stored the lines had been, and
now their eloquence was stored from those early flowers of Tennyson's
own.

With self-borrowing as with the more usual and less private kind of
allusion, what matters is that both the new and the old should be
independently yet interdependently respected. Tennyson does not envy
or patronise his past self, and he embodies a similar vital propriety when
he avails himself of the words of others. As in the section of *In
Memoriam* about leaving the family home at Somersby (CII, 5–8)

> We go, but ere we go from home,
>   As down the garden-walks I move,
>   Two spirits of a diverse love
> Contend for loving masterdom.

Tennyson commented: 'First, the love of the native place; second, this
enhanced by the memory of A.H.H.' Yet the lines are enhanced by a
further memory, of those poems so often remembered in *In Memoriam*:
Shakespeare's Sonnets with their evocation in Sonnet 144 of 'two loves'
and 'two spirits'. So the two spirits of Tennyson's stanza are not only—
though they are primarily—the family love and the Hallam love, but the
two spirits of Tennyson and of Shakespeare. Without any of the
parricidal melodrama of 'the anxiety of influence', Tennyson and
Shakespeare here benignly contend for loving masterdom (CII, 17–20).

> These two have striven half the day,
>   And each prefers his separate claim,

Poor rivals in a losing game,
That will not yield each other way.

Rivals, but not—even while still contending—foes; just as Tennyson is necessarily in some sense here the rival of Shelley but is his grateful friend and not his foe; for Tennyson is here having to prefer *his* separate claim with the help of Shelley's words from *Queen Mab*: 'mutual foes, forever play/A losing game into each other's hands'. Tennyson's is no losing game, but a victory (over rivalry and envy, not over Shelley). And so into the last stanza:

I turn to go: my feet are set
    To leave the pleasant fields and farms;
    They mix in one another's arms
To one pure image of regret.

The love of his family and the love of Hallam become one—even as Shakespeare, and then Shelley, and now Milton ('the pleasant Villages and Farmes'), mix in the hands of Tennyson to become one pure image. It is a pure image of the living, loving relationship—even after acknowledging rivalry and 'loving masterdom'—which is the art of allusion. And 'mix' is exactly the kind of word which should alert us to the creative relationship between these poems present and past.

Such allusions may animate the reader even while they soothe the writer. To the loneliness of the poet or of the man, they offer company, the company of dear dead poets, and they draw comfort while acknowledging despair—'Two loves I have of comfort and despair,/Which like two spirits do suggest me still . . . ' (Shakespeare: Sonnet 144).

All comfort will sometimes strike a chill, if only because it is privy to the need to be comforted. Yet Tennyson warmed even to cold comfort:

Cold comfort unto thee and me
    But yet a comfort, proving still
There lives a power to shape our ends
    Rough-hew them as we will!
                ('I loving Freedom', R 619, ll 53–6)

Not the 'divinity' called up by Shakespeare, but the power of Shakespeare. It is a power which helps us to shape not only our ends but our means, our words. So it is natural to find elsewhere both of the words 'comfort' and 'power' again in the immediate vicinity of literary allusion in Tennyson. ('For so great a poet', said Humphry House, 'for a man as intelligent as he was, he seems to have lacked to quite an extraordinary degree a genuine internal conviction of the value of what he was doing.'[6]) In a very early poem, 'The Coach of Death', 'comfort' and 'power' come together again, and again with the support of another poet's words.

> But some have hearts that in them burn
>   With power and promise high,
> To draw strange comfort from the earth,
>   Strange beauties from the sky. (R 74, ll 29–32)

For Tennyson is sensing his own power and promise high, while drawing strange comfort not from the earth but from the strange beauties of *The Ancient Mariner*:[7]

> This heart within me burns.
>
> I pass, like night, from land to land;
> I have strange power of speech.

We have powers of speech as a community, here in the present, only because we form a community with the past. All language holds communion with the dead, those dead who have no memorial except the language which they maintained, and those other dead who left the memorials of literature.

> How pure at heart and sound in head,
>   With what divine affections bold
>   Should be the man whose thought would hold
> An hour's communion with the dead.
>
> (In Memoriam, XCIV, 1–4)

'Communion with the dead', as a phrase, is part of the heritage of the language; it was also the language of the man honoured in *In Memoriam* who had written of

> Spirits that but seem
> To hold communion with the dead.

So, in his poem of 'divine affections', Tennyson holds communion with the dead Hallam. Perhaps, too, by a complementary public allusiveness, with an earlier writer; for 'hold/An hour's communion with the dead' suggests some communication with 'O that it were possible we might/ But hold some two days' conference with the dead' (*The Duchess of Malfi*), especially if we then sense a further union, a deeper communion, of those words and the great cry in *Maud* (R 1037, Part ii, ll 141–4):

> O that 'twere possible
> After long grief and pain
> To find the arms of my true love
> Round me once again!

—where the vista of long grief and pain becomes even longer in that it resumes 'Westron winde, when wilt thou blow . . .', the age-old human grief and pain returning once again, before circling back to Webster once more, with:

> Ah Christ, that it were possible
> For one short hour to see
> The souls we loved, that they might tell us
> What and where they be.

See them, we shall never, and yet they are indeed able to tell us something. We hold communion with the dead. 'The dead are not dead but alive' ('Vastness', R 1346, l 36).

> Behold a man raised up by Christ!
>   The rest remaineth unrevealed;
>   He told it not; or something sealed
> The lips of that Evangelist.   (XXXI, 13–16)

Once again, something is truly told. Tennyson's lips are not sealed, and that is because his words are raised up by an earlier poet whose lips were not sealed, Alexander Pope:

> rest ever unreveal'd
> Nor pass these lips in holy silence seal'd.[8]

Tennyson's power to speak of such holy silence makes this not the whole truth, then, that 'The rest remaineth unrevealed'. A truth and an admission remain revealed.

But thou and I have shaken hands,
Till growing winters lay me low;
My paths are in the fields I know,
And thine in undiscovered lands. (XL, 29–32)

Yet not simply undiscovered, since this truth was one which Tennyson could know because it had been discovered by a traveller who did return: Shelley. 'To seek strange truths in undiscovered lands'. It is not only Hallam and Tennyson, but Tennyson and Shelley who shake hands, meeting and parting, *ave atque vale*.

The word 'influence' itself can focus the relation between the 'strange power of speech' and the heartening example of those who have previously exercised the power. Wordsworth is often serenely and unmisgivingly influenced by Milton's evocation of 'sweet influence'. When Tennyson uses the word while in the adjacent lines under the influence of Milton, it is with a dark sense of how little the power of speech is to be relied on. In 'Armageddon' (R 64, Part i, ll 14–23), his earliest poem (preceded only by a translation from Claudian and by an unfinished play), he thanks the power of Prophecy.

I stood upon the mountain which o'erlooks
The valley of destruction and I saw
Things strange, surpassing wonder; but to give
Utterance to things inutterable, to paint
In dignity of language suitable
The majesty of what I then beheld,
Were past the power of man. No fabled Muse
Could breathe into my soul such influence
Of her seraphic nature, as to express
Deeds inexpressible by loftiest rhyme.

The 'inutterable' is uttered, in part at least, and this is because Milton comes to breathe influence into Tennyson's soul: 'to express/Deeds inexpressible by loftiest rhyme' has been made less impossible because nearby are Milton's 'Distance inexpressible' and his 'lofty rhyme'. Milton, like his Lycidas, knew to build the lofty rhyme—knew it, and could teach it.

Later in 'Armageddon' (ll 104–7), 'Witchcraft's abominations' can be imagined as 'Obscene, inutterable phantasies' with the help of Milton's imagining of the monsters of Hell as 'Abominable, inutterable', an utterance to which Tennyson in his old age could still owe some of his power to speak, through the mouth of 'Lucretius' (R 1206, ll 157–8): 'And twisted shapes of lust, unspeakable,/Abominable'.

One of the few occasions when Tennyson does what he was very reluctant to do (and Wordsworth and Byron, for very different reasons, delighted in doing), quote a phrase within quotation marks in a poem, comes when the unutterable is uttered with the acknowledged support of Milton in 'Perdidi Diem' (R 269, ll 9–15):

> My soul is but the eternal mystic lamp,
> Lighting that charnel damp,
> Wounding with dreadful rays that solid gloom,
> And shadowing forth the unutterable tomb,
> Making a 'darkness visible'
> Of that which without thee we had not felt
> As darkness, dark ourselves and loving night . . .

Tennyson wrote this poem when he was about twenty, and it is one of the earliest of his telling shudders at 'the unutterable tomb'. 'When I was about twenty, I used to feel moods of misery unutterable! I remember once in London the realization coming over me, of the *whole* of its inhabitants lying horizontal a hundred years hence.'[9]

The point is not so much that Tennyson has recourse to words of the *in——able* or *un——able* form, as that he often has recourse to the words of previous poets when engaged with the *in——able* or the *un——able*. 'Toiling in immeasurable sand' ('Will', R 1017, l 16) measures itself against, alongside, Shelley's 'Those deserts of immeasurable sand' (*Queen Mab*); as does 'Forward, backward, backward, forward, in the immeasurable sea' ('Locksley Hall Sixty Years After', R 1359, l 193), backward-forward measuring itself against Shelley's 'the immeasurable sea' (*Daemon of the World*), with Tennyson then continuing: 'Swayed by vaster ebbs and flows than can be known to you or me'. Yet the couplet is swayed by something known to Shelley, just as those 'undiscovered lands' were partly, thanks to Shelley, 'in the fields I know'.[10]

Not that such allusions, even when they are quiet to the point of reticence or privacy, can save those moments when something is askew or factitious. Thus, although Tennyson may sincerely say of Hallam 'I doubt not what thou wouldst have been' (CXIII, 8), he cannot truly imagine that career of Hallam's; Tennyson assumes the voice of Milton: 'A *potent voice* of Parliament', but what had been potent in *Paradise Lost* is here impotent. The truth of Tennyson's poetry is often in inverse proportion to its assurance (T. S. Eliot said of *In Memoriam*: 'Its faith is a poor thing, but its doubt is a very intense experience'),[11] which is why there is a narrowness in the line 'Drunk in the largeness of the utterance' (*The Lover's Tale*, R 299, Part i, l 462), actually compounded by Tennyson's recalling Keats's utterance, here the nemesis of allusion:

> Some mourning words, which in our feeble tongue
> Would come in these like accents (O how frail
> To that large utterance of the early Gods!)[12]

Tennyson, against the grain of his temperament, sought to turn Keats's sense both of frailty and of largeness, into a single confident impulse. To my ear, one of the few strikingly successful uses in Tennyson of such confident allusion (where finding utterance is itself alluded to) is a satirical one, the insinuating portraiture of 'A Character' (R 218, ll 13–18):

> He spake of virtue: not the gods
> More purely, when they wish to charm
> Pallas and Juno sitting by:
> And with a sweeping of the arm,
> And a lack-lustre dead-blue eye,
> Devolved his rounded periods.

The last line of the stanza gets its conclusive mordancy, its rounding-off the rhetorical falsity, from the way in which Horace's *verba devolvit* had devolved to James Thomson: 'Devolving through the maze of eloquence/A roll of periods',[13] which in its turn devolved to Tennyson, with Thomson's 'A roll of periods' authoritatively rounded into 'Devolved his rounded periods'. The line is full in its evocation of the finest empty verbalism, and this fullness is partly the cooperative presence of Thomson. It is the opposite of the emptiness of allusion in 'Eleänore' (R 367, ll 44–8):

> How may full-sailed verse express,
>   How may measured words adore
>   The full-flowing harmony
> Of thy swan-like stateliness,
>   Eleänore?

This breezily has Shakespeare's wind in its sails, not full (the repetition of 'full-' within two lines empties it) but empty of inspiration. Shakespeare's lines earned the right (which they then effortlessly waived) to congratulate themselves on how they met the challenge of a rival poet: 'Was it the proud full sail of his great verse . . . ';[14] Tennyson does not rise comparably to the challenge of Shakespeare.

His allusions rise when they speak, not of a fullness reasserted, but of an emptiness encouragingly peopled from the past, an emptiness defied by a poetic solidarity. In early Tennyson, such an allusion might gain the support of its own nature (allusion filling a hollowness) with the support of, among others, Milton. As in 'Ode: O Bosky Brook' (R 264, ll 55–8):

> In midnight full of sound,
> Or in close pastures soft as dewy sleep,
> Or in the hollow deep
> Of woods, whose counterchanged embroidery . . .

Compare *Paradise Lost*:[15]

> Abject and lost lay these, covering the Flood,
> Under amazement of their hideous change.
> He call'd so loud, that all the hollow Deep
> Of Hell resounded.

It is the opposite of a hideous change which has now been counterchanged, and the hollow deep does resound, full of sound. More deeply, in *In Memoriam*, 'hollow'—which has one kind of appropriateness to allusion (which can fill the hollow)—joins 'echo', which has another (an allusion being itself a kind of echo, as Pope appreciated in echoing Dryden's 'echoes').[16] Here Tennyson couches his phantom Nature and her music in the accents of Spenser (III, 9–12):

> 'And all the phantom, Nature, stands—
>   With all the music in her tone,
>   A hollow echo of my own,—
> A hollow form with empty hands.'

'From out waste places comes a cry', 'A hollow echo of my own': the cry becomes Tennyson's own, but it comes from a place which is not waste: Spenser's 'The hollow Echo of my carefull cryes' (*The Shepherd's Calendar: August*). A substantial continuity stands against the phantom of the hollow and the empty.

Similarly, the last line of section VII, 'On the bald street breaks the
blank day', is informed with something other than blankness, since the
lines by Wordsworth which had just proffered Tennyson the wise
innocent assistance of the words 'like a guilty thing' (themselves owed
by Wordsworth to *Hamlet*) also furnished Tennyson with the word
'blank' as a shield against misgivings: 'Blank misgivings of a
Creature . . .'.[17] With quite a different tone but with the same propriety
of self-reference in allusion (proper because the allusion's being in some
way about allusion is secondary to the line's sheer descriptive felicity),
Tennyson sees Lucretius's vision of the atom-streams of the universe,
'Ruining along the illimitable inane' (R 1206, l 40), his words supported
by the awe-filled precariousness which Shelley had given to the unusual
noun: 'Pinnacled dim in the intense inane'.[18]

The very workings of an allusion may reflect that which they explicitly
and primarily work upon:[19] 'And on the liquid mirror glowed/The clear
perfection of her face' ('Mariana in the South', R 361, ll 31–2). The glow
is not just in the strong delicacy with which 'perfection' replaces yet does
not expunge the expected reflection ('And on the liquid mirror
glowed/The clear reflection of her face'), but also in the way in which, by
its reflection from Shelley and his 'liquid mirror' (not his alone, of
course), the words reflect their own two-in-one meaning and nature. The
poignancy is of a loneliness contemplated in ghostly company, and
company is for Tennyson—as I suggested when speaking of 'They mix
in one another's arms/To one pure image of regret'—one pure image of
the art of allusion.

So a characteristic Tennysonian allusion is drawn to the words 'with
me', where the company called for includes a summoned spirit. 'The tide
of time flowed back with me' ('Recollections of the Arabian Nights',
R 205, l 3) is in the company of Arthur Hallam and his 'the tide of time'.
'Bathe with me in the fiery flood' ('Life of the Life', R 504, l 9) defiantly
delights in the company of the spirit of Shakespeare: 'And the delighted
spirit/To bathe in fiery floods' (*Measure for Measure*). 'Ah, bear me with
thee, smoothly borne' ('Move eastward', R 661, l 9) has the company not
only of the 'happy earth', but also of the poet who had so happily
imagined it: the earth, advancing from the west, 'beares thee soft with
the smooth Air along' (*Paradise Lost*). *In Memoriam* cries out not to be
divided from Hallam: 'Oh, wast thou with me, dearest, then', and it
moves to the hope that in death they are not divided (CXXII, 9–13):

> If thou wert with me, and the grave
> Divide us not, be with me now,

And enter in at breast and brow,
Till all my blood, a fuller wave,

Be quickened with a livelier breath . . .

If we ask what it is which enters and quickens the lines into a fuller wave, part of the answer is the intimate companionship of Hallam's own words in 'To One Early Loved': 'Tho' innumerable waves divide us now'. There is a turn akin to that in 'with me', in the fearful opening of section L:

Be near me when my light is low,
    When the blood creeps, and the nerves prick
    And tingle; and the heart is sick,
And all the wheels of Being slow.

Tennyson gains the courage to contemplate these fears because 'Be near me' is so magnificently unspecific an address; it speaks to God, and to Hallam, but also—since it avails itself of his words—to the supporting predecessor Shelley: 'My blood is running up and down my veins;/A fearful pleasure makes it prick and tingle:/I feel a giddy sickness of strange awe' (*The Cenci*); and 'urge/The restless wheels of being on their way' (*Queen Mab*).

In the face of lonely suffering and anxiety, these allusions embody the comfort of company: 'Be near me . . .'. Comfort is warm once again. 'Alone and warming his five wits/The white owl in the belfry sits' ('Song—The Owl', R 204, ll 6–7)—not alone, because of the blessed company of Shakespeare: 'Bless thy five wits! Tom's a-cold' (*King Lear*).

Knowledge is itself company and solidarity; and Tennyson's knowing, from Shakespeare's Sonnet 78, the phrase 'heavy ignorance', is one of the things shared by the lines in 'The Vision of Sin' (R 718, ll 191–4) travestying the brotherhood of man and the brotherhood of poets:

'Drink to Fortune, drink to Chance,
    While we keep a little breath!
Drink to heavy Ignorance!
Hob-and-nob with brother Death!'

Tennyson is lightly toasting a brother poet whose words are not dead, this being the proper counterpart to improper hob-nobbing 'with brother Death' or with Shakespeare.

II

I want now to consider Tennyson's allusions, and their often being in some way imaginatively self-referential, in relation to two longer vistas. The first is intrinsic to allusion as the use of the words of previous poets; the second is intrinsic to Tennyson's apprehension of what was most daunting even to the greatest poetry.

In a consideration of Dryden and Pope, called *Allusion: The Poet as Heir*, I took the cue of J. B. Broadbent's words: 'Literary allusion can be a lesson in the abuse of authority, as well as in the generous spending of an inheritance. We need an essay on "The poet as heir" '.[20] I believe that most allusions of subtlety and efficacy are likely to be related in some important way to inheritance. For Augustan poets, the essential or central inheritance was royal, political, legal, and literary; and the art of allusion in Augustan poetry was fecundated by a parallelism—one which acknowledged dissimilitude in the similitude—between its own nature as allusion (as a kind of inheritance) and its preoccupations (with particular forms of inheritance). So a paradigm of Augustan allusion is this:[21]

> Say from what cause, in vain decry'd and curst,
> Still Dunce the second reigns like Dunce the first?
>
> Alluding to a verse of Mr. *Dryden*'s not in *Mac Flecno*
> (as it is said ignorantly in the Key to the *Dunciad, pag.* 1.)
> but in his verses to Mr. *Congreve.*
> *And* Tom *the Second reigns like* Tom *the First.*

But what is seen as the central or essential inheritance may change in history, and this change both creates and is created by changes within literature and within its shaping spirit of imagination. Thus for Wordsworth, the essential inheritance is not royal, political, legal or literary, but perceptual and phenomenological. What we most importantly inherit is sense, including the eye and the ear.

> Therefore am I still
> A lover of the meadows and the woods,
> And mountains; and of all that we behold
> From this green earth; of all the mighty world
> Of eye, and ear—both what they half create,
> And what perceive . . .[22]

Wordsworth's note half-acknowledges Edward Young's perception: 'This line has a close resemblance to an admirable line of Young's, the exact expression of which I do not recollect'. Wordsworth's line is half-created from Young's 'Night Thoughts': 'And half-create the wondrous world they see'. This moment in 'Tintern Abbey' is for me a paradigm of literary allusion in Wordsworth, and elsewhere I hope to show why. Here I shall say only that Wordsworth's allusion is profoundly related to his deepest sense of the human inheritance, and is mightily or wondrously self-referential.

What then is central as inheritance for Tennyson? Only a small part is played by what for Byron and his poems had a central importance: the literal inheritance of wealth. Some part, though, for there is in Tennyson a sufficient memory of his father's disinheritance. Here Tennyson's debt to this same poem by Edward Young is very different from Wordsworth's, and is—in these lines from Tennyson's earliest original composition (*The Devil and the Lady*, R 7, I, i, ll 62–4)—exactly a matter of debt:

> Nor would I borrow of that usurer
> Procrastination, whose vast interest
> Is almost higher than his principal.

Tennyson borrows, from Young's 'Night Thoughts', 'Procrastination is the Thief of Time'. But as a borrower, not as a thief—that is, not as a plagiarist. ('Why, you might as well suspect the Rothschilds of picking pockets.')

The metaphor which would see allusion itself as an interest which accrues, this catches something beautifully anti-mercenary in *In Memoriam* (I, 5–8):

> But who shall so forecast the years
>   And find in loss a gain to match?
>   Or reach a hand through time to catch
> The far-off interest of tears?

For it is not a forecast, but a retrospect, which reaches a hand through time to catch the far-off interest of Shakespeare's tears.

> How many a holy and obsequious tear
> Hath dear religious love stolen from mine eye,
> As interest of the dead.
>   (Sonnet 31)

do not take away
My sorrow's interest; let no mourner say
He weeps for her.

(*Rape of Lucrece*)

The liquid drops of tears that you have shed
Shall come again, transformed to orient pearl,
Advantaging their loan with interest.

(*Richard III*)

Shakespeare's words come again, transformed, and advantaging their loan with interest, as 'The far-off interest of tears'.

The unworldly grief there in Tennyson's debt to Shakespeare has its satirical complement in another debt to Shakespeare, explicitly contrasting poetry and money, where Tennyson (in 'The Brook', R 1025, ll 1–8) borrows from that usurer Shylock (who says of money 'I make it breed'):

Here, by this brook, we parted; I to the East
And he for Italy—too late—too late:
One whom the strong sons of the world despise;
For lucky rhymes to him were scrip and share,
And mellow metres more than cent for cent;
Nor could he understand how money breeds,
Thought it a dead thing; yet himself could make
The thing that is not as the thing that is.

It would be unwise to make too much of the fact that one of the best collectors of Tennyson's borrowings is a man called Loane.[23] That there is something wrong with the critical sense of that earlier collector, Churton Collins, comes out in the lavish moneyed inappositeness of his metaphors for Tennyson's allusions:[24]

We live amid wealth as prodigally piled up as the massive and myriad treasure-trove of Spenser's 'rich strond', and it is now almost impossible for a poet to strike out a thought, or to coin a phrase, which shall be purely original.

As Virgil has, on a very large scale, drawn on the literary wealth of Greece and of his native land, so Tennyson has, on a corresponding scale, drawn not on that wealth merely, but on the wealth which has been accumulating since.

For it was exactly such metaphors which proved bankrupt when
Tennyson tried to expend them on Virgil: 'All the chosen coin of fancy
flashing out from many a golden phrase' ('To Virgil', R 131, 1 4).
Accumulated wealth crushes such tenderness as we hear in the far-off
interest of tears.

It is growth, not accumulation, which allusion must trust in. Happy
growth, though, is not often trusted by Tennyson, and it was imprudent
of him to appropriate Marvell's 'vegetable love' for 'The Talking Oak'
(R 675, ll 181–4):

> 'I, rooted here among the groves
>   But languidly adjust
> My vapid vegetable loves
>   With anthers and with dust.'

The words 'languidly adjust' and 'vapid' are all too self-referential.
Nothing grows, especially nothing more charming than Marvell's
original lines.

Growth may be thought of as digestive, and allusion may self-refer by
speaking of eating and drinking. Again Tennyson seems to me much less
successful when being happy at such a thought than when distressed by
it. Most of his best allusions embody a contrariety between a malign
force and a benign solidarity. I have said earlier that I think that
Tennyson's 'Drunk in the largeness of the utterance' is not supported
but felled by Keats's 'O how frail/To that large utterance of the early
Gods!', and I should add that 'Drunk' does nothing to help; it merely
suggests that Keats is on tap. Whereas Pope was able to 'draw light'
most exquisitely and sardonically from Milton's 'draw Light',[25]
Tennyson's affirmative line in 'Perdidi Diem' (R 269, 1 78) is too flatly
parallel to—and in competition with (insufficiently rotated from)—
Milton's line in the same passage ('And drink the liquid Light'): 'The
latest energies of light they drink' is not, to my ear, alive with singular
energy.

But Tennyson does indeed digest such allusions when the poem
speaks of the wrong kind of feeding while the allusion embodies the
right kind. The wrong kind, say, because unreflecting, ignorant, and so
less than fully human: 'a savage race,/That hoard, and sleep, and feed,
and know not me' ('Ulysses', R 560, ll 4–5).

> What is a man,
> If his chief good and market of his time

> Be but to sleep and feed? a beast, no more:
> Sure he that made us with such large discourse,
> Looking before and after, gave us not
> That capability and god-like reason
> To fust in us unused.

(Hamlet)

Tennyson, looking before and after, uses Shakespeare's words as part of a large discourse; the words are not hoarded, or slumbered on, but they are honourably fed upon, in contrast to the honourless daily round of which they speak. Once again the word 'know' is a quiet signal.

Or, to stay with the conjunction of sleeping and feeding, there is the sinister non-human predatoriness, deep below consciousness, of 'The Kraken' (R 246, l 12), 'Battening upon huge seaworms in his sleep'. Shelley had netted 'The dull weed some sea-worm battens on' (*Prometheus Unbound*); for his imagination, not dull at all, had fed—not battened—on *Hamlet*: 'Duller shouldst thou be than the fat weed/That rots itself in ease on Lethe wharf' ('Fat' fattened into Shelley's 'battens'.[26]) In 'The Kraken', Tennyson feeds—not battens—upon Shelley, swelling 'sea-worms' into 'huge seaworms' within this enormous enlargement by which the monstrous batteners become the even more monstrously battened-upon: from 'The dull weed some sea-worm battens on', to 'Battening upon huge seaworms in his sleep'. 'In his sleep', with its lethal calm and its own digestiveness, is a stroke of grim genius. It was left to T. S. Eliot to tame the Kraken—as he believed the Church of England to tame Christianity—down into the hippopotamus:

> The hippopotamus's day
> Is passed in sleep; at night he hunts;
> God works in a mysterious way—
> The Church can sleep and feed at once.

The numb comedy is not in the spirit of Tennyson, but the way with the allusion somewhat is, particularly in its use within a retrograde evolution or reversion (from the battener to the battened-upon; from the awe-inspiring Kraken to the outdone hippopotamus). So perhaps Tennyson would forgive Eliot; and forgive Robert Lowell, for what, as an heir of Tennyson, he did in 'Ford Madox Ford' with 'I the heir of all the ages, in the foremost files of time' ('Locksley Hall', R 688, l 178):

> The sun
> is pernod-yellow and it gilds the heirs
> of all the ages there on Washington
> and Stuyvesant, your Lilliputian squares,
> where writing turned your pockets inside out.[27]

Ford's pockets are not the only things that have been turned inside out, with the great vista of human history transformed into something moneyed, of the surface, and Lilliputian. Perhaps Tennyson would even forgive Geoffrey Hill[28] for his smouldering re-creation of the last line of *In Memoriam* ('To which the whole creation moves') as 'music's creation of the moveless dance,/the decreation to which all must move'.[29]

It was in the terms of health and disease that Arthur Hallam (whose words Tennyson was approaching there, the words 'The Love/Toward which all being solemnly doth move') characterised the progress or regress of poetry, in his essay 'On Some of the Characteristics of Modern Poetry, and on the Lyrical Poems of Alfred Tennyson' (*Englishman's Magazine*, August 1831). Englishmen had once 'imbibed' knowledge and power; but 'since that day we have undergone a period of degradation' and even 'the French contagion'; we are no longer 'untainted'. 'Hence the melancholy which so evidently characterises the spirit of modern poetry; hence that return of the mind upon itself and the habit of seeking relief in idiosyncrasies rather than community of interest'.

Yet allusion may resist such melancholy; allusion is the return of mind upon something other than itself, and is an honourable seeking of relief in community of interest. Many of Tennyson's allusions pit against disease or degradation or failure their own act of health-giving inheritance and continuity—in *The Princess* (R 741, Part vii, ll 195–200), for instance:

> let the wild
> Lean-headed Eagles yelp alone, and leave
> The monstrous ledges there to slope, and spill
> Their thousand wreaths of dangling water-smoke,
> That like a broken purpose waste in air:
> So waste not thou;

Nothing was left to waste purposelessly in air; something was preserved from John Armstrong's *The Art of Preserving Health* (a book in the

Tennysons' library): 'The virgin stream/In boiling wastes its finer soul in air'. In a later Tennyson poem, 'Lucretius (R 1206, 1 22), 'those tender cells', ravaged by poison, are likewise cells inherited from Armstrong's *Art of Preserving Health*: 'This caustick venom would perhaps corrode/ Those tender cells that draw the vital air.'

Armstrong's poem of 1744 was hardly well-known to Victorian England, and Tennyson's debt to him may have been a private arrangement, an intimate support. But when we hear that 'The woods decay, the woods decay and fall' ('Tithonus', R 1112, 1 1), we are to hold against this vision of decay one of Tennyson's favourite passages from Wordsworth, the undecaying vision of paradox: 'The immeasurable height/Of woods decaying, never to be decayed' (*The Prelude*). Yet the consolation is itself paradoxical, since Tithonus envies the woods which decay and fall, and is anguished at the thought that he is decaying, never to be decayed. Once again it is in the spirit of Tennyson's own allusions that William Empson should have imagined a dark redesigning of Tennyson's line, yet with allusion's endurance standing against the waste: 'The waste remains, the waste remains and kills'.[30]

One thing that must remain, a central inheritance, is heredity, both the common heredity of man and the particular heredity of men. The poet who thinks of himself ruefully as 'Fame's millionth heir-apparent'[31] has an intuitive sense of a relation between an art of allusion (itself an inheritance such as may be a heredity) and those pre-occupations with which such art is continuous. Whether human heredity or family heredity is to be praised—or, more usually, blamed—is often near the heart of a Tennyson poem, as it is near the heart of the Shakespearean tragedy which most often supported Tennyson, *Hamlet*. While still in his early teens, he knew that the Devil can cite *Hamlet* to his purpose.[32]

> I must be violent, fierce,
> And put that ugly disposition on
> Which is my portion by inheritance
> From my great grandsire Lucifer.
> > (*The Devil and the Lady*, R 7, I, v, ll 190–3)

What had been bitterly 'antic' ('To put an antic disposition on') is good-humouredly ugly.

But take Tennyson's description of *Maud*: 'This poem of *Maud or the Madness* is a little *Hamlet*, the history of a morbid, poetic soul, under the blighting influence of a recklessly speculative age. He is the heir of

madness . . .'. 'Morbid, poetic': it is an equivocal comma. The morbidity
is personal and historical (and age-old, too), and the influence of the age
is 'recklessly speculative' both as calling everything in doubt and as
mammonist. 'Did he fling himself down? who knows? for a vast speculation had failed' (*Maud*, R 1037, Part i, l 9). The narrator is 'the heir
of madness', and is under the blighting influence of the age; Tennyson
creates this highly allusive poem by being the heir of sanity, under the
fostering influence of previous ages. 'I the heir of all the ages, in the
foremost files of time': those are words which Churton Collins bent
upon Tennyson's allusions, characteristically mangling them: 'In his
own noble words, we moderns are "the heirs of all the ages"'.

The heir of madness: the poetic practice which seeks to be the heir of
sanity is a kind of therapy, and it has a direct parallel in the way in which
Arthur Hallam called upon literary allusion as an act of therapeutic love
towards Tennyson: 'Fare thee well. I hope you do fare well, and make
head against "despondency and madness"'. If Tennyson did make head
against them, it would be because of standing alongside, not only
Hallam's imaginative love, but Wordsworth's: 'We Poets in our youth
begin in gladness;/But thereof comes in the end despondency and
madness'.[33] Resolution and Interdependence, or, 'We Poets'. Hallam
had alluded in a similar spirit, but to a different poet, when he brought
to bear upon Tennyson's fear of blindness Milton's sense of what might
be involved in saying 'We Poets': 'Surely', wrote Hallam to Tennyson,
'you owe it to us all not to let yourself carelessly fall into the misery of
blindness. It is a hard and sad thing to barter the "universal light" even
for the power of "Tiresias and Phineus prophets old"'. Hallam then
continued at once, with an unforced sense of the supreme daily *writing*:
'Write to me yourself on this subject and speak openly and fully'.[34]

> . . . nor somtimes forget
> Those other two equal'd with me in Fate,
> So were I equal'd with them in renown,
> Blind *Thamyris* and blind *Maeonides*,
> And *Tiresias* and *Phineus* prophets old.
>
>   (*Paradise Lost*, iii, ll 32–6)

Insanity will speak insanely of heredity:

> And fair without, faithful within,
> Maud to him is nothing akin:
> Some peculiar mystic grace

Made her only the child of her mother,
And heaped the whole inherited sin
On the huge scapegoat of the race,
All, all upon the brother.

(*Maud*, R 1037, Part i, ll 483–6)

The inherited sin is both original sin and family malaise, and this in an
age when the human race is starting to plead diminished responsibility
('But if sin be sin, not inherited fate, as many will say . . .', 'The Wreck',
R 1334, l 85). 'This heir of the liar' (*Maud*, i, l 761): the words suggest
that mendacity is in the blood. 'Our sons inherit us' ('The Lotos-Eaters',
R 429, l 118)—they do not simply inherit from us. Tennyson, in
conversation, gave this as an instance of the real test of a man: 'Can he
battle against his own bad inherited instincts, or brave public opinion in
the cause of truth?'[35] And the public opinion might precisely be one
which told lies about the human or the family inheritance.

Tennyson asks how to confront sorrow (*In Memoriam*, III, 13–16):

And shall I take a thing so blind,
    Embrace her as my natural good;
    Or crush her, like a vice of blood,
Upon the threshold of the mind?

But the poet is not crushed (as in a vice) by a vice of blood; rather he
embraces the inherited virtues of Shakespeare ('I do confess the vices of
my blood', *Othello*) and of Shelley (in *Queen Mab*):

Let priest-led slaves cease to proclaim that man
Inherits vice and misery, when Force
And Falsehood hang even o'er the cradled babe,
Stifling with rudest grasp all natural good.
Ah! to the stranger-soul, when first it peeps
From its new tenement, and looks abroad
For happiness and sympathy, how stern
And desolate a tract is this wide world!
How withered all the buds of natural good!
No shade, no shelter from the sweeping storms
Of pitiless power! On its wretched frame,
Poisoned, perchance, by the disease and woe
Heaped on the wretched parent whence it sprung
By morals, law, and custom . . .

Tennyson would not have concurred with the religious or political insistences here, but his words show that he did look abroad, here in Shelley, for sympathy, and found some shelter.

'Proclaim that man/Inherits vice and misery': if man does, it may be with the help of the devil. What had been a diabolical lineage for Milton:

> And when Night
> Darkens the Streets, then wander forth the Sons
> Of *Belial*, flown with insolence and wine.[36]

was preserved by Dryden, with a true poetic lineage, as a collusive political family: 'During his Office, Treason was no Crime./The Sons of *Belial* had a glorious Time.'[37] Dryden here is acknowledging Milton, without 'insolence', as his poetic father.[38] What Tennyson preserved, as his portion of the inheritance, was exactly the wounding insolence; not explicitly the allusive lineage of 'sons of Belial' but its accompanying zeugma which transforms the sons into this brother who scorns the brotherhood of man (but who cannot destroy the brotherhood of poets):

> What if that dandy-despot, he,
> That jewelled mass of millinery,
> That oiled and curled Assyrian Bull
> Smelling of musk and of insolence,
> Her brother . . .
>
> (Maud, R 1037, Part i, ll 231–5)

It is blighting influence which Tennyson calls upon fostering influence to help him realise in his art. The fear that the world will become worse (even worse) than it is—this is politics and geology each seen under the other's aspect. Hallam might have helped to resist political destruction, but he could hardly have staved off all disaster, and the imagination of *In Memoriam* (CXIII, 8–20) goes out most to what it fears:

> I doubt not what thou wouldst have been:
>
> A life in civic action warm,
>   A soul on highest mission sent,
>   A potent voice of Parliament,
> A pillar steadfast in the storm,
>
> Should licensed boldness gather force,
>   Becoming, when the time has birth,

A lever to uplift the earth
And roll it in another course,

With thousand shocks that come and go,
   With agonies, with energies,
   With overthrowings, and with cries,
And undulations to and fro.

Yet within this vision of catastrophe something is steadfast; it is the acknowledgement of that which does not come and go, in the line 'With thousand shocks that come and go'. For Tennyson's alteration, in 1855, of 'many shocks' to 'thousand shocks' calls up *Hamlet*: 'The thousand natural shocks/That flesh is heir to'. Tennyson is heir to Hamlet's and to Shakespeare's strength, rather as the line to the yew-tree, 'Sick for thy stubborn hardihood' (II, 14), achieves its own hardihood by availing itself of the stubborn hardihood which Walter Scott had achieved within those two words.[39] 'With thousand shocks that come and go': because of what flesh is heir to, the line embodies a hope which disdains the cynical songs within 'The Ancient Sage' (R 1349, ll 146–9):

The poet whom his Age would quote
   As heir of endless fame—
He knows not even the book he wrote,
   Not even his own name.

Every man is an heir, and Tennyson tried to take his own advice, in his capacity as the Ancient Sage: 'Cleave ever to the sunnier side of doubt' (l 68). Another poem written in old age, 'By an Evolutionist' (R 1408, ll 13–14), strives to be grateful to old age for its evolutionary subjugation of the brute and the beast within man.

If my body come from brutes, though somewhat finer than their
      own,
   I am heir, and this my kingdom. Shall the royal voice be mute?

But the evolutionary heredity of man might be vitiated by the heredity of a particular man. Tennyson has an epigram, 'Darwin's Gemmule' (R 1228), on Darwin's hypothesis that a gemmule was thrown off from each cell, and transmitted from parents to offspring, thus being responsible for physical inheritance.

Curse you, you wandering gemmule,
  And nail you fast in Hell!
You gave me gout and bandy legs,
  You beast, you wanted a cell!
Gout, and gravel, and evil days—
  (Theology speaks, shaking her head)
But there is One who knows your ways!

Tennyson found intolerable both the prospect that man might improve beyond recognition and so be superseded, and the prospect that man might degenerate and so be superseded. T. S. Eliot's truthful joke about Whitman and Tennyson encompasses more than just the politics of Tennyson: 'Both were conservative, rather than reactionary or revolutionary; that is to say, they believed explicitly in progress, and believed implicitly that progress consists in things remaining much as they are'.[40]

'Contemplate all his work of Time': what helped Tennyson to contemplate (in *In Memoriam*) both the ascent and the descent of man was his being descended from (and ascending from) previous poets. Geology and evolution rolled on, 'Till at the last arose the man': and, thirteen lines later, the concept of arising arises again (CXVIII, 25–8):

Arise and fly
The reeling Faun, the sensual feast;
Move upward, working out the beast,
And let the ape and tiger die.

This moves upward from Shakespeare's 'sensual feast' (Sonnet 141), by an evolution which is paradoxical and mysterious: it does not arise and fly the words 'sensual feast'; it is not 'working out' Shakespeare; it does not claim to be Shakespeare's superior, with Shakespeare merely 'The herald of a higher race'; and so it is fortified against both an intolerable superseding and an intolerable unadvancingness, fortified by its creation of an evolution which is a type of true continuity, neither rising above nor sinking back upon.

'And let the ape and tiger die': but not let die such words themselves. '. . . I might perhaps leave something so written to after-times as they should not willingly let it die'. Milton's hopes are any poet's, and perhaps Edward FitzGerald remembered them when he expressed his hopes for Tennyson, doing so with a comically convoluted allusion to Shakespeare and to the whirligigs of the time machine: 'But with all his

faults, he will publish such a volume as has not been published since the
time of Keats: and which, once published, will never be suffered to die.
This is my prophecy: for I live before Posterity.'[41] 'This prophecy
Merlin shall make; for I live before his time' (*King Lear*).

It was the prophecy of sinking which most haunted Tennyson, and it
fused the geological, the evolutionary, and the social:

> A land of old upheaven from the abyss
> By fire, to sink into the abyss again
> ('The Passing of Arthur', R 1742, ll 82–3)

—even as the achievement of King Arthur is sinking into the abyss
again. The vision of 'then back into the beast again' made Tennyson
grateful for all the sounding words which are not just watchwords:

> Is there evil but on earth? or pain in every peopled sphere?
> Well be grateful for the sounding watchword, 'Evolution' here,
>
> Evolution ever climbing after some ideal good,
> And Reversion ever dragging Evolution in the mud.
> ('Locksley Hall Sixty Years After', R 1359, ll 197–200)

It is not just the word 'reversion' there, but the opening 'Is there . . .',
which makes me hear in Tennyson's lines a reversion to Pope's sounding
words: 'Is there no bright reversion in the sky,/For those who greatly
think, or bravely die?'[42] What had been bright and in the sky may be
dark and 'in the mud'. Yet the evil reversion has its sense of what a
bright reversion might be, grateful to Pope (and the word 'grateful'
perhaps precipitated by Pope's 'greatly'). Tennyson's lines are a dark
counterpart to Byron's bright reversion to Pope, Byron tacitly making
an exception for Pope within an 'Elegy to the Memory of a Fortunate
Gentleman':

> He that reserves his laurels for posterity
> (Who does not often claim the bright reversion)
> Has generally no great crop to spare it, he
> Being only injured by his own assertion . . .[43]

For Tennyson, the answer to the question 'Is there no bright
reversion in the sky?' is not merely 'No'. Worse, there is a dark reversion
in the sky. For it is the sky which brings home the nature of earth, our

earth doomed to an extinction manifest in the long vistas of geological and astronomical time and space. 'Man is as mortal as men': and poetry and nature and the very earth itself are all as mortal as man. Everyone who has read Tennyson knows how urgently and variously this sense of our dying earth pressed upon Tennyson. Humphry House seized as especially salient the late poem 'Parnassus' (R 1410, 1 16) in which there tower above the twin peaks of Parnassus two dark unignorable forms: 'These are Astronomy and Geology, terrible Muses!' The sight is worlds away from the Augustan confidence of Denham:[44] ''Twas this the Ancients meant, Nature and Skill/Are the two tops of their Parnassus Hill'.

In affectionate company, Tennyson could contemplate without terror 'The man in Space and Time'; the company of Horace and of a young girl lend equanimity, for instance, to Tennyson's tender dealings with geology and astronomy in the Epilogue to 'The Charge of the Heavy Brigade at Balaclava' (R 1307). But though the terrible Muses did not always strike terror into Tennyson, they often struck sadness (*Maud*, R 1037, Part i, ll 633–8):

> brought to understand
> A sad astrology, the boundless plan
> That makes you tyrants in your iron skies,
> Innumerable, pitiless, passionless eyes,
> Cold fires, yet with power to burn and brand
> His nothingness into man.

'Iron skies' is itself an extraordinary compacting of the terrible Muses of astronomy and geology. Perhaps his greatest contempt was for those who affected to be moved by this thought of 'nothingness', and the most cutting poem he ever wrote shows how early it was so ('A Character', R 218, ll 1–6):[45]

> With a half-glance upon the sky
> At night he said, 'The wanderings
> Of this most intricate Universe
> Teach me the nothingness of things.'
> Yet could not all creation pierce
> Beyond the bottom of his eye.

Tennyson's earliest verses (apart from schoolboy translations of Horace), his 'Translation of Claudian's "Rape of Proserpine"' (R 3), begin:

'The gloomy chariot of the God of night,/And the wan stars that sickened at the sight . . .'. Yet Claudian's words had not meant quite that; rather, 'the stars darkened by the shadow of his infernal chariot' (Loeb translation).[46] 'Wan' and 'sickened' are Tennyson's, or rather they are Milton's ('The blasted Starrs lookt wan') and Pope's ('The sick'ning stars fade off th' ethereal plain'). Tennyson aligns himself with Milton's vision of the hideous infection of the universe by Sin and Death, and with Pope's vision of the hideous extinction of the universe by universal darkness. The central impulse, even in these earliest lines of Tennyson, is less the imagining of 'the wan stars that sickened at the sight', than our sickening wanly at the sight of the stars. What saves Tennyson from being sickened into silence is the supporting presence of poets who have not faded off the ethereal plain.

This may seem too early, for Tennyson personally and for the age. But these Victorian pangs were eighteenth-century pangs, and the young Tennyson was aware of those poets who had tried to override their fears. When young, he imitated them, misguidedly, and he achieved their hollow hopefulness. So William Mason[47] described the earth's extinction:

> The time will come, when Destiny and Death,
> Thron'd in a burning car, the thund'ring wheels
> Arm'd with gigantic scythes of adamant,
> Shall scour this field of life, and in their rear
> The fiend Oblivion: kingdoms, empires, worlds
> Melt in the general blaze:

at which point Mason hey-presto'd the feats of fame:

> when, lo, from high
> Andraste darting, catches from the wreck
> The role of fame, claps her ascending plumes,
> And stamps on orient stars each patriot name,
> Round her eternal dome.

In 'Time: An Ode' (R 119, ll 51–6) Tennyson explicitly acknowledged a debt to Mason, but it was a bad debt, because it helped the young Tennyson to arrive at spirited vacancies, moving from what was felt:

> On, on they go along the boundless skies,
>   All human grandeur fades away

Before their flashing, fiery, hollow eyes;
    Beneath the terrible control
    Of those vast armèd orbs, which roll
Oblivion on the creatures of a day.

—lines which honourably anticipate the words 'boundless', 'skies'
'hollow', 'eyes' and even 'fires' ('fiery' here) within the 'sad astrology' in
Maud—moving immediately from this which was felt to what was not.

Those splendid monuments alone he spares,
    Which, to her deathless votaries,
Bright Fame, with glowing hand, uprears
Amid the waste of countless years.

'Live ye!' to these he crieth; 'live!
'To ye eternity I give—'

—and so for a further nine lines which four more times cry 'Live'.
Or there is Erasmus Darwin:

Roll on, YE STARS! exult in youthful prime,
Mark with bright curves the printless steps of Time;
Near and more near your beamy cars approach,
And lessening orbs on lessening orbs encroach;—
Flowers of the sky! ye too to age must yield,
Frail as your silken sisters of the field!
Star after star from Heaven's high arch shall rush,
Suns sink on suns, and systems systems crush,
Headlong, extinct, to one dark centre fall,
And Death and Night Chaos mingle all!
—Till o'er the wreck, emerging from the storm,
Immortal NATURE lifts her changeful form,
Mounts from her funeral pyre on wings of flame,
And soars and shines, another and the same.[48]

These are lines which imagined themselves to be an answer, half a
century later, to the end of *The Dunciad*, an answer set apparently to
culminate in *The Dunciad*'s final rhyme ('Thy hand, great Anarch! lets
the curtain fall;/And Universal Darkness buries all'): 'Headlong,
extinct, to one dark centre fall,/And Death and Night and Chaos mingle
all!' Yet not culminating there, because Darwin snatches from 'the
wreck' the reassuring figure of Immortal Nature. This too is a

reassurance which sought the support of allusion; for the last line, 'And soars and shines, another and the same', attempts (itself both another and the same, a type of the allusion) to do for Pope—'All as the vest, appear'd the wearer's frame,/Old in new state, another yet the same'⁴⁹—what Pope had done for Dryden: 'His Son, or one of his Illustrious Name,/How like the former, and almost the same'.⁵⁰ But Tennyson did not believe that Nature was Immortal. Not even the 'What if . . .' of a poet incomparably greater than Mason or Erasmus Darwin could convince Tennyson. Wordsworth's 'Vernal Ode' was 'composed to place in view the immortality of succession where immortality is denied, as far as we know, to the individual creature':

> What if those bright fires
> Shine subject to decay,
> Sons haply of extinguished sires,
> Themselves to lose their light, or pass away
> Like clouds before the wind,
> Be thanks poured out to Him whose hand bestows,
> Nightly, on human kind
> That vision of endurance and repose.⁵¹

Tennyson too believed in God, but not because in showing us the stars He bestowed a vision of endurance and repose; rather because He offered, against the desolating vision of the stars, a vision of endurance and repose. God's love would effect what human love must hope to find, 'The countercharm of space and hollow sky' (*Maud*, R 1037, Part i, l 641).

When the stars are merry in Tennyson, within this same imagining in *Maud* of the sad astrology which is modern astronomy, it is because he is attended by an unmodern poet, Spenser: 'All night therefore attend your merry play':⁵²'—And you fair stars that crown a happy day/Go in and out as if at merry play . . .'. When Tennyson himself writes an epithalamion, and there is a 'happy earth', this is because the love here and now is matched by a poetic companionship undaunted by astronomy. 'Ah, bear me with thee, smoothly borne' is, as I have said, a line borne along by the happy earth in *Paradise Lost*, which 'beares thee soft with the smooth Air along'. Or, still within an epithalamion, there is Tennyson's loving companionship with the poet Thomson, from whom Tennyson here inherited the right kind of gloom; the moon is to rise (*In Memoriam*, Epilogue, ll 117–24):

> And touch with shade the bridal doors,
>   With tender gloom the roof, the wall;

And breaking let the splendour fall
To spangle all the happy shores

By which they rest, and ocean sounds,
And, star and system rolling past,
A soul shall draw from out the vast
And strike his being into bounds . . .

The terrors of vastness ('Swallowed in Vastness, lost in Silence,
drowned in the deeps of a meaningless Past', 'Vastness', R 1346, 1 34),
of star and system, are happily mollified into 'tender gloom'. The
question of whether we should call *allusion* such a use of the words of a
previous poet seems to me much less important than the enduring
comfort which Tennyson found here, a solidarity with the unterrible
muse of Thomson against the terrible Muses. Even 'Parnassus' is
supported less by its final intervention from a divine outer space—'let
the golden Iliad vanish, Homer here is Homer there'—than by a smaller
muse than Homer's who furnished for Tennyson something which had
at least not vanished yet. Tennyson's hope at first, 'Lightning may shrivel
the laurel of Caesar, but mine would not wither', and his succeeding
despair, 'Poet, that evergreen laurel is blasted by more than lightning!',
are given the courage to contemplate the possibilities by their tribute to
Marvell's laurels, unblasted: 'And *Caesars* head at last/Did through his
Laurels blast'.[53] At last, perhaps, for the poet too; but not as yet. Which
is not a refutation of astronomy and geology, but is a paradoxical
inspiration in the face of them. Whereas Wordsworth had high hopes of

Art divine,
That both creates and fixes, in despite
Of Death and Time, the marvels it hath wrought,[54]

Tennyson placed his modest hopes in the Marvells that had wrought it.
   Geological catastrophe (more specifically, the geological theory of
catastrophism), death, and Tennyson's love for Hallam come together
in an early sonnet which Humphry House picked out as showing that
'the intensity of affection for Hallam, even in his lifetime, was linked to
the terrors of speculation':[55]

'Twere joy, not fear, claspt hand-in-hand with thee,
To wait for death—mute—careless of all ills,
Apart upon a mountain, though the surge

> Of some new deluge from a thousand hills
> Flung leagues of roaring foam into the gorge
> Below us, as far on as eye could see.
>   ('If I were loved, as I desire to be', R 353, ll 9–14)

What the ear hears, not drowned by the roaring foam, is that Tennyson's words—'some new deluge'—are clasped hand-in-hand with Marvell's: 'And Earth some new Convulsion tear', in another poem on 'two perfect Loves', 'The Definition of Love'.

The earth's convulsions are alive, too, in the 'Ode on the Death of the Duke of Wellington' (R 1007, ll 259–61), in lines created from Tennyson's continuity with both his own poetry and that of another.

> For though the Giant Ages heave the hill
> And break the shore, and evermore
> Make and break, and work their will . . .

For it is not just that in these lines Tennyson was working his will, making and breaking his own earlier lines from a draft of 'The Palace of Art':

> Yet saw she Earth laid open. Furthermore
>   How the strong Ages had their will,
> A range of Giants breaking down the shore
>   And heaving up the hill. (R 413–14)

If Tennyson can endure the sight of the hills as living heaving hills, it is by turning Wordsworth to a different purpose:

> Or caught amid a whirl of desert sands—
> An Army now, and now a living hill
> That a brief while heaves with convulsive throes—
> Then all is still.

But then Wordsworth himself had not been relying entirely, in this poem 'To Enterprise', on his own enterprise. *Note* (1822): ' "Awhile the living hill/Heaved with convulsive throes, and all was still". Dr Darwin describing the destruction of the army of Cambyses'.

The 'Ode on the Death of the Duke of Wellington' has tragic courage. 'The Golden Year' (R 714, ll 27–31) has comic courage.

'Ah, though the times, when some new thought can bud,
Are but as poets' seasons when they flower,
Yet oceans daily gaining on the land,
Have ebb and flow conditioning their march,
And slow and sure comes up the golden year.

Yet poets' seasons may still flower long after the poets, and conditioning
the march of Tennyson's lines is an old thought which newly buds:
Shakespeare's, 'the hungry ocean gain/Advantage on the kingdom of
the shore' (Sonnet 64). The poets' seasons do at least lessen the terror of
the aeons of astronomy and geology.

'We sleep and wake and sleep, but all things move;
The Sun flies forward to his brother Sun;
The dark Earth follows wheeled in her ellipse;
And human things returning on themselves
Move onward, leading up the golden year.

Even the darkest sounds may be lightened by these human things
returning on themselves (*In Memoriam*, XXXV, 8–12).

But I should turn mine ears and hear

The moanings of the homeless sea,
    The sound of streams that swift or slow
    Draw down Æonian hills, and sow
The dust of continents to be.

For 'the homeless sea' is not a friendless thought, since Shelley gave
those words his habitation and his name.

The hills are shadows, and they flow
    From form to form, and nothing stands;
    They melt like mist, the solid lands,
Like clouds they shape themselves and go.
                                    (*In Memoriam*, CXXIII, 5–8)

Nothing stands? Some words of Wordsworth stand, and help to shape
the line 'Like clouds they shape themselves and go': 'A thousand,
thousand rings of light/That shape themselves and disappear'.[56]
    Tennyson believed that only the divine miracle of personal immor-
tality would make it conceivable that there could be such things as

> jewels five-words-long
> That on the stretched forefinger of all Time
> Sparkle for ever . . .

> (*The Princess*, R 741, Part ii, 355–7)

Geological time, which made jewels, then made them valueless, ephemeral. Yet he was enabled to write, exquisitely and courageously, about such faith and such fears, not only by his religious belief but also by his taking up an inheritance, a various poetic inheritance with which he confronted our human inheritance: our inheriting the earth, and its being a dying earth.

The last poem which he finished, 'The Dreamer' (R 1456, 1 2), tells us that ' "The meek shall inherit the earth" was a Scripture that rang through his head'. To the wailing Voice of the Earth, whirling in space and time, with its 'iron Truth' and its 'Age of gold', the dreamer replies with the lyrical fervour of hope. The mighty J. Paul Getty was doubtless within his rights to say that 'The meek shall inherit the earth, but not its mineral rights', yet Tennyson sang of the fact that mineral rights are only as enduring as minerals themselves.

3 Tennyson and the Literature of Greece and Rome

Theodore Redpath

In the wake of his brothers, Frederick and Charles, Alfred Tennyson was sent by his father at the end of 1815, that is, at the age of six-and-a-half, to the Grammar School at Louth. Before that he had been to a village school not far from his father's rectory at Somersby; but that fascinating and gifted father of his, George Clayton Tennyson the younger,[1] had already been taking an active part in the education of all the three eldest boys, Frederick, Charles, and Alfred. Alfred used to tell in later years how, before his father considered him fit to go to the school at Louth, he had made him recite by heart on successive mornings all the four Books of Horace's *Odes*. That amounted to over one hundred poems, a good three months' autumn discipline! George Tennyson's insistence on Horace was to continue when Alfred returned home after over four years at Louth, one result being that he did not come to care for Horace till well over thirty years later. On the other hand, it is clear from the full annotations written by Alfred in the copy of Virgil which he received at the age of nine[2] that his study of that poet was comparably intensive, and yet there is no sign that it evoked any antipathy towards the Mantuan. George Tennyson had also started Alfred and his brothers off on Greek, and they evidently continued to receive some sort of education in both languages, with a ration of literature, at the Louth school; it is doubtful, however, whether the instruction there was at all substantial, and Alfred himself wrote, years later, the condemnatory words: 'In the little Louth school C[harles] and I learnt— well—*absolutely* nothing'.[3] Soon after the age of ten, however, Alfred fell under the spell of Pope's *Homer*, and wrote masses of couplets in Popean style. His reading of Pope's version may well have whetted his appetite for intensive study of the Greek original.

The really fruitful period for Alfred's classical education, in any case, began after he and Charles left Louth in 1820. From then on, for over seven years, they were educated at home by their father, whose teaching was however, supplemented by lessons in Classics from a Roman Catholic priest. George Tennyson had collected quite a good Classical library, both for his own purposes, and for educating his sons. He had, moreover, made himself into a good Latinist, and tolerable Grecian, and also acquired some knowledge of Syriac and Hebrew and one or two modern languages, during his years at St John's College, Cambridge, from 1796 to 1801. He evidently did not spend all his time swotting, however. According to family tradition, for instance, he at least took a second or two off to fire a pistol through one of the windows of his Chapel.[4] In subsequent years he went to considerable pains to further improve his Greek with the special object of giving his sons a thorough grounding in the language and acquainting them with the main landmarks in Greek literature. George Tennyson was evidently a stimulating and encouraging teacher, and, though there were interruptions through his physical and mental ups and downs, and periodic absences from home, the boys seem to have made good headway with their Classical studies. Alfred continued throughout his life to read and reread Greek and Latin literature, particularly poetry. He had his favourite writers: Homer, Theocritus, Pindar, Lucretius, Virgil, Catullus, and, in later years, the Horace he had so heartily detested.

My chief concern, however, is to consider the relation to Classical literature, not of the *man* Tennyson, but of his *poetry*. This relation seems to me to be *at least* four-fold. First, there are his translations of Classical poetry. Second, there are the touches of language, imagery and thought strewn through his work, which were probably taken consciously, subconsciously or unconsciously, from ancient writers. Third, there are the structural, formal and textural features *taken over from*, or, at least, *reminding one of* the work of one or other such writers. Fourth (and for me this is the most important topic), the treatment by Tennyson of Classical themes. I shall discuss each of the first three matters, dwelling rather more on the last.

At Lincoln there are some translations, dating from schoolboy days, of some of Horace's *Odes*. From what I have seen of these they seem competent and promising as one would naturally expect; but somewhat more interesting is Tennyson's free translation of the first 93 lines of the *De raptu Proserpinae* of the fourth century AD poet Claudian (R 1). I say 'somewhat more interesting' for several reasons. First, because it shows Tennyson already coming to grips, and remarkably successfully, with one of the more *recherché* poets included in his father's library, a poet who was, moreover, at least something of a stylist. Second, because the poem deals with the theme alluded to by Milton in the well-known lines in *Paradise Lost* (IV, 268–72), which may have had some special significance for Tennyson, and which were certainly one of the inspirations of his own late poem 'Demeter and Persephone'. Third, because Tennyson did it all in the Popean couplets in which he had already extensively exercised himself, and even adopted some very Popean diction, such as 'volumes' for the coils of a snake; and, moreover, that this was virtually his farewell to the Popean couplet. We find it no more in his translations and scarcely at all in his original poems.[5] In any case, that kind of apprenticeship was over.

More interesting still, though, are Tennyson's experiments in translating Homer—all from the *Iliad*, and probably all written in 1863–64. Two of them he published, that of VIII, 542–61, the end of the day on which the Trojans had driven the Greeks back close to their ships; and that of XVIII, 202–31, the passage where Achilles steps down from the wall to the edge of the trench, and roars a challenge at the Trojans. There are also two less successful pieces, from Books IV and VI, which Tennyson wisely left unpublished. These are in the Pierpont Morgan manuscript, which also contains two versions of eight more lines of the passage from XVIII.[6] Neither of these unpublished versions is really satisfactory. The two published translations, on the other hand, despite some interesting defects and sacrifices, are admirable. When I first looked into them carefully I was particularly struck with Tennyson's masterly resourcefulness in remaining generally faithful to the Greek and yet writing lines of real energy within the restrictions of blank verse, with its shortage of syllables as compared with the original. Later I was delighted to learn that Tennyson seems to have been aware of the value and at least part of the nature of his achievement: 'Must be judged by comparison with the Greek. Can only be appreciated by the difficulties overcome,' he said to John Addington Symonds. The two specimens make it a matter for regret that Tennyson did not do much more. Arnold was certainly wrong when he said that Tennyson's blank verse would not be suitable for translating Homer. Here, for example, is the first specimen:

So Hector spake; the Trojans roared applause;
Then loosed their sweating horses from the yoke,
And each beside his chariot bound his own;
And oxen from the city, and goodly sheep

In haste they drove, and honey-hearted wine
And bread from out the houses brought, and heaped
Their firewood, and the winds from off the plain
Rolled the rich vapour far into the heaven.
And these all night upon the bridge of war
Sat glorying; many a fire before them blazed:
As when in heaven the stars about the moon
Look beautiful, when all the winds are laid,
And every height comes out, and jutting peak
And valley, and the immeasurable heavens
Break open to their highest, and all the stars
Shine, and the Shepherd gladdens in his heart:
So many a fire between the ships and stream
Of Xanthus blazed before the towers of Troy,
A thousand on the plain; and close by each
Sat fifty in the blaze of burning fire;
And eating hoary grain and pulse the steeds,
Fixt by their cars, waited the golden dawn.[7]

Tennyson's rendering of the long final simile has been much admired, and it is certainly far superior to the halting hexameters which Arnold himself produced as a version. The simile is too long for me to compare with the original, but I feel bound to try to discuss the qualities, and try to measure the success of the opening lines. The first line: 'So Hector spake; the Trojans roared applause' is strong and economical. Tennyson has reduced the fourteen-syllable Greek line to ten, notwithstanding his addition of the word 'applause', which is only *implied* by the Greek κελάδησαν. The next line: 'Then loosed their sweating horses from the yoke', again reduces the fourteen-syllable Greek line to ten, by omitting an unnecessary relative pronoun, and not translating the word ὑπό ('under'), the literal but really redundant sense being 'from under the yoke'. For 'And each beside his chariot bound his own', the literal sense of the Greek is 'and each man bound [his horses] with thongs beside his own chariot'. Tennyson's line is somewhat elliptical perhaps, and omits the concrete Homeric detail 'thongs'; but it is adequate and compact. The next three lines and a bit are best taken together:

And oxen from the city, and goodly sheep
In haste they drove, and honey-hearted wine
And bread from out the houses brought, and heaped
Their firewood, . . .

Here '*goodly* sheep' seems a trifle precious; 'good fat sheep' might have been better, as in our New Year's Eve song 'And a good fat sheep to last you all the year'. 'In haste', again, does not seem 'spot on' for καρπαλίμως here: 'with speed' or 'swiftly' or perhaps, somewhat different, 'eagerly', might have filled the bill better. As for 'honey-hearted', it sounds splendid, and alliterates well with 'In haste', for which very reason Tennyson may have chosen 'In haste'; but what does 'honey-hearted' mean? Tennyson wrote a note 'Or, "wine sweet to the mind"; but I use the epithet simply as a synonym of "sweet"'. Now, μελίφρων is used elsewhere by Homer of sleep. I should not be surprised if it meant here something like 'heart-cheering', which would be much to the point after a hard day's fighting. Phonally, however, Tennyson's line is a success, and his use of the alliterated 'h's' and 'b's' in these lines is skilful. 'And bread from out the houses brought' is stately, and its inversion is reasonable in this somewhat Miltonic style. But what of 'and heaped their firewood'? Well, that is not what Homer said they did. He said they 'gathered' it—λέγοντο; but they would certainly need to 'heap' it too if they wanted to make the great fires whose 'vapours' were shortly going to rise to heaven. So 'heaped' is a reasonable licence, I think, for the sake of the sound, and perhaps also simply for the metre. And then the rest of the eight lines: 'and the winds from off the plain/Rolled the rich vapour far into the heaven'. Again the sound is magnificent; the alliteration 'rolled . . . rich' and the semi-alliteration 'vapour . . . far' make for a strong line, and perhaps it is not too fanciful to suggest that the 'f's' and 'p's' give a sense of the puffing of the rich smoke. As the passage stands in Tennyson's version, however, the cause of the 'rich vapour' remains a matter of implication. The text he has translated omits line 548, which tells that the Trojans offered 'perfect hecatombs to the immortal gods'. This line is omitted from the manuscripts, but it is preserved in a passage in the Platonic (or pseudo-Platonic) dialogue *Alcibiades II*. There is a certain abruptness, therefore, in the last clause of the passage in Tennyson's rendering; though the implication is possibly not all that hard to accept, and the resounding line carries the matter off with fair success. 'Rolled' is an interesting word. The Greek here is, however, φέρον, meaning 'carried' or 'bore', which in this context would suggest a lifting movement that 'rolled' does not involve. 'Rolled' and 'rich' are so strong, however, that with the addition 'far' (not in the Greek) they may perhaps just bring off the required meaning; ἡδύς means perhaps 'pleasant' or 'sweet' rather than 'rich'; but κνίση does mean the smell or vapour of a burnt sacrifice, and the form of its pleasantness could be its richness.

Given the text that he translated, then, Tennyson's version seems to me successful. It is energetic; and that a translation of the *Iliad* must be. The defects or sacrifices of accuracy or clear sense, such as they are (and they are not many) are for the sake of, or at least compensated by, the sound. The version of the lines is also economical. We have eight decasyllabic lines for the seven hexameters plus one word—eighty syllables for about a hundred. Why is this, it may be asked? Partly because of deliberate omissions of words; but partly because Tennyson's words are, on the whole, shorter than Homer's except for the Greek particles and prepositions. The seven Homeric lines contain six four-syllable and one five-syllable word. 'Honey-hearted' is the only word of more than three syllables in Tennyson's version. The result is a different pattern of sound; but the force and spirit and most of the concreteness of the original remain.

I must turn now to the touches of language, imagery, and thought strewn through Tennyson's work, and probably taken consciously, subconsciously or unconsciously from Greek and Roman writers. Among Greek writers these mainly come from Homer and Theocritus, but there are reminiscences of a wide range of lyric poets. There is rather little, on the other hand, from the tragedians or the philosophers. Among the Roman poets the main sources seem to be Lucretius, Catullus, Virgil and Horace, though Ovid, Juvenal, Persius and Claudian make their contributions. A good deal of sleuthing was done in this field in Tennyson's own lifetime and shortly after his death.[8] John Churton Collins became a kind of *bête noire* for the poet through his articles in the *Cornhill* in 1880 and 1881, and subsequently his *Illustrations of Tennyson* (1891), following Tennyson's 'reminiscences' of earlier poets, largely Classical, through his volumes. Actually, Churton Collins, who was clearly a pretty learned man, produced considerable numbers of convincing instances of these 'borrowings'. Some were, however, less convincing intrinsically. Others were categorically denied by the poet to be 'borrowings' at all. Among this last variety is the case of line 24 in 'Oenone': 'For now the noonday quiet holds the hill', which is, as Churton Collins said, 'a curious literal translation of a line in Callimachus': 'μεσαμβρινὰ δ'εἶχ' ὄρος ἀσυχία'.[9] When Tennyson saw Collins' statement in the *Cornhill*, he wrote in the margin of his copy 'not known to me'; but, as Christopher Ricks has pointed out (R 386), in the *Eversley* edition Tennyson simply quotes the Callimachus line in his own note on the 'Oenone' line. There is, however, a general note at the beginning of the poet's annotations stating that 'many of the parallelisms' which he gives in his notes are 'accidental'. He does not say which; and 'accidental' is, in any case, a rather nebulous term, which could certainly cover cases of subconscious or unconscious reminiscence, as well as sheer coincidence. What nettled Tennyson was that Churton Collins was trying to demonstrate that he was not a great original poet like Homer, Dante, Chaucer or Shakespeare, but a poet like Virgil, Horace, Tasso and Gray, supremely artistic assimilators and adaptors of earlier literature. Tennyson could, I believe, have afforded to rest on his real originality; but it is, I suppose, understandable that he should have been sufficiently moved to permit himself to call Churton Collins 'a louse on the locks of literature' or 'a jackass', whichever, if either, was the description of Collins that he communicated to Edmund Gosse at that tea-party at Aldworth in the summer of 1886.[10]

Whether 'borrowings' or not, some of Tennyson's parallelisms are often highly felicitous, and sometimes positively creative. When, for instance, Ulysses tells of having 'drunk delight of battle' with his 'peers', 'far on the ringing plains of windy Troy', the Homeric parallel to 'delight of battle', χάρμη, so often used in the *Iliad*, must be a reminiscence, but it is very happily Anglicised; and 'windy' is a stock Homeric epithet for Troy, Ἴλιος ἠνεμόεσσα; yet the striking total line: 'Far on the ringing plains of windy Troy' is Tennyson's own admirable creation. Likewise, there is, as is well enough known, 'borrowing' in Ulysses' command to his men later in the poem: 'push off, and sitting well in order smite/The sounding furrows . . .'. One is readily reminded of the line which occurs more than once in the *Odyssey*: ἑξῆς δ᾽ ἑζόμενοι πολιὴν ἅλα τύπτον ἐρετμοῖς (e.g. IV, 580; IX, 104)—'And sitting in order they smote the gray sea with their oars'. Tennyson is again not just lifting. Apart from 'well in order', it is not simply the 'gray sea' that his men are to smite, but 'the sounding furrows', a fine broad phrase in its own right, but also one achieving consonantal harmony with 'off', 'sitting' and 'smite'.

Yet Tennyson was not always so happy in his 'borrowings'. When, in *In Memoriam*, he calls the British kingfisher 'the sea-blue bird of March', he is borrowing from Alcman's description of the halcyon, ἁλιπόρφυρος εἴαρος ὄρνις,[11] 'the sea-purple bird of Spring'; but the naturalisation is, I feel, of dubious value, given the regrettably frequent deviation from the imputed colour on the part of our 'distant Northern sea'.

Nevertheless, the great majority of the 'borrowings' or 'reminiscences' are either enriched or at least expressed in finely perceptive language. What is more, there sometimes occurs a phenomenon fairly similar to that noticed by Sir Charles Tennyson and elaborately exemplified more recently by Christopher Ricks.[12] As they have rightly shown, Tennyson often finds an uncannily appropriate context for words, phrases, or lines which he also used elsewhere less strikingly, sometimes in work written much earlier, sometimes in work written at much the same time. Somewhat similarly, in the case of the Classical 'borrowings' Tennyson often finds for them a deeply impressive context.[13] A context of any kind may be wholly or virtually absent in the original, as in the case of the eight lines of Pindar's description of Elysium,[14] which Tennyson closely renders at the end of 'Tiresias' (R 568) in especially fine blank verse, and in the potent context of the longing of the blind old prophet (and, of course, his nineteenth century counterpart) to be 'gathered to [his] rest',

> And mingled with the famous kings of old,
> On whom about their ocean-islets flash
> The faces of the Gods.
>   (ll 163–5),

Tennyson was fond of quoting the final lines (167–77) of the poem (so close to Pindar) as a 'sample' of his blank verse,[15] and it is, indeed, worth reminding ourselves of them:

>   . . .—and these eyes will find
> The men I knew, and watch the chariot whirl
> About the goal again, and hunters race
> The shadowy lion, and the warrior-kings,
> In height and prowess more than human, strive
> Again for glory, while the golden lyre
> Is ever sounding in heroic ears
> Heroic hymns, and every way the vales
> Wind, clouded with the grateful incense-fume
> Of those who mix all odour to the Gods
> On one far height in one far-shining fire.

Yet we need also to bear in mind the added richness that Tennyson has given to these lines by the context into which he has put them, a context in which the death of Arthur Hallam in 1833, shortly after which the poem originated, is attempted to be seen by the poet as a 'sacrifice' for some great purpose. It was originally one of Tennyson's *diverse* poignant attempts to adjust himself to the terrible taking of his friend, before the subtler reflective distillation of his grief over the long creation of *In Memoriam* was to enable him to emerge into something of a serenity tinged with ultimate hope and even triumph. As you will remember, 'Tiresias' was not published until 1885, over fifty years later. It is hard to be sure why. Perhaps Tennyson felt it incongruous to think of Arthur

Hallam as actively sacrificing himself as the prophet urges Menoeceus to to do in the poem. Perhaps, on the other hand, he thought that the whole idea verged on blasphemy; or might seem to do so. In any case, when he came to revise the poem in 1883, it seems to have been intended to bear a more general reference—to be something of an appeal to the finest of the young not to be afraid to sacrifice themselves for great causes. At all events, that Tennyson's purpose was now evidently in part didactic is evidenced by his wife's writing to Edward Lear at the time: 'Ally has been finishing one of his old world poems begun about the *Ulysses* period and discarded as what Carlyle called "a dead dog" but Ally has come to think that the world will receive lessons thus when it discards them in modern garb'.[16] The final lines of the poem, which I quoted just now, were added during that revision, and they seem to express nothing didactic, but rather a yearning for the kind of rest which involves a nostalgic *contemplation* of the glory of old times—the times, possibly, when Arthur Hallam and their friends achieved those intellectual glories and that nobility here transformed into the physical idiom of the chase, the games, the contests, and the sacrifices of ancient Greece.

I wanted to say these few things about 'Tiresias'; but you will remember that the point from which I started was that in these final lines of the poem we have lines which have no context in Pindar, but which Tennyson takes over and gives a context.

Most often Tennyson simply takes over phrase or passage, and context, but in other cases he takes a classical phrase or passage which already had a context and gives it a new one. In several places in Virgil we find the phrases 'lacrimae inanes' (for example *Aeneid* IV, 449; X, 465) or 'fletus inanes' (for example, *Georgics* IV, 375), and no doubt the phrases were familiar to Tennyson from boyhood; but, although there is a powerful context in each of the Virgil passages, there is nothing to compare to the strange, complex, and evasive contexts which Tennyson provides in that brilliant song in Book iv of *The Princess* (R 741, ll 21–40):

> 'Tears, idle tears, I know not what they mean,
> Tears from the depth of some divine despair
> Rise in the heart, and gather to the eyes,
> In looking on the happy Autumn-fields,
> And thinking of the days that are no more.
>
> 'Fresh as the first beam glittering on a sail,
> That brings our friends up from the underworld,
> Sad as the last which reddens over one

That sinks with all we love below the verge;
So sad, so fresh, the days that are no more.

'Ah, sad and strange as in dark summer dawns
The earliest pipe of half-awakened birds
To dying ears, when unto dying eyes
The casement slowly grows a glimmering square;
So sad, so strange, the days that are no more.

'Dear as remembered kisses after death,
And sweet as those by hopeless fancy feigned
On lips that are for others; deep as love,
Deep as first love, and wild with all regret;
O Death in Life, the days that are no more.'

There are further possible cullings in this poem, such as with regard to the casement, from Leigh Hunt's 'Hero and Leander' (ll 284–5) at the point when Hero is about to kill herself; and 'Dear as remembered kisses after death' may well be a reversing reference to Moschus's 'Lament for Bion' (ll 68–9), where Aphrodite is said to long for Bion more than for the kiss which she gave to Adonis when he died 'the other day'. Some of the context here is therefore *literary*; but in the case of Moschus Tennyson's feelings have even wrenched the literary reminiscence right round into the current of his own drift of passion and thought in that memorable line.

Before passing to my next topic I should like to express the opinion that in so far as the language of a poet can receive direct influence from the language of poets who have written in tongues other than his own, it is scarcely possible to exaggerate the permeating influence of the *language* of the Greek and Latin poets on Tennyson's poetical style. Even, indeed perhaps especially, one notices the influence of Horatian phrases, turns, and tones. However much Tennyson found Horace distasteful for years through having been overfed on him, even then the ingrained habits moulded his style very considerably; and later on, as I have said above, he even came to have a real affection for Horace's work. Yet much of the pervasive influence of Tennyson's style is not from single writers but from common classical practice. Tennyson's language was, however, naturally enough, most directly influenced by that of the poets of his native language—first by Thomson, then by Pope, Scott, Elizabethan drama, Shakespeare's poems, Byron and Milton, Moore, Crabbe, Coleridge, Shelley, Keats, Browning, and a host of other writers; and of these some, for example, Milton, Coleridge, and Shelley, were close readers of the ancient poets in the original.

I must now say a few words on structural, formal and textural relations between Tennyson's work and the Classics. From early days Tennyson hankered after writing an epic. Pope's *Iliad*, Virgil's *Aeneid*, *Paradise Lost*, all exerted their urges; and Milton had left free the theme of Arthur. Tennyson started on an Arthurian epic in twelve books in 1833, the year of Arthur Hallam's death. But he began the epic at the end.[17] The deep psychological problem of the relation of this fact to Hallam's death, and to the death of Tennyson's father in 1831, I shall not attempt to discuss. What Tennyson did do, in any case, was, as we know, to publish the 'Morte d'Arthur' in his 1842 volume, curiously cushioned by a half self-deprecating introduction and conclusion, 'The Epic', which had not existed when Tennyson read the poem to Edward FitzGerald in 1835.[18] The 'Morte d'Arthur' received some very favourable reviews;[19] but Leigh Hunt and John Sterling were both critical;[20] and, according to Tennyson's own testimony, years later, in conversation with William Allingham in 1867, it was Sterling's comments that stopped him from writing the Arthurian epic in twelve books.[21] What Tennyson said, according to Allingham, was: 'I had it all in my mind, could have done it without any trouble. The King is the complete man, the Knights are the passions.' In the 1842 volume, however, the 'Morte d'Arthur' had been placed at the head of a number of *English Idyls*. And this, naturally, is where Theocritus comes in. The dominant structure for narrative, monologue and dialogue poems or parts of poems (such as of *Maud*) by Tennyson are the Theocritan Idylls. The Theocritan Idylls, you will remember, are of different kinds, only a few being strictly narrative. Tennyson's choice of the Idyll as a dominant form for his various purposes was a wise and deliberate one. It suited Tennyson's variety, length of wind, scope, penchant for description, and meticulous textural work, exceptionally well. Into the much disputed question about the genre and structure of *Idylls of the King*—whether it is, after all, an epic, or a tragedy, or simply a series of idylls—I cannot here enter. I must content myself with the dogmatic suggestion that it is not an epic, but a series of idylls with some order (about which Tennyson exercised himself considerably), which has something of an overall tragic pattern, though one which is to a fair degree episodic. The units of which the whole is composed fall, in any case, within the category of idylls, as Tennyson himself was rightly aware when he rejected the alternative and stricter title Edmund Lushington suggested, *Epylls of the King*,[22] because he did not like the sound of the word 'Epylls'.

To say that the dominant structure of Tennyson's narrative, monologue, and dialogue poems or parts of poems derives from the Theocritan Idylls is not to say that Tennyson did not create new structures, such as the total structure of the 'monodrama' *Maud*, or of the meditative struggle and resolution of *In Memoriam*.

Besides the larger structures, moreover, there are the lyrics, and the short epistles such as the delightful poem to Edward FitzGerald on his seventy-fifth birthday. There is something playfully and warmly Catullan about that affectionate missive from one septuagenarian friend to another; though it is also at times not altogether diverse in tone from the well-known poem of Callimachus to his friend Heracleitus.

As far as the *texture* of Tennyson's verse is concerned, it derives very little metrically from the ancient poets. Metrically it is in general an ever more complex, and ever more distinctively Tennysonian, metric creation. Tennyson did deliberately imitate some classical metres, rather wryly in the case of hexameters, more seriously in the case of the more successful alcaics on Milton; but the bulk of his work is in the characteristically English blank verse, which he developed to such a high degree of sophistication. Yet there are occasionally passages of great distinction directly based on classical metres, for instance, these haunting lines from *Maud* (R 1037, Part i, ll 88–101):

> Cold and clear-cut face, why come you so cruelly meek,
> Breaking a slumber in which all spleenful folly was drowned,
> Pale with the golden beam of an eyelash dead on the cheek,
> Passionless, pale, cold face, star-sweet on a gloom profound;
> Womanlike, taking revenge too deep for a transient wrong
> Done but in thought to your beauty, and ever as pale as before
> Growing and fading and growing upon me without a sound,
> Luminous, gemlike, ghostlike, deathlike, half the night long
> Growing and fading and growing, till I could bear it no more,
> But arose, and all by myself in my own dark garden ground,
> Listening now to the tide in its broad-flung shipwrecking roar,
> Now to the scream of a maddened beach dragged down by the wave,
> Walked in a wintry wind by a ghastly glimmer, and found
> The shining daffodil dead, and Orion low in his grave.

Stanzaically, again, though Tennyson admired Sappho's fragments, Horace's alcaics and Pindar's complex forms, he did not attempt to reproduce them. He created stanzaic forms of his own, helped to some degree by knowledge of the work of his English predecessors.

And now for my final topic: Tennyson's treatment of Classical themes.

Let us start with 'Oenone' (R 384) first published in 1832, and much revised and improved for the first 1842 volume. The main source is the letter from Oenone to Paris in Ovid's *Heroides* V, where she begs her childhood playmate and lover to come back to her. Yet there her appeal is to Paris himself, and it is, moreover, largely an argumentative one in Ovid's alert, intelligent style, mingled with a far from hopeless pathos. Tennyson's poem is much more emotional, and much more despondent, but also far fuller of concrete detail. The combination of these features is found in many passages, for instance in the first stanza of the Song (ll 25–32), whose physical detail Tennyson claimed to have observed at first hand in the Pyrenees:

> The grasshopper is silent in the grass:
> The lizard, with his shadow on the stone,
> Rests like a shadow, and the winds are dead.
> The purple flower droops: the golden bee
> Is lily-cradled: I alone awake.
> My eyes are full of tears, my heart of love,
> My heart is breaking, and my eyes are dim,
> And I am all aweary of my life.

The poem is, however, not merely wonderfully passionate, lyrical and concrete, but it bears deeper meanings. It tells graphically the whole story of the Judgment of Paris (to which Ovid only alludes), and endorses Oenone's condemnation of Paris's choice of sensuous love against Pallas's offering of 'self-reverence, self-knowledge, self-control', which she claimed 'alone lead life to sovereign power'; but, still more important, would alone enable one to follow right without fear, which is the highest thing a human being can do. Tennyson joins Oenone's appeal to Pallas's cause, but Paris is deaf to it: and the disaster does not simply befall Oenone or Paris, but Troy and Mycenae. It is the disaster from unlicensed sex that Tennyson (somewhat like Tolstoy) shows to be an ever-threatening peril. The poem is thus a wonderfully integrated whole, precise in physical detail, rich in musical resonance, allusive to Greek myth, and a marvellous expression of passionate despair, addressed to 'many-fountained Ida', and not to the infatuated and unhearing Paris. In this poem Tennyson has created out of the ancient materials something highly successful, and splendidly new. Ovid's poem was also well integrated, and full of delightful touches; Tennyson's is not only more expansive, but a richer achievement both in its well-defined sensuousness and in its moral force and depth. It would be rewarding to compare the two poems in more detail; but that would need considerably more space.[23]

Let us now turn to 'The Lotos-Eaters' (R 429). Like 'Oenone' Tennyson published it in his 1832 volume, but also revised and improved it for the first volume of his 1842 *Poems*. The revisions were less extensive than those of 'Oenone', the main ones being the addition of the brilliant section VI (ll 114–32) and the powerful rewriting of ll 150–73. The brilliance of adding section VI consists largely in the introduction of the uncanny transformation of the attitudes of the tainted men towards their wives, their homes, their countrymen, and homeland, once so dear to them; and the sense that they would be superannuated misfits were they to return home, and that if their home countries were in disorder they would be too tired to put things right. The rewriting of ll 150–73 transforms a comparatively commonplace and rather repetitive insistence on remaining 'in the golden vale/Of the Lotos-land, till the Lotos fail', expressed in largely lightweight lines, into a heavily oppressive cumulation of weighty lines in which the infected sailors swear to achieve the terrifying mirage of living the lives of the gods, 'careless of mankind', lying in 'their golden houses' (ll 159–73):

> Where they smile in secret, looking over wasted lands,
> Blight and famine, plague and earthquake, roaring deeps and fiery sands,
> Clanging fights, and flaming towns, and sinking ships, and praying hands.
> But they smile, they find a music centred in a doleful song
> Steaming up, a lamentation and an ancient tale of wrong,
> Like a tale of little meaning though the words are strong;
> Chanted from an ill-used race of men that cleave the soil,
> Sow the seed, and reap the harvest with enduring toil,
> Storing yearly little dues of wheat, and wine and oil;
> Till they perish and they suffer—some, 'tis whispered—down in hell
> Suffer endless anguish, others in Elysian valleys dwell,
> Resting weary limbs at last on beds of asphodel.
> Surely, surely, slumber is more sweet than toil, the shore
> Than labour in the deep mid-ocean, wind and wave and oar;
> Oh rest ye, brother mariners, we will not wander more.

The main source of the poem is, of course, the *Odyssey*, IX, 82–104; but Tennyson also drew touches of his deceptive Paradise from Washington Irving's *Life of Columbus*. With Irving I am not here concerned; I *am*, however, concerned with Tennyson's transformation of the Homer passage. In the *Eversley* edition Tennyson's own note modestly reads: 'The treatment of 'Oenone' and 'The Lotos-Eaters' is, as far as I know, original'. In both cases, in point of fact, the treatment is superbly creative. The twenty-odd lines of the *Odyssey* contain no song; they simply tell the short tale. Tennyson's poem, like his 'Oenone', starts with narrative, but continues over a great span with modulated lyrics gathering in momentum of incantatory power. This is structurally interesting; but there is, of course, more to be said. It is probably worth my first offering a translation of the brief Homeric passage. Odysseus is telling his adventures to Alcinous:

> From there for nine days I was swept along by death-dealing winds across the fish-filled ocean; but on the tenth we reached the land of the Lotos-eaters, who feed on the fruit of flowering shrubs. There we went ashore and drew water, and my men and I at once took a quick meal near the ships. But when we had had our food and drink I sent some of my men to go and find out what sort of people the inhabitants were, detailing two men for that task, and a third as a herald. So they went off, and soon made contact with the Lotos-eaters. Now, interestingly enough, the Lotos-eaters had no intention of being the ruin of my men, but they did give them lotos to taste, and each man who ate the honey-sweet fruit of the lotos no longer had any wish either to report back or to return, but all they wanted to do was to stay with the Lotos-eaters, feeding on lotos, and forget all thought of going back home. I had them dragged back blubbering to the ships, hauled into the hold and bound fast. But the rest of my trusty crews I ordered to look sharp and get aboard the swift ships, for fear anyone might eat some lotos and forget about returning home. And they went on board at once, sat down on the benches in proper order, and struck the gray sea with their oars.

Tennyson starts his poem by making Odysseus cheer his men on with the hope of shortly striking land. It is the only appearance of Odysseus in the whole poem: but it is important, because the 'courage' which he urges, is just the thing that the men are going to lose under the insidious influence of the lotos. But then, as you will remember, after the first two lines of encouragement, Tennyson launches on that spellbindingly soporific description in Spenserian stanzas (vaguely evoking Spenser's Bower of Bliss and Thomson's *Castle of Indolence*) of the nature of the land 'In which it seemèd always afternoon', and again 'A land where all things always seemed the same', reminding one of Lucretius's *eadem sunt omnia semper* (III, 945) and *eadem tamen omnia restant* (III, 947), parts of an argument urged by Nature for putting an end to one's life if one is discontented with it. The land and its fruit are against life and effort. The 'mild-eyed melancholy Lotos-eaters' are pale in the 'rosy flame' of the sunset. The lotos branches they offer to the sailors are magically in 'flower and fruit' at the same time; the existence of a Lotos-eater is a deep sleep, although paradoxically he is awake. Time no longer seems to count, and the Lotos-eater's dreams, though 'sweet', they are too weary to realise. *One* of the drugged sailors *says* 'We will return no more', and that moves the whole company to sing the Choric Song. Tennyson has caught—or should we say 'created'?—the details of the land's atmosphere, and also of the psychological and physical changes in the men, with their utter sense of weariness and refusal of effort; and all this was only barely *mentioned* in Homer.

There was, of course, no choric song in Homer, while the rest of Tennyson's poem consists of just that. The stanza forms are complex. It is a long lamentation about toil, and a yearning for contemplative detachment, which is ultimately seen to be a longing for the possibility of being callously superhuman. At one point the sailors appeal for the alternative of death: 'Give us long rest or death, dark death, or dreamful ease' (1 98), but ultimately it is the life of the gods (the Homeric gods—the Olympians) that they wish for. But there is no sign that they achieve it—that it is anything more than itself an idle dream; and there are signs, I suggest, that they ought not to achieve it. For Tennyson could surely assume that his readers would remember that these dreamers were shortly to be dragged back to the ships and tied up. Tennyson is no more ultimately taken in by the wonderful melodic arabesques in which he articulates the sense of weariness of life and refusal of effort than Spenser was by the attractions of the Bower of Bliss or the powerfully urged arguments of Despair for self-destruction; though, like Spenser, he seems to feel keenly the disturbing urge towards the hallucinating but ultimately pernicious possibility.

Great as are Tennyson's achievements in 'Oenone' and 'The Lotos-Eaters', however, I personally believe that the two finest of his Classical poems—indeed, possibly, of all his poems, are 'Ulysses' (R 560) and 'Tithonus' (R 1112). This may be connected with the fact that both 'Oenone' and 'The Lotos-Eaters' were originally written before the searing experience of the loss of Arthur Hallam, and, although, in their final forms, they incorporate the deeper feelings and thoughts as well as aesthetic improvements, they did not grow integrally from the mind and heart of the poet who had suffered that disaster. We need, I think, always to bear in mind that 'Ulysses' *and* 'Tithonus' (in its original form) were both written very soon after Hallam's death; and we need also to take account of two things that Tennyson himself said of 'Ulysses' in relation to *In Memoriam*. The first was this: 'The poem was written soon after Arthur Hallam's death, and it gave my feeling about the need of going forward and braving the struggle of life perhaps more simply than anything in *In Memoriam*.'[24] The second was a later comment, to James Knowles, when talking about *In Memoriam*: 'There is more about myself in *Ulysses*, which was written under the sense of loss and that all had gone by, but that still life must be fought out to the end. It was more written with the feeling of his loss upon me than many poems in *In Memoriam*.'[25] 'Tithonus', in its original form 'Tithon' (R 566), was a different response to the same grief, together perhaps with the grief of Tennyson's sister Emily to whom Arthur Hallam had been betrothed.

I will first consider 'Ulysses'. There has been much discussion, particularly in the last thirty years or so, as to how the poem should be interpreted, and how the character of Ulysses himself should be regarded. I have strongish, but not necessarily right, views on these points—of which more below. Meanwhile, let us recall what Tennyson himself names as his sources, the *Odyssey* XI, 100–37, and Dante's *Inferno* XXVI, 90 to the end of the Canto. In the *Odyssey* passage Tiresias prophesies to Odysseus that he will kill Penelope's suitors, and later go off and encounter some men who know nothing about ships, and there he is to sacrifice to Poseidon, then leave for home, and there offer sacred hecatombs to all the gods in turn; eventually death will come to him, either 'far from the sea' or 'from out the sea' (there are unfortunately reasonable arguments for both translations); and, in any case, it will be when he is very old, rich and comfortable, and his countrymen are prosperous. There is nothing there about any great *longing* on Ulysses's part to leave home, and make further voyages, nor do we know how he is to die. The Dante source is more informative in relation to Tennyson's poem. Dante places Ulysses and Diomedes in the Eighth Circle of Hell, among the thieves, for having gone out by night, cheated and killed Dolon, and stolen the Palladium of Troy, which was essential to the city's safety (*Iliad*, X). Virgil asks Ulysses to tell what happened to him in the end. Ulysses says that after he left Circe neither fondness for his son, nor reverence for his old father, nor the love which he owed Penelope and which ought to have given her joy, could overcome his eagerness to know the world, and human vice and worth, and so he set off on the deep open sea, with only a single ship and the small company which had not deserted him. They sailed West as far as Spain and Morocco, and by the time they reached the Straits of Gibraltar, beyond which Hercules had placed his pillars as landmarks to stop men from going farther, they had become old and slow. But at that point Ulysses appealed to his men: 'O my brothers, who through a hundred thousand dangers have reached the West, do not deny to this brief vigil of your senses that remains, experience of the unpeopled world that lies beyond the sun. Consider your origin: you were not created to live like brutes, but to follow virtue and knowledge'. That made the men enthusiastic for the voyage, and they set off, following a course West by South, reached the Equator, and after five months sighted a high mountain—the Mount of Purgatory. They were at first overjoyed to see it; but their joy was soon turned to misery, for a storm arose from the new land, struck the forepart of the ship, whirled it round three times, and then at the fourth blow raised the stern and sank the poop, according to God's will, and the sea closed over them.

In the Dante account there is this great longing for experience on Ulysses's part, which reappears in Tennyson's poem; but there is no indication that Ulysses ever went home before the final voyage. Moreover, he seems to have a guilty conscience that he did not allow his feelings for his son, his father, and especially Penelope, more weight than he did. On the other hand, the ultimate fate of Ulysses is made abundantly clear: and it is a good deal less comfortable than in the *Odyssey*. Yet the enthusiasm of Ulysses for the final voyage does not seem to be condemned by Dante. In the *Odyssey* no attitude is expressed towards the further journeys after the killing of the suitors; and Ulysses does return home.

Tennyson, as I said, takes more from Dante than from Homer; but he starts the story quite differently, and his characterisation of Ulysses is not the same.[26] Ulysses has come home and presumably killed the suitors, has grown old, and become bored with an inactive life. Penelope is no longer as attractive as she was, and ruling savages is not very interesting. He is restless for further adventure. He has had many experiences, but experience is inexhaustible, and he must have more. He is insatiable for life, and it would be monstrous not to live out the little that remains to him as fully as he can, and 'To follow knowledge like a sinking star,/Beyond the utmost bound of human thought' (ll 31–2). He will leave Telemachus to rule the land, which he is well fitted to do. Some critics complain that this is utterly selfish and irresponsible,[27] Ulysses indulging excessively his own lust for life,[28] condemning Telemachus to a mode of life he himself despises,[29] and denying him the chance of adventure. But the poem nowhere says this; and even if that *were* the implication, does not the poem make us more concerned for the satisfaction of Ulysses's aspirations than for those of Telemachus, who has, in any case, a good deal more of his life before him, and, if we are to believe Fénelon,[30] had neither been, nor was to be, starved of experience? Ulysses in Tennyson's poem is, indeed, obsessional; but that is a great part of his attraction. It involves some rough talk at the start of the poem, but that is quite like the Homeric Odysseus. Tennyson's Ulysses is not the Dantesque figure troubled with conscientious scruples about staying with blood-relations and wives. One modern critic has suggested that this Odysseus (Homeric, I believe, though possibly also somewhat Byronic) is inconsistent with the man of noble aspirations portrayed at the end of Tennyson's poem.[31] I am not convinced of the inconsistency. The Homeric Odysseus was also something of an obsessional voyager, though a voyager, admittedly, whose ardent aim was to get home. Yet this was a far from ignoble aspiration. Another modern critic has taken Tennyson to be attacking his Ulysses as caring for nothing but earthly experience, and lacking the preoccupation with and hope for immortality which provide such a bulwark for Tennyson in *In Memoriam*.[32] I cannot believe that those magnificent lines which end Tennyson's 'Ulysses' (R 560, ll 54–70) could lend themselves to such an interpretation:

> The lights begin to twinkle from the rocks:
> The long day wanes: the slow moon climbs: the deep
> Moans round with many voices. Come, my friends,
> 'Tis not too late to seek a newer world.
> Push off, and sitting well in order smite
> The sounding furrows; for my purpose holds
> To sail beyond the sunset, and the baths
> Of all the western stars, until I die.
> It may be that the gulfs will wash us down:
> It may be we shall touch the Happy Isles,
> And see the great Achilles, whom we knew.
> Though much is taken, much abides; and though
> We are not now that strength which in old days
> Moved earth and heaven; that which we are, we are;
> One equal temper of heroic hearts,
> Made weak by time and fate, but strong in will
> To strive, to seek, to find, and not to yield.

It is in this connection that we must try to arrive at what Tennyson meant when he said that the poem 'gave [his] feeling about the need of going forward and braving the struggle of life perhaps more simply than anything in *In Memoriam*'. Could not 'perhaps more simply' mean *without considering the matter of personal immortality*? Just going on with this earthly life and living it out with all its struggles? And in the words to James Knowles, again, there is no mention of anything other-worldly. The sense of loss, and that everything worthwhile in life was over, was cruelly oppressive, and yet the poem embodied the feeling 'that still life must be fought out to the end'. And where in the poem is that feeling embodied except in the dynamic determination of the 'gray spirit', Ulysses, and the 'heroic hearts' who remain with him? Such an attitude to the loss of Hallam may not have been one which, for one reason or another, Tennyson was able to sustain over the years. He evidently came to need more consolation; but it is an attitude possible to many people, and one that was seemingly possible to Tennyson himself then, and which he has moreover expressed in poetry which has already caught the imagination of many thousands of readers. There is, however, one possible velleity which ought perhaps to be taken account of. This occurs in those three admirable lines:

> It may be that the gulfs will wash us down:
> It may be we shall touch the Happy Isles,
> And see the great Achilles, whom we knew. (R 560, ll 62–4)

To be 'washed down' by the 'gulfs' was, of course, the fate that Dante's Ulysses said ultimately befell them. But what about 'touching' the Happy Isles? Does it mean that they will at least have a *glimpse* of a life beyond death (a pagan one, of course) in the Islands of the Blest? Possibly, but it is an alternative to being 'washed down', and so it is within the bounds of their earthly lives. The only consolation for Ulysses and his men would be that they would realise that their great hero was receiving his due reward beyond the grave; and even that is only stated as a *possibility*. It is hard not to think of 'the great Achilles, whom we knew' as an Arthur Hallam figure, who, in the words of Pindar (*Olympian* II, 68–70), was one of those who had 'three times stood out in keeping their souls pure from all wrongful acts'. There *may* be a tenuous feeling towards that further consolation; but it is a brief moment, and it carries no certainty.

'Tithonus' (R 1112), though written in its original form under the immediate shadow of Arthur Hallam's death, was not published until 1860. Thackeray was starting the *Cornhill*, and in 1859 badgered Tennyson for a poem for his first number. Tennyson found 'Tithon'

(R 566) among his 'old books', and revised it towards the end of 1859.[33] Tennyson called 'Tithon' 'a pendent' to 'Ulysses'. In the ancient myth Tithonus was Priam's brother. He was loved by Eos (Aurora), and by her begat Memnon. Eos begged Zeus to make Tithonus immortal. This was granted; but she forgot to ask for him also to have eternal youth, and he withered away into a shrunken and miserable old age, like one of Swift's Struldbrugs. In the Homeric *Hymn to Aphrodite*, from which the story is derived, Eos actually locked Tithonus up when he grew unbearably old. This does not happen in Tennyson's poem, which is, in any case, like 'Ulysses', a monologue. Tithonus, in Tennyson's poem, originally asked *Aurora* to give him immortality, and *she* granted it to him, but her 'strong Hours' 'beat [him] down' and 'marred' and 'wasted' him, leaving him 'maimed'

> To dwell in presence of immortal youth,
> Immortal age beside immortal youth,
> And all I was, in ashes. (R 1112, ll 21–3)

He begs her to take back her gift, which was an unnatural one for a man. Tennyson evidently makes Aurora sorrowful that she cannot take back the gift. She sheds tears, and that makes Tithonus fear that 'The Gods themselves cannot recall their gifts'. I am not convinced by a distinguished modern critic's suggestion that here 'recall' also bears the sense 'remember'.[34] It seems that Aurora remembers her gift only too clearly.

In a superb paragraph Tithonus recollects the vitality of their early days of love (ll 50–63), but Aurora's glorious Eastern rising now only strikes cold into him, and he cries out (ll 72–6):

> Release me, and restore me to the ground;
> Thou seest all things, thou wilt see my grave:
> Thou wilt renew thy duty morn by morn;
> I earth in earth forget these empty courts,
> And thee returning on thy silver wheels.

The courts are 'empty', I think, because his nature can no longer mix with Aurora's, and he cannot travel with the 'wild team' which 'love' her, and which 'arise' 'And shake the darkness from their loosened manes,/And beat the twilight into flakes of fire' (ll 41–2). And he will forget also the melodious sound and pale hue of the wheels of her returning chariot, now so poignant to him, before so joyful. The ending of the poem is great poetry, and so is the beginning (ll 1–10):

The woods decay, the woods decay and fall,
The vapours weep their burthen to the ground,
Man comes and tills the field and lies beneath,
And after many a summer dies the swan.
Me only cruel immortality
Consumes: I wither slowly in thine arms,
Here at the quiet limit of the world,
A white-haired shadow roaming like a dream
The ever-silent spaces of the East,
Far-folded mists, and gleaming halls of morn.

And there is a melancholy quietness about both passages. There is none of the excitement and energy we find in 'Ulysses'. Yet in both cases the poet has chosen as the speaker an old man; and no doubt after Arthur Hallam's death he in some way felt an old man, to some degree devitalised. Yet if we wish to interpret the poem in relation to Hallam we may encounter ambiguities. If we consider Aurora, roughly, as the life-giving glow which came from this inspiring relationship; and the request to Aurora, roughly, that life, if it be like this, shall continue for ever, then the poet's survival when joy has gone is deeply depressing. That seems fairly clear. If, however, we think of the immortality as, in any sense, Hallam's, then Hallam would need to become Aurora, and the picture would be skewed. The sorrow and diminution must surely, in any case, be that of the *poet*; and *Hallam* had suffered no diminution by *survival*. It is safer, then, in my view, to eschew any attempt to identify Hallam as a character in the poem. Indeed, it could well have been a fear on Tennyson's part that people would be tempted to make such identifications (with the possibility, moreover, of undesirable frills) that partly caused him not to publish the poem with 'Ulysses'; though the strength with which the death wish is expressed, may also have seemed to him something to be rejected, and certainly not to be exposed. But the diction and movement of the poem, and the wonderful contrast pictorially and spiritually between, on the one hand, the vitality of Aurora and of their old relationship, and, on the other hand, the pathetic wraithlike figure with his longing to be buried in the earth, make this poem, in my view, with 'Ulysses', Tennyson's supreme achievement in a wholly serious vein. It is interesting that ancient literature could enable him to express his deepest preoccupations with such density and perfection.

We do not know how well acquainted Tennyson was with Lucretius before Hugh Munro brought out his great edition, and his translation, in

1864. It may well be that he had pondered parts, at least, of the *De rerum natura* when he was contemplating suicide *before* Arthur Hallam's death, and writing 'The Grave of a Suicide' (R 123), and it is virtually certain that Lucretius's discussion of death in Book III was one of the influences behind the final version of the struggle 'between Faith and Scepticism' in 'The Two Voices', completed after Hallam's death, and published in 1842 (R 522). An 1807 copy of Creech's edition (1695) is listed among the books in his father's library,[35] and so is a copy of the 1813 edition of Wakefield (1796–97).[36] Tennyson himself possessed a copy of the 1821 edition of Wakefield,[37] and he later obtained a Teubner text dated 1852.[38] But he also acquired a copy of Munro's 1864 edition,[39] and was evidently *given* by Munro a copy of the second edition of his *translation*, published by Deighton Bell in Cambridge in 1866.[40] Early in October 1865 Emily Tennyson wrote in her diary: 'A. read me some Lucretius', and noted that he was at that time working on 'his new poem of "Lucretius"'. On 2 May 1868 the poem (R 1206) was published in New York in *Every Saturday*; and in the same month, with some toning down of sensuality, in *Macmillan's Magazine*. As is well known, the poem derives its story from the reference to Lucretius's death in Jerome's statements in his addition to the Eusebian chronicle that Lucretius was driven mad by drinking a love-potion, wrote some books during lucid intervals, and eventually killed himself at the age of forty-four. A subsequent tradition attributed to Jeróme the further assertion that it was Lucretius's wife, who loved him greatly, who killed him with a philtre designed to regain his love. This tradition appears in Lyly's *Euphues*, where the wife is called Lucilia.[41] Without questioning for the moment either this later augmentation or the truth of Saint Jerome's words,[42] written, in any case, some 400 years or more after Lucretius's death (though the account *may* date back to the time of Suetonius), let us consider what Tennyson achieved in his poem.

'Lucretius' starts with twenty-five lines describing Lucilia's sense of outrage that after 'the morning flush of passion' had died, Lucretius did not respond even to her kisses of greeting, but was immersed in his philosophical thinking and poetic creation, and his continual study of 'those three hundred scrolls/left by the Teacher, whom he held divine'— Epicurus, of course. She fancied there was another woman in the case, and found a 'witch' who brewed a love-philtre for her. This she mixed from time to time with her husband's drink, and ruined his brain. The rest of the poem, save for the last seven lines, is a long monologue by Lucretius. This shows very close reading by Tennyson of the *De rerum natura*. One recognises readily enough such cullings from Lucretius's great poem as the powerful description of the storm in Book VI, the references to the Sullan Reign of Terror, the momentary glance at the invocation to Venus, the admiring mention of Empedocles, the empathic sense of the fullness of animal life, the description in Book III of the remote and peaceful habitations of the gods (itself an imitation of Homer), the inclination of men to attribute to gods effects whose causes they cannot observe, the power of images to cause consternation, the potency of dreams and their relation to waking life, the indication of the satisfying character of the simple Epicurean life, the reiterated Lucretian intention to wrap up harsh truths in honeyed words, the view of inanimate objects changing into animate and into feeling beings without any design on the part of gods, the banishment of Tartarus from the realm of possibility, hell being simply an earthly phenomenon. There are, however, many subtleties in the Lucretian original which do not appear in Tennyson's poem. This is no reproach, since Tennyson's purpose was very different from that of Lucretius. Tennyson is concerned to show Lucretius in a final phase of insanity, on the very day when, according to Jerome's account, he is going to do away with himself.

I want now to consider a view taken shortly after the poem appeared, that 'the Lucretius whom it describes has a true resemblance to the real Lucretius, as revealed in his own work'. The words are those of the distinguished Classical scholar, Richard Jebb, in a fine article on the poem in *Macmillan's Magazine* a month after the poem appeared.[43] I have not time to do full justice here to that article. Jebb rightly stresses the prophetic earnestness and intensity of the Roman poet, and also his feeling for the life and beauty of nature. He also rightly recognises, however, that what Tennyson had performed was 'the difficult task of translating' Lucretius's intensity into 'a morbid phase'. Tennyson had shown the bafflement of an eager mind. I think Jebb's comments pinpoint an important part of Tennyson's achievement in the poem. There are a number of powerful moments at nodal points in the work expressing the sense of mental disintegration, for example, when Lucretius affirms that he meant, like his master, to prove that there are immortal gods, and then hesitates:

> Meant? I meant?
> I have forgotten what I meant: my mind
> Stumbles, and all my faculties are lamed. (R 1206, ll 121–3)

(There is something Browningesque in the tone and movement here, I feel.) And again, much later in the poem, when he says that he thought that he himself lived as 'securely' as the gods, with 'Nothing to mar the sober majesties/Of settled, sweet, Epicurean life' (ll 217–18), but immediately reveals the agony of the present (ll 219–22):

> But now it seems some unseen monster lays
> His vast and filthy hands upon my will,
> Wrenching it backwards into his; and spoils
> My bliss in being.

A haunting question is, I believe: Why did Tennyson do this translation into the 'morbid phase'? My own tentative answer is that it was perhaps because he was horrifyingly impressed by the thought that such a firm attitude to life as we find in the *De rerum natura* could, after all, be at the complete mercy of a physical poison, a 'wicked broth' confusing 'the chemic labour of the blood', and 'tickling the brute brain within the man's' (ll 19–23). At all events, if that is the drive behind the poem, it is, I suggest, a better poem than it otherwise would be.

I should have liked to have had time to say something about the two poems on classical themes which Tennyson wrote in old age. First, 'Demeter and Persephone' (R 1373, written 1886–87 and published in 1889), which his son Hallam suggested to him, and which he agreed to write, saying, illuminatingly, 'but when I write an antique like this I must put it into a frame—something modern about it. It is no use giving a mere *réchauffé* of old legends.'[44] What Tennyson seems to offer as a 'frame' is the retrieving power of love. Secondly, the 'Death of Oenone' (R 1427, written 1889–90 and published in 1892), less interesting, closely following the story in Book X of Quintus Calaber's *Fall of Troy* (fourth century AD), in which Paris, shot by a poisoned dart, begs Oenone to save him. She refuses, but soon after, in passionate remorse, throws herself on his burning funeral pyre. Tennyson tells the tale movingly, and endorses the value of forgiveness. In his short poem 'To the Master of Balliol' (R 1426), to his close friend Jowett, Tennyson calls his own poem on Oenone's death

> a Grecian tale re-told,
> Which, cast in later Grecian mould,
> Quintus Calaber
> Somewhat lazily handled of old. (ll 5–8)

Tennyson cut Quintus's treatment down to less than half. Tennyson had since the 1830s been concerned to avoid diffuse writing. Of his aims at that time he wrote: 'I felt certain of one point then; if I meant to make my mark at all, it must be by shortness, for the men before me had been so diffuse, and most of the big things except 'King Arthur' had been done'.[45]

I shall have to reserve any discussion of those two late poems for a mythical future essay. I will end simply by supposing someone were to raise the question which of the poets of Greece and Rome Tennyson most resembles. Many people might say 'Virgil'. Tennyson's dedication to the details of his art matches that of Virgil; but Tennyson's total *oeuvre* is far more various than Virgil's. Again, the relations of Tennyson and Virgil to the moral, political, scientific, philosophical, and religious conditions of their time bear certain important resemblances.[46] Yet, despite this, and despite that admirable tribute 'To Virgil' which Tennyson wrote for the Mantuans in 1882, to the question which of the ancient poets Tennyson was most like, I personally would want to answer 'None'. He is sometimes like one poet, sometimes like another; and the width and depth of his knowledge of the ancient poets enabled him both to introduce special touches of great variety into poems not concerned with classical themes, and also to make out of classical themes themselves new creations sometimes deeper and sometimes of more permanent value than the specific sources on which he drew.

4 Tennyson In and Out of Time

Philip Collins

My title recalls T. S. Eliot's 'the moment in and out of time' (*The Dry Salvages*, v) but I shall not be adding to the recent spate of enquiries into his relationship with Tennyson,[1] fascinating though it would be to compare their treatments of Time in, particularly, *In Memoriam* and *Four Quartets*. Nor indeed am I using Eliot's phrase in quite the meaning it bears in its context, where it refers to the saint's, or the mystic's, apprehending 'The point of intersection of the timeless/With time'. Tennyson had, and wrote about, such experiences, and we shall be concerned with them: moments, from his boyhood through to his latest years, when (as he said) he got 'carried away out of sense and body, and rapt into mere existence', and when, as he put it in that remarkable poem 'Armageddon' (written, Sir Charles Tennyson argued, at the age of fifteen or less), 'All sense of Time/And Being and Place was swallowed up and lost . . . (R 64, ii, ll 43–4).[2] Such moments provided, for those privileged to experience them, a brief but unforgettably convincing knowledge of 'The vanities of after and before', as he put it in another early poem, 'The Mystic' (R 229)—a release, to quote from a poem written half a century later, from the myopia which normally afflicts humanity: for 'with the Nameless' (God) there

> is nor Day nor Hour;
> Though we, thin minds, who creep from thought to thought,
> Break into 'Thens' and 'Whens' the Eternal Now . . .
> ('The Ancient Sage', R 1349, ll 103–4)

But all, mystic and earthbound alike, will eventually be carried by death 'from out our bourne of Time and Place' and, to quote the familiar words (from 'Crossing the Bar', R 1458) which, on Tennyson's instructions, come at the end of every volume of his collected poems, 'I hope to see my Pilot face to face/When I have crost the bar' (ll 15–16). For Tennyson was of course much concerned with his hope, or assurance, of immortality, with being 'out of time' and into Eternity. In 1842 he had given prominence to 'The Poet's Song', using it to conclude his *Poems in Two Volumes*, which established him as a major author, and its final lines were: 'For he sings of what the world will be/When the years have died away' (R 736).

At about this time, he was writing to his future wife, 'The far future has been my world always', and in two other letters to Emily the same year (1839), he writes (*Mem.*, i, 168, 171–2):

> Annihilate within yourself these two dreams of Space and Time. To me the far-off world seems nearer than the present, for in the present is always something unreal and indistinct, but the other seems a good solid planet, rolling round its green hills and paradises to the harmony of more general laws . . .
>
> Dim mystic sympathies with tree and hill reaching far back into childhood. A known landskip is to me an old friend, that continually talks to me of my own youth and half-forgotten things, and indeed does more for me than many an old friend that I know . . .

Here he is concerned with experiences '*in* time'—and, conspicuously, not with the present but 'the far future' or that other 'far-off world' for which he had a favourite phrase, 'the passion of the past, the abiding in the transient', which, he said, 'I used to feel when a boy' (*Mem.*, i, 253; ii, 319). He writes of this in that late poem, 'The Ancient Sage' (R 1349), which has already been quoted:

> Today? but what of yesterday? for oft
> On me, when boy, there came what then I call'd,
> Who knew no books and no philosophies,
> In my boy-phrase 'The Passion of the Past.'
> The first gray steak of earliest summer-dawn,
> The last long stripe of waning crimson gloom,
> As if the late and early were but one—
> A height, a broken grange, a grove, a flower
> Had murmurs 'Lost and gone and lost and gone!'
> A breath, a whisper—some divine farewell—
> Desolate sweetness—far and far away—
> What had he loved, what had he lost, the boy?
> I know not and I speak of what has been. (ll 216–28)

'What had he loved, what had he lost . . . ? I know not': the puzzlement, and that alliterative juxtaposition, will call to mind two of his most familiar sentences: 'Tears, idle tears, I know not what they mean' (R 784, iv, l 21) and ''Tis better to have loved and lost Than never to have loved at all' (*In Memoriam*, XXVII, 15; LXXXV, 3). Memories, and their meaning, are a frequent theme in Tennyson, but so is the future. In his poems he, or his characters, often 'dip into the future far as human eye can see' (R 688, l 15), or 'rise upon a wind of prophecy/Dilating on the future' (R 764, ll 154–5). The 'Ring out, wild bells' section of *In Memoriam* (CVI), another obvious example of this, manages in its thirty-two lines to refer to his own personal and poetic development ('Ring out the grief that saps the mind, . . . Ring out, ring out my mournful rhymes, But ring the fuller minstrel in') and also to a wide range of hopes for improvement in society, politics, manners, medicine; it reverts to his passionate belief in a League of Nations ('Ring out the thousand wars of old, Ring in the thousand years of peace'); it ends on 'the Christ that is to be'—'the broader Christianity of the future', as he glosses it.

Now Tennyson was not of course the first poet to be concerned with such themes of Mutability, *tempus fugit*, calling back yesterday, 'looking before and after', nor am I the first commentator to remark on this preoccupation of his. To make only three references: among his immediate predecessors, Keats and Shelley, both influences on him, were in their different ways much concerned with Time; and many recent critics have quoted and descanted upon Humphry House's observation that Tennyson 'was an Aeonian poet; one on whom the consciousness of time bore like a burden; that is why Geology and Astronomy were[in his late poem, 'Parnassus', R 1411] "terrible Muses".'[3] We shall return to those Muses: but to mention them reminds one of further enormous ranges of Time which Tennyson, as poet, uniquely made his own. *In Memoriam*, his most ambitious and inclusive poem on our theme, has the word 'immortal' in its opening line, and its closing words are: 'one far-off divine event,/To which the whole creation moves'. It is concerned with eschatology and teleology, but also with the past, present and future at a multitude of levels—Tennyson himself as man and as poet, his friend Hallam whom the poem celebrates, the embryo's development within the womb, the progress of the nation and the nations, and of human beliefs and knowledge, the inheritance and the prospects of mankind, the evolutionary process in the animal kingdom and in plants, the evidence and implications about the universe provided by recent discoveries and theories in astronomy and geology. No English poem explores so many dimensions of time, besides treating of those two modes of being 'out of time', memorably connected in section XCV when, experiencing a 'trance' which removes him from the temporal world and body, 'The dead man touched me from the past' and the poet

> came on that which is, and caught
> The deep pulsations of the world,
>
> Aeonian music measuring out
> The steps of Time—the shocks of Chance—
> The blows of Death . . . (ll 39–43)

Here he simultaneously gains the assurance that 'the dead man' lives and has memory of him, and that Godhead exists—'that which is'[4]—what elsewhere in the poem he describes more tentatively as 'That which we dare invoke to bless; . . . The Power in darkness whom we guess' (CXXIV, 1–4).

Tennyson of course had available to him ranges of time unsuspected by earlier generations. Geology, remarked J. A. Froude in 1864, 'is not a century old, and its periods are measured by millions of years'.[5] It was geology, 'above all other sciences', wrote the influential geologist Poulett Scrope in 1826, that makes us aware of the 'important but humiliating fact' that the historical periods which appear to us as 'of incalculable duration, are in all probability but trifles in the calendar of Nature': and, he continued, 'The leading idea which is present in all our researches, and which accompanies every fresh observation, the sound which to the ear of the student of Nature seems continually echoed from every part of her works, is—Time!—Time!—Time!'

Charles Lyell begins his magisterial *Principles of Geology* in 1830 with the stress that this is an historical, not a merely descriptive, science ('Geology is the science which investigates the successive changes that have taken place in the organic and inorganic kingdoms of nature'); he claims that the 'connexions brought to light' by it are 'far more astonishing and unexpected' than those discovered in human history, and comments that 'Never, perhaps, did any science, with the exception of astronomy, unfold, in an equally brief period [as the last thirty years], so many novel and unexpected truths, and overturn so many preconceived opinions'.[6] Not everyone abandoned the opinions being thus challenged. In 1859, the year of Darwin's *Origin of Species* (which owed much to Lyell), the Bampton Lecturer, Canon George Rawlinson, was solemnly explicating Bishop Ussher's 4004 BC chronology: Moses' mother Jochebed had probably met Jacob, who could have known

Noah's son Shem; and Shem probably knew Methuselah, who had for 243 years overlapped with Adam.[7]

But Rawlinson was an Oxford man, a Fellow of Exeter. At Tennyson's Cambridge, the intellectual atmosphere was more liberal and progressive (as Basil Willey, of Cambridge, remarks), though the sciences which Tennyson began to absorb were for him, as for his exact contemporary Darwin, extracurricular studies. In his sonnet addressed to Cambridge in 1830, Tennyson informs the University that 'your manner sorts/Not with this age wherefrom ye stand apart' (R 287, ll 10–11), and in *The Princess* he sketches a more modernistic syllabus than existed anywhere in Britain in 1847; the ladies study geology, biology, chemistry and physics, though they draw the line at surgery as liable to 'Encarnalize their spirits' (R 741, l 298). Later, as a father, he kept his boys up to date in science (*Mem.*, ii, 408).

Now Canon Rawlinson cannot be taken as a complete, or eminent, embodiment of the Oxford mind, but one appreciates why one of Tennyson's fellow Apostles at Cambridge (who on principle used a lower-case 'o' for the rival university) used to say: 'I often wonder what we have done to deserve being so gifted, as we are, so much above those cursed idiotic oxford brutes'.[8] Certainly when in 1842 young G. G. Bradley, an Oxford man later to become Dean of Westminster and a close friend of Tennyson's, first met him in the company of other ex-Apostles, he was greatly struck by the differences between the two universities' preoccupations: 'The [Tractarian] questions that so deeply stirred our seniors and ourselves at Oxford . . . were scarcely mentioned, or, if mentioned, were spoken of as matters of secondary or remote interest' (*Mem.*, i, 204). That past which concerned the Tractarians never much exercised Tennyson's mind, and indeed the newly discovered geological past was a more intelligent preoccupation. G. M. Young, in his lecture on 'The Age of Tennyson', quoted Matthew Arnold's criticism that Tennyson 'lacked intellectual power', but drily comments on that Oxford view: 'I cannot recall any passage in Arnold's writings which suggests that he had ever given a thought to the ichthyosaurus'.[9] Tennyson had; and these prehistoric beasts had featured in the Apostles' slang. Thus, Arthur Hallam, revisiting Cambridge a year or so after going down, found the customs, topics and slang so altered that he felt he could not now reside there with pleasure. As he wrote to Tennyson: 'I should feel like a melancholy Pterodactyl winging his lonely flight among the linnets, eagles and flying fishes of our degenerate post-Adamic world' (10 April 1832; *Mem.*, i, 85). Tennyson's interest in these 'monstrous efts' (R 1037, i, 132) was lifelong; on his last visit to London, at the age of eighty-two, he insisted on revisiting the geology rooms at the Natural History Museum 'and seeing again his old friends the Ichthyosaurus, the Plesiosaurus, and the Giant Sloth' (*Mem.*, ii, 413). More to the point, he had so far absorbed this geological, biological and astronomical knowledge into the whole texture of his mind that it was richly available to his poetry; geology and astronomy might be intellectually and spiritually terrifying, but they were for him the greatest of the sciences, and they were Muses that inspired him. It was partly for such reasons that T. S. Eliot judged that '*In Memoriam* is not only a greater technical achievement than any of Arnold's poems, but a more complex and comprehensive expression of an historic phase of thought and feeling, of the grandeur and the tragedy of the Victorian age'.[10]

Eliot thought of using as an epigraph to his *Four Quartets* a sentence from Tennyson's great contemporary Dickens—the philosophical reflection of Mr Roker, in the Fleet Prison in *Pickwick Papers* (chapter 42), 'What a rum thing Time is, ain't it, Neddy?'[11] He thought better of it (this being the second time Dickens missed out in Eliot's headings, for *The Waste Land* had originally been entitled, from another snatch of Dickensian dialogue, *He Do the Police in Different Voices*)—but Tennyson would never have contemplated using such a jaunty epigraph. It would have been as out of character as his saying, with Oscar Wilde, that no one can ever be certain of the afterlife or the end of the Cromwell Road. He was more solemn on serious matters, and when once he tried to transpose his concern about Time into a lighter key, in 'The "How?" and the "Why"', the result was not felicitous and he got slapped down by John Stuart Mill:[12]

> The world is somewhat; it goes on somehow;
> But what is the meaning of *then* and *now*?
>   I feel there is something; but how and what?
> I feel there is somewhat; but what and why?
> I cannot tell if that somewhat be I . . . (R 186, ll 21–5)

I mention Dickens, however, to contrast him with Tennyson rather in matters of preoccupation than of tone. Dickens's mind was not broodingly philosophical, nor was he much more interested than Arnold in the ichthyosaurus—though he does imagine a megalosaurus 'waddling like an elephantine lizard up Holborn Hill' in an antediluvian London, and Susan Shatto has related his vision of these 'monstrous efts' to Tennyson's.[13] If we were concerned only with present Time, with their *times*, there would be much point in writing about these authors as eminently 'The Two Voices' of the age, for in their different ways and kinds they are fuller witnesses to it than any of their rivals; and indeed they often coincide, in their pathos, for instance, or their adulation of domesticity,[14] and even in areas of their politics. Contemporaries praised them both for combining genius with English commonsense. They even looked alike, as Tennyson's friend Edward FitzGerald averred (*Mem.*, ii, 104)—a point brought home to me when the *Radio Times* illustrated a Dickens feature of mine with a photograph of the poet. During the years when Tennyson was writing *In Memoriam*, Dickens's Scrooge was arriving, by a different route and to different effect, at a declaration which the protagonist of that poem might have made, 'I will live in the Past, the Present, and the Future!' and, Time being now such a fashionable guest at literary colloquia, the novelist's concern with the tenses has lately been almost as much discussed as the poet's.[15] But here is a time-reference characteristic of Dickens, which lies out of Tennyson's range; it comes from one of those remarkable evocations of urban change in *Dombey and Son* (1846–48), when he is describing how Staggs's Gardens, in the north of London, has disappeared in the track of the new railway line going into Euston, and the whole area has gone over to the railway spirit: 'There was even railway-time observed in clocks, as if the sun itself has given in' (chapter 15). Tennyson did not have that anthropomorphic wit, nor that concern with the paraphernalia of modernity—for Dickens was referring here to the new standardised time (our Greenwich time) adopted in 1840 because railway timetables could not be constructed on the assumption that noon was the moment, whether you were in London or Land's End, when the sun stood highest in the sky; there was seven minutes' difference between the two.

Inevitably the railway became the main symbol of the age's rapid changes; it was indeed a main or contributory cause of many of them. 'How times [have] changed in the last forty years', exclaimed Froude in 1881, introducing an essay on religious practices and beliefs, and unbelief; 'we [have] been travelling on a spiritual railroad'.[16] Tennyson reached for the same metaphor at the end of 'Locksley Hall', when the protagonist (a figure not very distant from his creator) after the switchback of exaltation and depression about the prospects of enjoyment 'in this march of mind/In the steamship, in the railway, in the thoughts that shake mankind' (R 688, ll 165–6), eventually opts for the present and future and not for 'some retreat':

Forward, forward let us range,
Let the great world spin for ever down the ringing grooves of
change (R 688, ll 180–1)

That line was written in 1830, twelve years before the poem was
published (but Tennyson, as Professor Ricks has shown, was frugal with
and tenacious of his most fragmentary creations[17])—written when the
poet, very enterprisingly, went by that momentous first train from
Liverpool to Manchester (I wonder how this obscure young man from
Lincolnshire managed to get a ticket) and, as he later explained,
'thought that the wheels ran in a groove. It was a black night and there
was such a vast crowd round the train at the station that we could not see
the wheels' (*Mem.*, i, 195). Tennyson's mistake strikes one as significant;
for by 1842, when the poem was published, he had had opportunities to
observe railway wheels better, by daylight, and by 1892 had had ample
time to tinker with this line as he did with many others. He was capable
of suppressing a poem because he had got the gnat's behaviour in it
wrong (R 185) or holding one up because the camel's colouring in the
moonlight was inappropriate (R 300), or for some other fault in its
natural history (R 284), and remained vexed for decades because one
poem of reminiscence had 'two and thirty years ago' when he should
have written, 'one and thirty' (*Mem.*, i, 475). So obviously, by contrast, it
did not seem important to him to get railway wheels right—a cavalier
attitude towards this dominant symbol of the age. It was salutary to
protest in his poem 'Mechanophilus (In the Time of the First Railways)'
against the cockiness of the age—the assumption that, because it had
invented railways and other such mechanical wonders, it was also the
first human generation to 'stand and understand,/And sunder false from
true', that 'All other times were but the shade—The preface unto this'.[18]
Nevertheless there is no merit in getting those railways wheels wrong:
not that he often writes, or writes very effectively, about railways or such
topics. In a conversation, indeed, he remembered his old friend, and
'fancied, standing by a railway at night, the railway must be like some
great Ichthyosaurus' (*Mem.*, i, 277); in a poem he writes, with what may
now impress us as prophetic aptness, about railway vandalism:
'Wrecked—your train—or all but wrecked? a shattered wheel? a vicious
boy' (R 1359, l 214). He makes momentary incursions into the regions
explored by the social novelists of his age—'the giant-factoried city-
gloom' (R 1095, l 5), 'When a Mammonite mother kills her babe for a
burial fee' (R 1037, Part i, l 45), and the like. Such lines, however, rarely
engage his major poetic skills; they do not rise above the level of

journalistic clichés, they lack the verbal felicity, and that sense of the eye on the object, so abundant in his natural observations—'When rosy plumelets tuft the larch' (*In Memoriam*, XCI, l), 'A full sea glazed with muffled moonlight' (R 741, l 244).

Tennyson's difficulty in treating poetically the material texture of his age, rather than its spiritual atmosphere, was not unique to him, of course. One might read the whole of his poetry, remarks G. Robert Stange, 'without becoming conscious of modern London. The city that one feels is most real to him is the Camelot of the *Idylls of the King*'—but Stange is offering Tennyson as an example of 'The Frightened Poets' (the title of his essay in the Dyos/Wolff collection *The Victorian City*[19]). The novelists, led by Dickens, notoriously found it much easier than the poets to accommodate the city and the railway and such into their imaginative vision, and Tennyson was both a participant and a major exhibit in the critical debate about whether, how far and how the poets should try to compete: and he worrried about it. As House remarks, 'For so great a poet, for a man as intelligent as he was, he seems to have lacked to quite an extraordinary degree a genuine internal conviction of the value of what he was doing'.[20] This appears in those modern frame-poems used as prologues or epilogues to some of his poems set in the past. In one of these, 'The Epic' (R 582) preluding 'Morte d'Arthur', he uses a dummy-figure, the supposed poet Everard Hall, to express his own doubts about reviving anything like epic grandeur:

> 'Why take the style of those heroic times?
> For nature brings not back the Mastodon,
> Nor we those times . . .' (R 582, ll 35–7)

—though in a manuscript version Everard Hall's credentials are deliberately tarnished by his expressing that cockiness about today which Tennyson so hated: 'Old things are gone; we are wiser than our Sires' (R 583 n). His reference to the fossil-record may be paralleled from John Stuart Mill's essay on 'Theism', written in the 1850s: 'Religions tend [now] to be discussed, at least by those who reject them, less as intrinsically true or false than as products thrown up by certain stages of civilisation, and which, like the animal and vegetable productions of a geological period, perish in those which succeed it from the cessation of the conditions necessary for their continued existence.'[21]

Tennyson was very much a man of his time in adopting this historicist, and specifically this evolutionary, approach:

The old order changeth, yielding place to new,
And God fulfils Himself in many ways,
Lest one good custom should corrupt the world
                    (R 585, ll 240–2; 1742, ll 408–10)

—the first line of which was so crucial to Tennyson's meaning in the
Idylls that it was repeated from the final one to the first one (R 1469,
l 508). Or recall: 'Our little systems have their day;/They have their day
and cease to be . . . ' (*In Memoriam*, Prologue, 17–18). There of course
he is considering religious systems, but he applies the idea elsewhere to
literary forms, or political arrangements, as in 'Love thou thy Land'
(R 613):

> For Nature also, cold and warm,
>   And moist and dry, devising long,
>   Through many agents making strong,
> Matures the individual form.
>
> Meet is it changes should control
>   Our being, lest we rust in ease.
>   We all are changed by still degrees,
> All but the basis of the soul. (ll 37–44)

Change, he recognised, was inevitable. Stagnation, he said, was 'more
dangerous than Revolution' (*Mem.*, ii, 339), or, fifty years earlier,
'Byron and Shelley, . . . however mistaken they may be, did yet give the
world another heart and new pulses, and so we are kept going. Blessed be
those that grease the wheels of the old world, insomuch as to move on is
better than to stand still' (*Mem.*, i, 141).

It was a cliché, but none the less true for its being one, that his was
eminently an Age of Change—rapid and manysided change, 'an awful
moment of transition', as he later put it (*Mem.*, ii, 337). It was so from his
youth. Three times in *In Memoriam* he evokes the discussions he had
held with Arthur Hallam and other Apostle friends at Cambridge,
and every time it is change that preoccupies them (LXXI, 9–11;
LXXXVII, 21–4; LXXXIX, 35)

> we talked
> Of men and minds, the dust of change, . . .
> The days that grow to something strange . . .
>   . . . we held debate . . .
>   . . . on mind and art,

And labour, and the changing mart,
And all the framework of the land . . .
We . . . touched the changes of the state.

'Yesterday,' Hallam wrote to him in 1832, 'I saw (perhaps) the last king of England go down to open the first assembly of delegates from a sovereign people' (*Mem.*, i, 92). And the previous year Hallam had written, alarmedly, about 'the lurid presages of the times that are coming; . . . the awful commotions of society, which few of us do not expect,—the disruption, it may be, of those common bands which hold together our social existence, necessarily followed by an occurrence on a larger scale of the same things that were witnessed in France forty years ago'.[22] Tennyson too abhorred the French Revolution, and feared a repetition of it in England or across Europe. Towards the end of *In Memoriam* (CXXVII, 1–8), however, he looks more hopefully at even the apparently disturbing developments in theology and in politics, present and impending:

And all is well, though faith and form
  Be sundered in the night of fear;
  Well roars the storm to those who hear
A deeper voice across the storm,

Proclaiming social truth shall spread,
  And justice, even though thrice again
  The red fool-fury of the Seine
Should pile her barricades with dead.

And after further dire predictions he ends this section with Hallam, who from his point of vantage above has a better perspective on these disturbances, and can hear that 'deeper voice across the storm':

While thou, dear spirit, happy star,
O'erlook'st the tumult from afar,
And smilest, knowing all is well. (ll 18–20)

Professor Ricks notes that some current optimistic implications of geology underlie this section, and quotes remarks by Lyell on volcanoes which are, in fact, 'agents of a conservative principle above all others essential to the stability of the system', and contending that 'the general tendency of subterranean movements, when their effects are considered

for a sufficient number of ages, is eminently beneficial' (R 976n).
(Inevitably, Tennyson was quoted in the funeral sermon on Lyell in
Westminster Abbey—not *In Memoriam*, as it happens, but the
'Locksley Hall' lines about 'one increasing purpose' and 'heir of all the
ages'.[23]) I would add that Tennyson's reformist-conservative political
opinions found analogies in, and support from, the outcome of the great
pre-Lyell debate between the Catastrophists and the Uniformitarians:
had geological and biological change occurred through a series of one-
off catastrophes, or through a long slow uniform process of erosion and
other such causes? Uniformitarianism triumphed: by analogy, revolution belonged with the old discredited catastrophist theory of
change, and thus was 'against Nature'. If only men would 'Let Nature
be [their] teacher', they would learn, from Tennyson's interpretation of
it, what Sidney Webb was to proclaim to the Labour Party Conference
in 1920, 'the inevitability of gradualness'. 'Regard gradation', Tennyson
advises (R 613, l 67), make 'seasonable changes fair/And innovation
grade by grade' (R 480, ll 151–2). Referring, in 1833, to the coming
year's 'new developments' in 'the changeful West' and the possibility of
violence, he again uses the slow progress of Nature, in the seasons, as a
model (R 475, ll 105–9):

> A simpler, saner lesson might he learn
>   Who reads thy gradual process, Holy Spring.
> Thy leaves possess the season in their turn,
>   And in their time thy warblers rise on wing.
> How surely glidest thou from March to May

and so on. In another poem ('An Idle Rhyme', R 662) he explains why he
is reluctant to write poems on topics of the day, because he is concerned
with the longer perspectives of time:

> The muse would stumble from the tune,
>   If I should ask her 'Plump my purse,
> Be for some popular forenoon
>   The leading article in verse'. . . . (ll 5–8)

> For, though she has her hopes and fears,
>   She dwells not on a single page,
> But thrids the annals of the years,
>   And runs her eyes from age to age. (ll 13–16)

'What's near is large to modern eyes', he continues, but not always as important as we take it to be: and he ends on his preferring to attend to 'The deep pulsations of the world' (R 662, 1 40)—a line later transferred to *In Memoriam*, XLV.

This long-term perspective inevitably had conservative implications, as was pointed out by Edward Dowden in his admirable essay on Tennyson as the poet of law (1878):

> No one so largely as Mr Tennyson, has represented in art the new thoughts and feelings, which form the impassioned side of the modern conception of progress. His imagination is ever haunted by 'the vision of the world, and all the wonder that would be'. But the hopes and aspirations of Mr Tennyson are not those of the radical or movement character. He is in all his poems conservative as well as liberal . . . [Dowden contrasts Shelley's more radical and Utopian poems about the regeneration of society, and continues—] Now Mr Tennyson's conception of progress, which he has drawn from his moral and intellectual environment . . . is widely different. No idea perhaps occupies a place in his poems so central as that of the progress of the race . . . [a concern which Dowden proceeds to illustrate, from nine poems]. But . . . the progress of mankind is . . . represented as taking place gradually and slowly, and its consummation is placed in a remote future . . . [And after citing examples of this, he comments] These days and works of the crowning race are, however, far beyond our grasp; and the knowledge of this . . . puts a check upon certain of our hopes and strivings. He who is possessed by this faith will look for no speedy regeneration of men in the social or political sphere, and can but imperfectly sympathise with those enthusiastic hearts whose expectations, nourished by their ardours and desires, are eager and would forestall futurity.[24]

This is well said. Still, it was a conservatism founded on an awareness of change, of 'Eternal process moving on' (LXXXII, 5); it belonged to its time, and had roots quite different from, say, Dr Johnson's conservatism a century before. Tennyson might be 'Sick of the coming time and coming woe' (R 472, 1 3), but he knew that it would be different from today, and there were many occasions when he pictured the future, at least in the longer run, as better—though it might be more comfortable to sleep through the harder intervening years of struggle and confusion, as he prettily puts it in the 'Envoi' (R 632) to his retelling of the Sleeping Beauty story:

Well—were it not a pleasant thing
To fall asleep with all one's friends;
To pass with all our social ties
To silence from the paths of men;
And every hundred years to rise
And learn the world, and sleep again;
To sleep through terms of mighty wars,
And wake on science grown to more,
On secrets of the brain, the stars,
As wild as aught of fairy lore;
And all that else the years will show,
The Poet-forms of stronger hours,
The vast Republics that may grow,
The federations and the Powers;
Titanic forces taking birth
In divers seasons, divers climes;
For we are Ancients of the earth,
And in the morning of the times. (ll 3–20)

These lines survey a characteristic sample of his curiosity about the future—political and international, and scientific and literary, developments: and his first long poem, *The Princess*, sets itself to explore, however imperfectly, the future of the relations between the sexes, particularly when—as was not then the case—women had access to higher education. And note those secrets unravelled by science, 'As wild as any fairy lore'—a notion echoed in 'Locksley Hall': 'With the fairy tales of science, and the long result of Time' (R 688). Tennyson found science wonderful and exciting, and his was no ignorant or innocent wonderment; he was, as every student knows, exceptionally well informed, and commanded the respect of such professionals as the biologist T. H. Huxley and the astronomer Sir Norman Lockyer. Indeed, he was more intelligently aware of scientific advances, and more openminded about them, than he was about the literary developments during his long life.

Thus, it was intelligent of him, as an undergraduate, to seize upon the new embryology developed in Germany, showing that the human embryo passes through stages during which it resembles fishes, birds and lower mammalia, and thus to propound to a college discussion the theory that 'the development of the human brain might possibly be traced from the radiated, vermicular, molluscous and vertebrate organisms'[25] (*Mem.*, i, 44). It was precisely these discoveries which

Herbert Spencer, twenty-five years later, generalised into his evolutionary Law of Progress.[26] Spencer was excited by the embryologists' theory of the development of the organism as a progress from homogeneity to heterogeneity; and Tennyson in an early poem makes this point. The soul in 'The Palace of Art' (1832 version) speaks (R 409n, ll 13–20):

'From change to change four times within the womb
    The brain is moulded,' she began,
'So through all phases of all thought I come
    Into the perfect man.

'All nature widens upward: evermore
    The simpler essence lower lies.
More complex is more perfect, owning more
    Discourse, more widely wise . . .'

—lines he was right to suppress, for he might have remarked about them, as Wordsworth did of his poem 'Character of the Happy Warrior', 'It does not best fulfil the conditions of poetry: but it is a chain of extremely *valooable* thoughts'.

Tennyson was twenty-three when he wrote those lines. At that age, Dickens (to revert to that comparison), who was three years his junior and another early starter, was publishing *Sketches by Boz illustrative of Every-day Life and Every-day People*. Both men were to dominate their chosen literary form for several decades. Tennyson had little literary capacity for exploring the everyday; Dickens's knowledge of science was negligible and mostly incorrect, and he had no discernible theory of the ranges of development, from the nebula's or the species' or the embryo's, to the nation's or mankind's, which preoccupied Tennyson. Dickens has no consciousness that our sun is 'dying' and 'will pass' (III, 8; R 1359, l 182) or that, as Tennyson knew when a teenager, the 'rays of many a rolling central Star,/Aye flashing earthward have not reached us yet' (R 166, ll 3–4). In his *Christmas Books* Dickens plays around—but much more mundanely—with literary time-machines ('in a whimsical kind of masque': Author's Preface), but he has no real interest in futurity, whether it is that of Britain a generation or so ahead, or that of the human race when it is—what? extinct (R 1367), just another fossil 'blown about the desert dust' (LVI, 19)? caught up in one of the 'vast eddies in the flood/Of onward time' (CXXVIII, 5–6)? or still moving upward, 'working out the beast' and letting 'the ape and tiger die'

(CXVIII, 27–8; R 1454, 1 2)—not that they will die easily, as Huxley remarked in a witty allusion to *In Memoriam*?[27] or when it arrives at being that 'crowning race . . ./No longer half-akin to brute' (*In Memoriam*, Epilogue, 128, 133)? 'But, how much of the Future? . . . Did Louisa see these things?' (*Hard Times*, 'Final' chapter)—no, nor did any of Dickens's characters in his final chapters, nor did he. Of the afterlife, his conception—very unlike Tennyson's, as we shall see—was conventional, uninsistent, unanxious, incurious. 'The number of great subjects in which Dickens took no interest whatever,' observed Dean Inge, 'is amazing.'[28] Nevertheless Dickens was very knowledgeable, and on important matters; and, for many of our purposes in trying to make the mid-nineteenth century comprehensible, it makes sense to call it 'the age of Dickens'. 'CITY TYPISTS WORK IN DICKENSIAN CONDITIONS' runs a headline in our local paper, and readers understand. Typists cannot work, though, in *Tennysonian* conditions. 'But the age of Tennyson! The notion is, of course, preposterous', wrote Alfred Austin, the future Poet Laureate, in a sprightly denigration of the present incumbent in 1870: 'How do we note the past ages? We speak of the age of Homer, the age of Dante, the age of Shakespeare. Can anybody in his senses imagine posterity speaking of our age as the age of Tennyson? Posterity will be too kind to do anything so sardonic. It will speak of it as the age of Railways, the age of Destructive Criticism, or the age of Penny Papers.'

But Austin acknowledged that 'he thinks with us of this particular day, feels with us of this day, and is the exponent of such poetical feelings as in this day we are capable of . . . he shares our littleness with us': for, agreeing that 'The age is scientific or it is nothing', Austin maintains that 'science and all its processes, its aims and its methods alike, are antagonistic to poetry, and its aims and methods'.[29]

Tennyson's poetry had its weaknesses and its pusillanimities, but here surely it was stronger and more intelligent than the post-Romantic commonplace expressed by Austin. Tennyson found in science a suggestive analogy to other forms of change, individual and social, and he could render its findings with a feeling and brilliance unequalled in any English poetry inspired by recent science since those eighteenth-century poets surveyed by Marjorie Nicolson in her *Newton Demands the Muse* (1946). The anti-scientific bias of Romanticism had been an intellectual liability, though necessary perhaps in its poets' explorations of other forms of truth. Perhaps only Tennyson, in his time, remarks Gertrude Himmelfarb,[30] would instinctively have seen a train as an ichthyosaurus. Certainly no poet of the period would have seen—as he did, in the same conversation, quoted above—the weald of Kent as the 'delta of a great river flowing from as far as Newfoundland' (*Mem.*, i, 277) and have made, out of such a consciousness, lines such as these (*In Memoriam*, CXXIII, 1–8), which demonstrate the shallowness of Austin's poetic:

> There rolls the deep where grew the tree.
> O earth, what changes hast thou seen!
> There where the long street roars, hath been
> The stillness of the central sea.
>
> The hills are shadows, and they flow
> From form to form, and nothing stands;
> They melt like mist, the solid lands,
> Like clouds they shape themselves and go.

At levels rarely coinciding with Dickens's, and not only in the history of nineteenth-century poetry, this *was* 'the age of Tennyson'—and not least because of his preoccupation with time. Jerome Buckley begins his admirable book *The Triumph of Time: A Study of the Victorian Concepts of Time, History, Progress, and Decadence* from the proposition that 'The Victorians, at least as their verse and prose reveal them, were preoccupied almost obsessively with time and all the devices that measure time's flight. The clock beats out the little lives of men in *In Memoriam . . .*'[31] In this respect, certainly, their Poet Laureate was a 'Representative Man': and here is another.

I quoted Froude on 'the spiritual railroad' of the years between the 1840s and the 1880s. In a more famous passage making the same retrospect, he surveys the years when Tennyson emerged as a major author: 'It was an era of new ideas, of swift if silent spiritual revolution'. And after instancing changes in the political sphere, in religion, in science and technology, in philosophy, and in the understanding of the past, he has his famous purple-passage about the intellectual and spiritual disturbance these caused:

> Thus all around us, the intellectual lightships had broken from their moorings, and it was then a new and trying experience. The present generation [he is writing in 1884] which has grown up in an open spiritual ocean, which has got used to it and has learned to swim for itself, will never know what it was to find the lights all drifting, the compasses all awry, and nothing left to steer by but the stars.

The best and bravest of his contemporaries, Froude continues, faced that open sea and tried to find what certainties remained: 'Tennyson became the voice of this feeling in poetry; Carlyle in what is called prose', and Tennyson's poems—up to *In Memoriam*, Froude specified—'became part of our minds, the expression in exquisite language of the feelings which were working in ourselves'.[32]

Tennyson's reluctance to engage creatively with the present, at the material and topical level of the railway, the city, or the leading-article, was (I remarked) not unique to him. Mid-nineteenth-century poetry in general makes a poor showing here, virtually ceding this territory to prose fiction. But the cultural tendency in this direction was confirmed, in him, by strong personal obsessions: positively, by his preference for what was distant in space and in time (past or future), and his inclination to brood philosophically on the years, the ages and Eternity rather than the day; negatively by his distaste for the present, whether the current state of his nation or civilisation or, during crucial phases of his life, his own immediate situation. His predilection for 'the far-off world', for the remembered landscape, has been quoted above. 'The words "far, far away" had always a strange charm for me', he remarked, talking about his boyhood (*Mem.*, i, 11), and as an old man he wrote a poem with this title (R 1405). In his teens he had written a poem beginning 'Oh sad *No more!* oh sweet *No more!*/Oh strange *No more!*' (R 161)—an early attempt at a familiar theme (and the workings of this 'passion of the past' in his poetry are such a familiar concern of Tennyson criticism that I shall noł discuss them further here). But his old Cambridge friend James Spedding, scholar and acute critic, also wrote in 1835 about Tennyson's 'almost personal dislike of the present, whatever it may be' and, in another letter of that year: 'he is a man always discontented with the Present until it has become the Past, and then he yearns towards it, and worships it, and not only worships it, but is discontented because it is past' (*Mem.*, i, 154).[33] Again this personal inclination was allied to a cultural inheritance; there are analogies to this sentiment in Wordsworth and in Keats, and in Shelley's 'To a Skylark':

> We look before and after,
> And pine for what is not: . . .
> Our sweetest songs are those that talk of saddest thought.

The Romantic poets, said Matthew Arnold, 'did not know enough', they turned their back on too much, they did not 'apply modern ideas to life' ('The Function of Criticism', 'Heinrich Heine'). Well, some of this—

some of Dean Inge's imputation—could be levelled against Tennyson. But like Dickens, though in very different areas, he was very knowledgeable. Thackeray, meeting him again in 1841, remarked: 'His conversation is often delightful, I think, full of breadth, manliness and humour: he reads all sorts of things, swallows them and digests them like a great poetical boa-constrictor as he is'.[34] One remembers those formidable worklists he drew up in his early manhood (*Mem.*, i, 124), for all the world like Milton preparing over decades 'by labour and intent study . . . [that] I might perhaps leave something so written to aftertimes, as they would not willingly let die':

Monday.	History, German.
Tuesday.	Chemistry, German.
Wednesday.	Botany, German.
Thursday.	Electricity, German.
Friday.	Animal Physiology, German.
Saturday.	Mechanics.
Sunday.	Theology.
Next Week.	Italian in the afternoon.
Third Week.	Greek. *Evenings.* Poetry.

The sciences here offer a new interpretation of that part of the world which occupies Tennyson's creative attention; the equivalent—entirely missing from his reading—for the social novelists would be the Blue Books and Parliamentary Reports which provide analogues (and sometimes even a source) for their fiction. As Ulysses says of his son Telemachus, left to cope with the quotidian and mundane: 'He works his work, I mine'. The novelists, like Telemachus, could stay usefully 'centred in the sphere/Of common duties'; Tennyson felt rather the Ulyssean ambition 'To follow knowledge like a sinking star/Beyond the utmost bound of human thought' (R 560, ll 39–40, 31–2).

I will finish on a range of his poetical speculations in just that area, beyond the ordinary bounds of human thought: those 'out of time' experiences, whether mystical or in the life beyond the grave. The tragic early death of his brilliant, beloved and revered friend Arthur Hallam not only provoked his greatest poem but also focused what had always been and would always remain an obsession with him, the question of immortality. The life after death, he never tired of maintaining, was the cardinal point of Christianity, and he was specially pleased when he could get a bishop to agree with him on this (*Mem.*, ii, 420). Another kind of authority, that of those nearing their own investigation of the matter, was often consulted. 'With the country folk he loved to converse,' recalled his son Hallam, 'especially seeking out the poor *old* men, from whom he always tried to ascertain their thoughts upon death and the future life' (*Mem.*, ii, 211). He became a founder member of the Society for Psychical Research, though he never believed in Spiritualism. He never tired, either, of asserting the meaninglessness of this life unless another followed it, or of detailing the ways in which he might commit suicide if he ceased to believe that one existed. 'If I ceased to believe in any chance of another life,' he said in 1872, 'and of a great Personality somewhere in the Universe, I should not care a pin for anything'—a confession which the pious Humphry House found appalling. He would chloroform himself, or jump off Richmond Bridge (even if it might look comic), or, with poetical vagueness choose 'To drop head-foremost in the jaws/Of vacant darkness and to cease' (XXXIX, 15–16). In a rather quaint expression, he said that the idea of regarding the individual life as a mere preparation for the life of more perfect beings in a future human race was wholly unsatisfactory to him: 'I should consider that *a liberty had been taken with me* if I were made simply a means of ushering in something higher than myself' [my italics].[35] It is a theme of many poems besides *In Memoriam*— 'Vastness', 'Locksley Hall Sixty Years After' and others—well discussed by Sir Charles in his essay 'Tennyson's Religion' (*Six Tennyson Essays*). He had a Mrs Gummidge-like conviction that, however others might yearn for or feel about immortality, he 'felt it more . . . Yes, yes, I feel more than other people do, I do show it more. It's my misfortun' (*David Copperfield*, chapter 3). This appears in William Allingham's comic anecdote about when Tennyson told him, 'In my boyhood I had intuitions of Immortality—inexpressible! I have never been able to express them. I shall try some day'. Allingham made the mistake of concurring; he too had felt something of the kind. But the poet jealously rejected this confirmation: 'I don't believe you have. You say it out of rivalry.'[36] He became much identified with his convictions on this question. Moved by the letters he received on his eightieth birthday, he said: 'I don't know what I have done to make people feel like that towards me, except that I have always kept my faith in Immortality' (*Mem.*, ii, 359).

All this is familiar knowledge; but what I had not realised until I read Geoffrey Rowell's *Hell and the Victorians* (1974) was that in this preoccupation with the afterlife Tennyson was, again, the age writ large, for though, as Dr Rowell remarks, 'eschatology was not a new subject of controversy in the nineteenth century, . . . there is little doubt that it was discussed more publicly, and perhaps with more vehemence, than in any previous age'. So it is not surprising, he comments, that '*In Memoriam*, with its hope of a future life, and its awareness of the difficulties caused to a belief in immortality by the new scientific theories, should have enjoyed such popularity', and he quotes the great preacher F. W. Robertson as saying that the poem contained 'the *most* satisfying things that have been ever said on the future state' (*Mem.*, i, 298n; italics Robertson's).[37] Certainly the poem contains much speculation about what happens in the afterlife, and scholars such as Eleanor Mattes and Dwight Culler have assessed the possible influence upon Tennyson's thinking in various recent books on the matter.[38] I have nothing to add, in detail, to what they say, but I want to remark how very mid-Victorian his Heaven is. It has often been remarked that, though *In Memoriam* begins with the invocation 'Strong Son of God', it contains hardly any specifically Christian doctrine; indeed Coventry Patmore thought that no modern work had 'done so much to *undermine* popular religion'.[39] What is less often noticed is that it contains no Day of Judgement, and that its Heaven has no angels and virtually no God. Nor is the possibility of Hell contemplated—though indeed Tennyson's speculations are concerned mainly with Hallam and himself, who have led tolerably virtuous lives. But all of this coincides with the theological developments surveyed by Dr Rowell, which included the phasing out of Hell. Tennyson's great unease about the 'everlasting fire' (*Matthew*, xvv, 41) was widespread, as Dr Rowell shows; there was much controversy about the translation of αιωνιος here, and Tennyson was disappointed that the Revised Version retained 'everlasting'.[40]

His friend the Reverend F. D. Maurice, whom he regarded as 'the truest Christian he knew in the world', was dismissed from his Chair at King's College, London, for the revisionism on this text and doctrine in his *Theological Essays* (1853); this volume was, significantly, dedicated to Tennyson, and *In Memoriam* is quoted in its Dedicatory Letter on 'the Christ that is to be'.[41] Tennyson showed public support for Maurice by publishing in 1855 his elegantly sympathetic verse epistle to him (R 1022), and similarly comforted his friend Jowett during the *Essays and Reviews* (1860) brouhaha which famously ended with the Privy Council's reversing the condemnation of another contributor on the same issue of everlasting punishment—'Hell dismissed with costs', in Bowen's quip.[42]

Dr Rowell's description of the increasingly popular view of the afterlife accords very closely with *In Memoriam*: 'It was an immortality of self-realisation, rather than an immortality of salvation, to which men looked forward, and so we find that in many nineteenth-century works on eschatology the future life is envisaged as a time of ever-increasing powers of mind and knowledge of the universe, attendance at some celestial university'. It was a secularisation of Heaven, obviously influenced by current ideas of change and progress: and Tennyson participates too in another anxiety, more man-oriented than God-oriented, which Dr Rowell discusses: 'In particular the question whether friends would recognise each other in heaven exercised many writers and preachers'.[43] The 'celestial university' idea appears in *In Memoriam* in such contentions as that Tennyson on earth is still 'following with an upward mind/The wonders that have come to thee [Hallam]' (XLI, 21–2), that the dead have 'larger eyes than ours' (LI, 15), and that Hallam has already been shown 'All knowledge that the sons of flesh/Shall gather in the cycled times' (LXXXV, 27–8). In a conversation, indeed, Tennyson argued that the newly ascended soul would begin in a celestial school (later to graduate to the celestial university?): 'We shall have much to learn in a future life, and I think we shall all be little children to begin with when we get to heaven, whatever our age when we die, and shall grow on there from childhood to the prime of life, at which we shall remain for ever'.[44] Elsewhere he imagines Hallam winning the responsibility, promotion and 'acclaim' (LXXV, 20) of which he was robbed on earth by his early death: he becomes, perhaps, a sort of celestial Cabinet Minister (XL, 17–20):

> And, doubtless, unto thee is given
> A life that bears immortal fruit
> In those great offices that suit
> The full-grown energies of heaven.

Christopher Ricks aptly comments that the word 'those' is sheer bluff— 'oh, *those*'.[45] One applauds Tennyson for avoiding the banality of the twanging of harps and endless singing of hymns through Eternity; but one notes the complete absence of God from his Heaven. He is reduced to being an offstage invisible Guarantor of one's getting there and meeting one's friends again.

The other eminently nineteenth-century feature of Tennyson's afterlife is the continuance 'out of time' of the progressive evolutionary processes observable 'in time'. 'I can hardly understand,' he said, 'how any great, imaginative man, who has deeply lived, suffered, thought and wrought, can doubt of the Soul's continuous progress in the after-life'

(*Mem.*, i, 321). He was fond of quoting his poem 'Wages' on the subject (R 1205, ll 8–10): the virtuous soul

> . . . desires no isles of the blest, no quiet seats of the just,
> To rest in a golden grove, or to bask in a summer sky:
> Give her the wages of going on, and not to die.

Or these lines from 'The Ring' (R 1383, ll 41–3; *Mem.*, ii, 365)

> Aeonian Evolution, swift or slow,
> Through all the Spheres—an ever opening height,
> An ever lessening earth . . .

But as his references to the 'isles of the blest' and other concepts of the afterlife remind us, many great imaginative men have not thought of 'continuous progress' as a feature of the afterlife. Tennyson was predisposed to do so because of the date of his birth. Again Dr Rowell offers many apposite comments and illustrations, for 'The notion of progress had also been taken up into some of the thinking concerning immortality, where the destiny of man was conceived as an unending progress rather than an arrival at a static perfection'.[46]

A similar secularity may, finally, be observed in Tennyson's accounts of his experiences 'out of time' during those trances which, as he said, 'I have frequently had, quite up from boyhood, when I have been alone' (*Mem.*, i, 320). His several accounts of these are very similar to one another, and to his verse rendering in 'The Ancient Sage' (R 1349, ll 229–39):

> And more, my son! for more than once when I
> Sat all alone, revolving in myself
> The word that is the symbol of myself,
> The mortal limit of the Self was loosed,
> And past into the Nameless, as a cloud
> Melts into Heaven. I touched my limbs, the limbs
> Were strange not mine—and yet no shade of doubt,
> But utter clearness, and through loss of Self
> The gain of such large life as matched with ours
> Were Sun to spark—unshadowable in words,
> Themselves but shadows of a shadow-world.

The prose account I began by quoting from the *Memoir* in fact began— Hallam omits the first few words in his transcription—'I have never had any revelations through anaesthetics'. Tennyson was replying to a cranky American, Benjamin Paul Blood, author of *The Anaesthetic Revelation and the Gist of Philosophy* and other works including *Tennyson's Trances and the Anaesthetic Revelation*.[47] Blood was a forerunner of Aldous Huxley and other such believers in a quick chemical trip into the extrasensory world. Such mechanical short cuts were not for Tennyson—too much like lotos-eating. But was 'repeating my own name two or three times'—'revolving in myself/The word that is the symbol of myself'—spiritually much more respectable? Such hypnotic mantras more usually, and traditionally, refer to the non-self, the other-worldly. Tennyson did not 'Abba, Abba' cry, but 'Alfred, Alfred'—or was it his surname that was invoked? The question seems to admit of debate. Dwight Culler entitles his opening chapter 'Tennyson, Tennyson, Tennyson' but cites no authority for the assumption (though he does usefully relate this trance-inducing device to the trick of hypnotic repetition in the poems). Harold Nicolson is more circumstantial: 'he . . . would sit upon the damp moss of Holywell Glen saying, "Alfred, Alfred", to himself, and again "Alfred", until every thing became very poignant, mystical and hazy'[48]—but this seems to owe more to Lytton Strachey than to documentary sources. Whichever name Tennyson used, such a self-regarding technique may strike us as a form of spiritual masturbation, and certainly as an extreme example of the Romantic poets' concern with the self. Tennyson went 'out of time', as he apprehended the Eternal Life, in ways that smacked of the time in which he wrote. He escaped beyond the usual 'bounds of human thought' by means more human than divine: but this was not inappropriate in an age that felt it was experiencing the death, or at least the disappearence, of God.

5 The Timing of *In Memoriam*

Michael Mason

In Memoriam, of all the really important long works of Victorian prose or poetry, is probably the one about whose composition the least information survives. Of the poem's 133 sections—131 numbered sections plus the so-called 'prologue' and 'epilogue'—less than one-fifth can be dated with certainty. A further third can be assigned dates of composition which are more or less tentative. And the growth of the general design of the poem is also controversial. We have Tennyson's own word for the fact that the earliest component sections were written without any idea of 'weaving' them together (to use his own striking term), but we do not know when Tennyson started to compose verses consciously designed for inclusion in a long poem about Hallam's death.

There is thus a kind of discrepancy or imbalance between *In Memoriam* as a body of MSS and as a published text, between the private imperfectly known poetic activity that these MSS represent and the very familiar, highly public phenomenon which was the published poem. Several literary reputations were made overnight in the Victorian period, but with *In Memoriam* Tennyson migrated beyond the mere success of extraordinary sales to the special kind of celebrity conferred by the laureateship. The composition of *In Memoriam* is a dim episode occasionally lit by remarks in letters, diaries and reminiscences of Tennyson's immediate circle; the volume that resulted, and its reception, are matters of national history.

Of course the contrast between Tennyson before 1850 and after can be drawn too sharply. It is always hard to say anything incontrovertible about literary reputation—partly because the very notion is multiform—but it seems certain that Tennyson's stock (especially on the strength of the 1842 volumes) was already high in several quarters before

1850. On the other hand this high estimate was a sufficiently parochial or cliquish matter for it to escape the attention of Lord John Russell when he advised Queen Victoria on the candidates for succession to Wordsworth as Poet Laureate, and told her that Henry Taylor, Sheridan Knowles, John Wilson and Tennyson were 'of nearly equal merit'. The public dignity of the office was also— as became well recognised during Victoria's reign—partly of Tennyson's own making. The title of Laureate was not in itself sufficient to confer the strikingly unchallenged reputation that Tennyson enjoyed for the next forty-two years. Moreover there was much about Tennyson in those years which continued to seem reclusive and withdrawn from the public gaze and this, indeed, enhanced his interest for the public. A striking continuity of temper is illustrated by the fact that Tennyson seems to have had no enthusiasm for writing poetry for the Queen or about Royal events, and scarcely did so, until the death of Albert in 1861 excited a purely personal concern about Victoria.

It remains true that the publication of *In Memoriam* produced a change in Tennyson's standing, whereby he abruptly became a very conspicuous public figure, of a kind that very few writers can have experienced. The contrast between obscurity and celebrity has an obvious kind of parallel in *In Memoriam* itself. Of all the extended elegies written in English (and there are not many) Tennyson's springs from a more personal loss, more intensely felt, than any other. But nor is there a long elegy which concerns itself so directly and extensively with matters of common concern for its readership: questions about the nature of man and his society, the place of man in the physical universe, and the nature of that universe. The transformation of Tennyson's standing brought about by *In Memoriam* was remarkable, but so was the process by which the poem's material was transformed from something inexpressibly crushing and personal into something which communicated a private grief in a fashion that seized the attention of thousands of readers. Unfortunately the story of this adjustment by Tennyson is generally unrecoverable because of the sparseness of the surviving facts about his work on *In Memoriam* and on other poems to do with Hallam. Generally we have to deduce its nature, or guess at it on the strength of indirect evidence.

II

A good deal of attention has been paid, for example, to Tennyson's published poetry of the period between Hallam's death and 1850 in the

light of reviewers' remarks about it. There is a well-known argument to
the effect that the revisions made by Tennyson to poems reissued in the
1842 collection, and the new poems in these volumes together with *The
Princess* (R 741) of 1847, show an unusual responsiveness to opinions
expressed about Tennyson's poetry in the periodicals. Broadly speaking
the case is convincing. It does seem that Tennyson consciously sought to
comply with certain preferences about poetry expressed by these
reviewers. The greater metrical orthodoxy in the last section of 'The
Lotos-Eaters' (R 429) as reissued in 1842, for example, seems to be
directly due to reviews of the 1832 volume in which the poem first
appeared. And the new material in this portion about social ills—in
effect a picture of 'two nations'—may be a response to the very strong
urgings towards relevance and topicality that were consistently being
sounded in reviews of new poetry, Tennyson's included. A poet who
complies with this preference admits, of course, a responsibility to his
public of two kinds: to its aesthetic standards and to its current
preoccupations. If Tennyson had not respected the call to topicality he
would not have written *The Princess*, or many passages in *In Memoriam*.
The Princess is also a long poem—the first that Tennyson had
attempted. Thus although it is 'A Medley' it has the weight, the
portentousness, that might be expected in the work of a candidate for
the laureateship. *In Memoriam* is even more strikingly, indeed wholly, a
long poem made out of short ones—though the apparent contradiction
of forms involved was brilliantly solved by Tennyson.

Looking directly at the poetry inspired by, or concerned with,
Hallam's death, we at once come up against certain important
complications inherent in the relationship between personal feeling and
its artistic expression, some peculiar to the experience of grief and others
more general. Tennyson famously said of the first poem he wrote that
relates to Hallam's death (comparing it to *In Memoriam*): 'There is more
about myself in *Ulysses*, which was written under the sense of loss and
that all had gone by, but that still life must be fought out to the end'
(R 560). This reminds us how artificial is the notion (a notion which *In
Memoriam* itself in a special way and quite legitimately exploits on
occasion) of the poetic utterance of overwhelming grief. An overwhelming grief will overwhelm utterance along with everything else. To achieve
an utterance concerning it, such as 'Ulysses', the poet must write directly
about the conquest of grief ('still life must be fought out to the end'
expresses a necessity for survival, not a fact about grief), and only
indirectly about the grief itself. 'Ulysses' shares this kind of obliqueness
about grief with other poems of the period which are directly inspired by

Hallam's death such as 'Youth' (R 577), 'On a Mourner' (R 557), 'Oh! that 'twere possible' (R 598), and 'Hark! the dogs howl' (R 555). In 'Ulysses' Tennyson also secures obliqueness in relation to actual persons and events through the use of a fictitious or legendary situation—the method also of 'Tithon' (R 566), 'Tiresias' (R 568), and 'Morte d'Arthur' (R 585) (though in the last Tennyson's alibi, so to speak, is so good that he can permit himself, in the name of his hero, a startlingly straightforward reference to real circumstances).

But it was not just the cruelly unmentionable character of the experience that required a degree of detachment in Tennyson before he could write directly about Hallam's death. We would not feel inclined to say that a poet was expressing feelings about such an experience or any other unless we were also prepared to say that he had in some sense made us aware of the character of those feelings. Otherwise we would be trapped in a contradiction. The notion of 'expressing' a feeling includes the idea of securing a certain effect in the listener or spectator. In this context the grammar of 'express', as some philosophers would put it, is more like the grammar of 'communicate' than that of 'release' or 'discharge'. Lyric poetry, John Stuart Mill had written in the 1830s, is 'overheard' feeling, but Mill was simply noticing the convention that presides in respect of this literary form. Instances of the form are in reality uttered to the reader as published texts, not overheard by him. Most of the sections of *In Memoriam* operate at one level like conventional lyrics, and involve the degree of conscious simulation of an 'overheard' quality perfectly proper to the form. But the poem is, on its own showing, self-conscious and sophisticated about these matters, and there is another kind of artifice at work which is more unusual and which supervenes on ordinary lyric expressiveness. It springs naturally from the method both of the uncommunicative (but emotion-discharging) poems such as 'Ulysses', and of the lyrics in which Tennyson sought to communicate his grief.

In Memoriam makes use, for example, of the angle of deflection away from certain concerns to betray the very power of these concerns—just as the wide angle of deflection away from Hallam's death in 'Ulysses' betrayed (not, in this case, deliberately) 'the sense of loss and that all had gone by'. The mourner in *In Memoriam* is quite explicit at several points about the difficulty he has experienced, hitherto, in contemplating various distressing topics. The fact of the loved one's death, his leading qualities and even his identity, the circumstances that brought him into contact with the mourner, and the whereabouts of his death, all this information is withheld for varying lengths of time in the poem. One of the patterns in the carpet of *In Memoriam* created by Tennyson's 'weaving' together of his elegies (though the modern reader in possession of all the facts about Hallam and Tennyson might not notice this) is simply the progressively revealed occasion of the poem: the story of Arthur Hallam's death.

This is one of a number of procedures in *In Memoriam* which may be thought of as 'ironical', as long as that term is not understood to imply a humorous or disparaging effect. The construction and bringing forward of these ironies must have been among the chief possibilities that became available to Tennyson once he had decided to assemble his elegies into a work of some length. So the decision thus to assemble them constituted a step in the transition from private to public in a double sense. To make a long poem was one aspect of the conversion of a personal grief into a publicly notable utterance; it was supplemented by the poet's detachment of himself from the mourning hero of the poem by various ironical connections between its parts.

It is probable that the idea of combining the elegies into a long poem occurred to Tennyson a good deal earlier than used to be supposed. Tennyson's recollection about this, as ascribed to him in the *Memoir* (i, 304–5) had tended to suggest a relatively late date for the plan: 'The sections were written at many different places, and as the phases of our intercourse came to my memory and suggested them. I did not write them with any view of weaving them into a whole, or for publication, until I found that I had written so many.' Even if this is what Tennyson said (which is perhaps doubtful in view of the reminiscental character implied for the early lyrics) the 'many' sections he spoke of may not have amounted to a large number. He had definitely decided on a collection of elegies by November 1842, the date which appears on the Lincoln MS and which must be at least its starting date. The Lincoln notebook contains versions of the great bulk of the *In Memoriam* lyrics, though by no means all are in fair copy form and hence datable to before November 1842. But the plan for a sequence of lyrics may, on various grounds, be fairly confidently pushed back a good deal further. If Tennyson used long ledger-like notebooks for drafts of parts of *In Memoriam* because they 'assisted him to arrange the poems in due order by bringing many of them at once before his eye' (as one contemporary account has it) then the idea of a sequence may date from as early as 1834—the date at which Ricks conjectures that Tennyson started to compile the Trinity MS (which is in the long ledger format (R 857).

This rather tenuous reasoning is given support by an obvious and, to my mind, persuasive consideration which seems to have been neglected.

Tennyson's decision, whenever it occurred, to reserve the special ABBA stanza for all poems on Hallam's death, and only those poems, must have followed on some kind of plan to assemble these as a group. The stanza had been used several times by Tennyson in poems which can be dated to the early 1830s. It was quite consistent with his evident interest in it at the time that he should have adopted it for some of the early poems about Hallam's death (though the other poems in which it had been used were all on political topics). The latest of the non-*In Memoriam* poems cast in the stanza, either 'Love thou thy land' (R 613) or 'Of old sat Freedom' (R 617) cannot be dated after 1834. And the last stanzaic poem relating to Hallam's death that does *not* use the *In Memoriam* rhyme scheme is probably 'Break, break, break' (R 602), ascribed by Ricks to the spring of 1834.

III

These are guesses about the early history of *In Memoriam* which can be made with some confidence. Thereafter the picture becomes almost entirely blank until quite soon before publication in 1850. And the story of the closing stages of *In Memoriam*'s development shows how persistent were the tensions between the private and public aspects of the poem. Tennyson may have conceived the idea of one long poem about Hallam's death as early as 1834, and it is likely that he soon started to arrange its components so that the 'moods of sorrow' were 'dramatically given', as he put it, but sixteen years later he could still exhibit signs of ambivalence about coming before the public with the poem that was to prove such a decisive success. In early 1850 he issued to friends the very small corpus of printed copies of the poem which is usually called the 'trial' edition, though it is hard to see what could have been tried by this procedure. More likely Tennyson required, psychologically, to take the steps through printing to publication one by one. In other words he needed to surmount the transition from MS to printed page before he could undertake the further transition to unrestricted release of his poem in printed form.

Further contradictions attended the eventual publication in May 1850. Although the work was anonymous—at Tennyson's firm insistence—there was little secret about the author's identity, which was mentioned in several of the early reviews, and in at least three announcements at the time of publication. It is interesting that Moxon seems to have brought the publication date forward from Christmas, because this must suggest that there was an attempt (though of course

Tennyson may have been unaware of it) to strengthen Tennyson's candidacy for the laureateship, left empty by Wordsworth's death in April. Moxon himself may not have been at all certain what kind of investment he had on his hands. The contract with Tennyson seems very cautious, for the poet bore the whole cost of production—which in turn suggests a surprising avidity to publish on his side. Yet the first printing was sizeable: 5000 copies. The history of tergiversation in 1850 is crowned by the episode of Tennyson's drafting both an acceptance and a rejection of the Laureateship when it was offered to him in November.

The trial edition represents the last prepublication version of the poem that we have. The divergences between it and the published text, though limited in number and only relating to a brief phase of the poem's growth, seem to confirm that the tendency of Tennyson's work on the poem was towards a sequence of lyrics that are to be thought of rather like the soliloquies of a dramatised character. Consequently the reader should not always take at face value the accounts of his feelings which this mourning character offers, but consider them also for what they might betray about feelings which are unacknowledged by him (this is the sense in which the lyrics are ironical). And where there is no such discrepancy between the explicit and the implicit content of the lyrics it will still not be safe to assume that Tennyson's own feelings are being expressed.

It is a striking fact, and a kind of evidence of Tennyson's sure instinct about his public, that the poems added after the trial edition include some of the best known in the poem. The 'Dark house' lyric (VII) and its companion 'Doors where my heart . . .' (CXIX) were added in the first proper edition, as was lyric LVI (in which Nature is 'red in tooth and claw'), XCVI (in which it is asserted with hesitant hyperbole that 'There lives more faith in honest doubt/ . . . than in half the creeds'), and CXXI (the 'Hesper-Phosphor' lyric). The second 'yewtree' lyric (XXXIX) was added as late as 1869 (the only other addition after the first edition being lyric LIX, which first appeared in the fourth edition of 1851). It has been said, chiefly on the strength of lyric LVI, that one tendency of these additions was to intensify the pessimism of the poem (though it is hard to think that Tennyson ever intended LV to remain without its sequel, so direct a rejoinder is the one to the other). But Tennyson's aim seems to have been rather to heighten the contrast of tones generally, for in 1850 he also added lyric CXXVIII with its confidence that 'all, as in some piece of art/Is toil cooperant to an end'. The marked optimism of this lyric means that it is probably a case in

which the distance between Tennyson and his mourner is particularly
great, in which, more than usual, 'it's too hopeful, this poem, more than
I am myself' (*Mem.*, i, 304–5).

Three of the 'pendant' pairs which are such a conspicuous feature of
the poem's general design were created by additions in the published
version and are not found in the trial edition: the 'Dark house' and
'yewtree' pairs, as mentioned, and the two 'Oh Sorrow' lyrics (III and
LIX). The construction of the last of these pairs very clearly contributes
to the ironically revealed secret history of the mourner's feelings, and in
a way that well illustrates the subtlety of Tennyson's understanding of
the psychology of mourning, that is, of the condition of being
griefstricken and trying to give this emotion some utterance. A less
thoughtful poet might have made the first apostrophe to sorrow
welcoming in tone, and the second more resentful. Tennyson does the
opposite, and so the very early resistance to sorrow expressed in lyric III
(which might strike the reader even at the time as surprisingly
inconsistent with the evident power of the grief which grips the
mourner) is seen as a brittle, ineffectual, but required strategy to prevent
the mourner's mind being quite overmastered by grief. For his own
psychic survival he must deal with sorrow as if it were a kind of
hereditary insanity, a 'vice of blood'. The acceptance of sorrow as a
'wife' in lyric LIX, by a convincing psychological paradox, betokens
greater security of mind. One of Tennyson's own nine 'natural' divisions
of the poem is meant to start with this lyric. The idea that to mourn more
is to grieve less is most important for the poem. The consolation
achieved at the end of *In Memoriam* has several aspects, but it consists
chiefly in the mourner's ability to mourn or, more precisely, to state his
loss without being intolerably distressed by it.

A similar idea is promoted by the very fascinating pair of 'Dark house'
lyrics. The 'dark house' of the first of these (VII) is joined with its 'doors'
as the double subject of the verb 'behold', which may be in either the
indicative or imperative mood. The syntax is characteristically fluid and
unassertive, and hence provisional in feeling, but it does, if only
provisionally, express self-centredness: the mourner wishes, or imagines, the house and its doors to behold 'me'. The resoundingly
alliterative adjectives that he flings at the approaching dawn in the
lyric's last line are also tokens of his enthralment in his own despair:
'On the bald street breaks the blank day'. Baldness and blankness
(and, in the previous line, ghastliness) are being forced upon Wimpole
Street, where they can only find a shallow foothold in the facts of the
street's emptiness and pallor. And of course the outer world cannot win

at this stage, as far as the mourner is concerned. It is *also* a cause for misery that Wimpole Street is about to become a peopled, urban thoroughfare: 'far away/The noise of life begins again'. 'Far away/ . . . life begins again'; the undermining, ironical suggestion is quiet but unmistakable. Even less to be mistaken by a Protestant audience is the allusion to new life achieved by the first words of this last verse: 'He is not here'. 'For he is risen' comes in unspokenly to complete the familiar, momentous words of the angel at Christ's sepulchre.

Lyric CXIX has its own plosively alliterating group of adjectives:

> I see
> Betwixt the black fronts long-withdrawn
> A light-blue lane of early dawn,
> And think of early days and thee,
>
> And bless thee, for thy lips are bland,
> And bright the friendship of thine eye.

But they are attached in the right places. Adjectives of sensory fact are used for the outer world, which is 'black' (not bald) and 'blue' (not blank) (the only epithet with figurative force at this point, 'long-withdrawn', is firmly planted in the literal and is thus a pun of a kind of quite common in *In Memoriam*: Hallam, and his hands, have been withdrawn long ago, and Wimpole Street is a long, straight street in which the buildings diminish in perspective). Adjectives with affective force ('bland', 'bright') are restricted to the image of the lost Hallam. They are not wrenched away and foisted on the outer world, as they were in the companion lyric. And this image is now known by the mourner to subsist only within himself. Through this recognition—the recognition of his loss—he can recover Hallam and his handclasp: 'in my thoughts . . ./I take the pressure of thine hand'. Again the mourner is not learning to find Hallam (any more than he finds him with any certainty in lyric XCV) but learning to lose him.

Procedures such as these in *In Memoriam* have increasingly attracted the notice of critics in recent years. It is characteristic of the poem that the store of ironical linkages that can be found is, for practical purposes, inexhaustible. Tennyson's weaving together of the elegies is so dense—so many points are attached to so many others—that *In Memoriam* becomes for its reader a poem with a quite exceptionally plastic, protean character. No two readers assemble its constituent parts in the same way, and perhaps no individual can read it in the same fashion on any two occasions. *In Memoriam* only differs by degree from other long poems in interconnectedness, but this difference of degree is enough to make it in practice a quite special object. It is not farfetched to think of the analogy of the human brain, an organ which only differs in degree of complexity from more primitive central nervous systems, but which as a result is effectively different in kind.

It is important, however, to keep the nature of irony of *In Memoriam* clearly in view. The case of lyric VII, with its bold allusion to Christ's resurrection, is not representative. This irony, it may be said, is an 'absolute' one. Any lyric about death written in Protestant England which included the words 'He is not here' without intending some allusion to the conquest of death would be a poor one, short on verbal alertness. But usually in *In Memoriam* there is no sense in which one may reasonably speak of the mourner as absolutely wrong or right, and certainly not the former. After all, the wrongness of grief—most people would agree—is a relative matter. A sense of equanimity about a death, if it is achieved, may be adjudged a more desirable state of mind than a preceding episode of grief, but it is only when this comparison is made that it is possible to think of the grief as regrettable—and then only in a restricted sense. Indeed if this were not the case *In Memoriam* could not have evolved as it did in its early stages. There was certainly a time when the grief of many of the elegies was a straightforwardly heartfelt thing for Tennyson. Only subsequently, as each of the elegies became more and more richly attached and connected in the weaving of the poem, would the grief they expressed assume a different aspect for the poet. Grief is only regrettable relative to consolation, but consolation itself is not a simple state of feeling, rather an evolving one, and as a result the dividing line between it and an undesirable state of grief tends to get brought forward in time continuously in *In Memoriam*. The poem gives the appearance of ending several times, and even when its tally of numbered lyrics is made up Tennyson adds the further two resting or ending points described in the epilogue and prologue. The latter draws the grief-consolation line between itself and the *whole* of the rest of the poem.

Hence *In Memoriam* is a very different sort of dramatic poem from such contemporary specimens of dramatic poetry as Browning's monologues. Indeed, given the striking failure of some of the latter to be 'dramatic' in the sense of communicating a state of mind and feeling different from the author's, they may be said to be antithetical to *In Memoriam* in character. *In Memoriam* is a personal poem which became impersonal, while 'Bishop Blougram's Apology',[1] for instance, is an apparently impersonal poem which fails to exclude the personal. The development, in Tennyson's case, must have been more or less irresistible. In a long series of lyrics which sets itself to deal with two such contrasting attitudes as grief and equanimity about the death of a beloved person it would be very hard to insulate the component poems from each other, to prevent a particular section from suggesting a slightly adjusted evaluation of an earlier one. It is because a sequence of lyrics in this situation will tend so strongly towards the condition of drama that *In Memoriam* is reminiscent in its procedure of the lyric sequences of the German poet Mueller (familiar in their settings as song cycles by Schubert) of which Tennyson had no knowledge.

IV

The component lyrics of *In Memoriam* are generally both truthful and fallacious, according to the frame of reference. The efforts of John Ruskin to deal with such effects in Tennyson's poetry as examples of 'pathetic fallacy'[2] (a rhetorical category which, one may suspect, he devised partly in response to just these Tennysonian instances) are an interesting testimony to the complicated, elusive character of what is involved. Ruskin makes things harder for himself by neglecting to consider at all systematically the difference it would make for poetic fallaciousness if a poem were dramatic rather than straightforwardly lyrical. He gets into a serious muddle over his first major example of pathetic fallacy, which is taken from 'O Mary, go and call the cattle home' in *Alton Locke*[3] (a novel in which Tennyson is often quoted and extolled): 'They rowed her in across the rolling foam,/The cruel crawling foam'. 'The foam is not cruel, neither does it crawl' writes Ruskin. But such mistakes, according to the theory of pathetic fallacy, are supposed to be the mark of a relatively 'weak' writer, and it is not to the literal writer, Charles Kingsley, that the weakness can be imputed in this case. For Kingsley wrote this poem as an example of the work of the imaginary poet, Alton Locke. Would *he* be a weak poet, if he existed? Alton Locke might very plausibly defend himself by saying that 'the speaker' (an agency that Ruskin himself brings into play in discussing pathetic fallacy) is one of the mourners for Mary the cowgirl.

Even if Ruskin had considered more carefully whose 'character' was shown to be 'weak' by Kingsley's poem he would not have got to the bottom of the question of its fallaciousness. Foam does not 'crawl' he complained in 1856, but seventeen years later he praised Kingsley's epithet for its 'precision'[4], and linked it in this respect with Tennyson's epithet in 'the climbing wave' ('The Lotos-Eaters', R 429, 195). Clearly the degree of figurativeness (and hence imputed animation in the sea) the reader finds in the phrase 'crawling foam' is arbitrary. It is the juxtaposition, in context, with 'cruel' which has encouraged Ruskin, in his first account of the epithet, to read it as strongly figurative. This is like Tennyson's pair of adjectives, 'bald . . . blank', in lyric VII of *In Memoriam*. The dawn may be thought of as literally 'blank', but the clearly non-literal force of 'bald' encourages us to apprehend instead the figurative sense of the epithet, defined by the *Oxford English Dictionary* as 'void of interest or event'. And Kingsley's poem has a character, broadly speaking, like that of a component section of *In Memoriam*. It does not depend on its context in *Alton Locke* to be intelligible and effective (and so may stand quite well on its own as a lyric) and yet its meaning and force are likely to seem quite different when it is read within that context.

So Ruskin is not, as he supposes, noticing an unequivocal 'fallacy' in Kingsley's poem. Rather he is obediently reading Kingsley in a univocal, figurative sense at the latter's behest. The idea that Ruskin is not noticing a figure of speech, but instead noticing that he is supposed to notice one, would explain a puzzling feature of the theory of pathetic fallacy, namely, that this figure—which must, on any reckoning, have a long and rich history in poetry—was not identified and discussed until the middle of the nineteenth century. It is true that Ruskin does not cite any examples from before about 1800, as if they did not occur—but he nowhere makes this assumption explicit or justifies it. And the fact (though it may be doubted how interesting a fact it is) that Victorian poetry when sampled and surveyed by Josephine Miles[5] seems to use affective metaphors about the outer world *less* frequently than Romantic poetry is no longer surprising if the theory of pathetic fallacy is a theory about the fashion, and not the fact, of such usages.

Ruskin exhibited similar, interesting confusions about his new rhetorical discovery when he discussed examples from Tennyson. In a footnote to the chapter on pathetic fallacy he gives two quotations from *Maud* (then a very recently published work). He clearly feels excited and delighted by these examples, in contrast to his severity, in his general theorising, on the 'falseness' of pathetic fallacy. 'I cannot quit this subject', he interjects eagerly, 'without giving two more instances, both exquisite.' One is from the last section of Part One, with its crying red rose, weeping white rose, listening larkspur, and whispering lily. The other is from the very first section (R 1037, Part i, 9–12)—I give Ruskin's wording and punctuation:

> For a vast speculation had fail'd;
> And ever he mutter'd and madden'd, and ever wann'd with despair;
> And out he walked, when the wind like a broken worldling wail'd,
> And the *flying gold of the ruin'd woodlands drove thro' the air.*

What Ruskin found 'exquisite' here, and identified with his italics, is clearly the clever dramatisation of the hero's pain and revulsion about his father's financial failure and suicide (and about mercantilism in general) through the device of making him perceive autumn leaves as coins, and the bareness of the trees as poverty.

But the irony here is an absolute one, of a kind unusual in *In Memoriam*. The phrase 'flying gold of the ruin'd woodlands drove thro' the air' would be odd and obsessive-seeming even in an isolated lyric. Indeed the reader encounters it with virtually no context, as it occurs so early in *Maud*, and it must direct his attention to the possibility of something pathological in the hero's state of mind at this point. *Maud* is a 'Monodrama', and it employs these emphatic ironies much more freely than *In Memoriam*, but it also contains many examples of the less clearcut variety of pathetic fallacy. Ruskin commented on such a case some years after *Modern Painters* Vol. III, in *Sesame and Lilies*:[6] 'For her feet have touched the meadows/And left the daisies rosy' (R 1037, Part i, ll 434–5). 'Only a lover's fancy', Ruskin said, 'false and vain'. This prompted Tennyson to one of his gruff, fantastic jokes: 'The very day I wrote it, I saw the daisies rosy in Maiden's Croft, and thought of enclosing one to Ruskin labelled "A pathetic fallacy"' (*Mem.*, i, 511). Of course such a missive would not have met the case, because Ruskin's point is presumably that it is mistaken of the hero to attribute the colour of the daisies to the influence of Maud's feet. But the spirit of Tennyson's retort—drawing attention to what is literally true in the image—is appropriate. Ruskin would almost certainly not have spoken as he does about this lover's 'fancy' if he had not been given his cue to do so by the dramatic context which Tennyson has constructed. 'False', 'vain'—both epithets are exact for the hero of the poem in his depression before he falls in love with Maud. Various kinds of alleged dishonesty in the world are the main focus of his despair, and they induce a conviction of the futility of his life. But he is to discover that his relationship with Maud, which at first seems likely to introduce truthfulness and purpose into his life, *cannot* bring this about. He can only put falseness and vanity behind him in the patriotic endeavour of war. This is the central irony of the narrative of *Maud*, and Ruskin shows a good instinct in picking it up (unconsciously) early in the poem[7]—but it was Tennyson who had the wit to devise it.

6 One Word More— on Tennyson's Dramatic Monologues

William E. Fredeman

I

If 1850, because of the concatenation of Tennyson's laureateship and his marriage to Emily Selwood and the publication of *In Memoriam*, is the *annus mirabilis* of the poet's life, 1842 is at least pivotal in his development as a poet, for the appearance in that year of the two volumes of *Poems* firmly established Tennyson's reputation, paving the way for his subsequent elevation as the 'official' poet of the Victorian era.

Of the two volumes, it was the second that was distinctly new, for while the first contained six new titles and important revisions of earlier poems from the 1830 and 1833 volumes, most notably of 'The Lady of Shalott' (R 354), the second, beginning with 'The Epic' (R 582) and ending with 'The Poet's Song' (R 736), established the boundaries of Tennyson's future career. Containing several of his major poems, the volume was experimental and original. In 'The Gardener's Daughter' (R 507), 'Audley Court' (R 704), 'Edward Gray' (R 726), 'The Lord of Burleigh' (R 603), and three or four others, Tennyson refined the form of the domestic (or English) Idyl that he had launched in 'The Miller's Daughter' (R 371) a decade earlier; and in 'Morte d'Arthur' (R 585), 'Sir Galahad' (R 610), and 'Sir Launcelot and Queen Guinevere' (R 502) he secured his claim on the Arthurian materials first staked out in 'The Lady of Shalott'. Tennyson seems also, to judge from the closing lines of 'The Poet's Song' and of the volume—'For he sings of what the world will be/When the years have died away' (R 736, ll 15–16)—finally to have reconciled his inner struggles concerning the artist and to have accepted

169

the role of the public poet. As central as these three aspects of the volume are, however—relating to form, theme, and poetic commitment—the most striking innovation of the 1842 *Poems* is the introduction, in 'Ulysses' (R 560) and 'St Simeon Stylites' (R 542), of the earliest examples of the dramatic monologue. Both poems were composed in 1833, the year of Browning's 'Pauline', and their publication roughly coincided with Browning's 'My Last Duchess' and 'Count Gismond', the first of Browning's poems to evince his own mastery of the form. 'Ulysses' and 'St Simeon Stylites' are very different in that they exemplify the rhetorical and ironic extremes of Tennyson's handling of the form throughout his writing, but they are central to the dramatic concerns that dominate his poetry, almost from the beginning.

'Subjectivity', Robert Langbaum writes in *The Poetry of Experience*, 'was not the program but the inescapable condition of romanticism',[1] and both Tennyson and Browning were attracted to the dramatic monologue as a means of masking their essential subjectivism. Tennyson's monologues, like his other dramatic narratives and lyrics, reflect his lifelong struggle for certainty and his preoccupation with dualities and tensions that in the poetry take the form of reiterated thematic polarities: love and loss, past and present, youth and age, faith and doubt, life and immortality. This struggle, which Martin Dodsworth[2] has called the 'central mystery' of Tennyson's poetry, is closely linked to his morbidity, the most obtrusive aspect of his personality and the most difficult to sublimate or to exclude from the poetry. By disguising his subjective feelings in these dramatic modes, Tennyson was able to achieve both an aesthetic and an emotional distancing that enabled him to approach that condition of the dramatic monologue, which Langbaum describes, whereby the poet can talk about himself by talking about something else (and vice versa).

Tennyson's major[3] monologues follow mainly rhetorical rather than ironic patterns, which means not that the speakers are merely transparent mini-Tennysons—'exercises in ventriloquism' as David Shaw calls them[4]—but that they employ a language, invariably in blank verse, that is characterised by the formalities of structure—balance, repetition, hortatory constructions, and the like—rather than a language that is essentially, and appropriately, colloquial, which is Browning's great achievement. In Browning's monologues, the speakers converse in a language that, whether formal or informal, creates its own dynamic and reinforces not only the verisimilitude of the situation but also the poet's paramount concerns with point of view and the revelation of character. It is an oversimplification to say that Browning's monologues are more realistic, and Tennyson's more 'poetic'; however, since the *dramatic* quality of the dramatic monologue depends at least as much on its linguistic effects as it does on the reversal of the Aristotelian tragic formula, emphasising, as Browning observes in the Preface to *Strafford*, action in character rather than character in action,[5] the distinction may partially explain Browning's capacity to achieve a more convincing immediacy of incident (or action) and a greater dimensionality of character than is apparent in most of Tennyson's monologues.

There are of course other explanations, the most important of which involves what may be called the fiction of the form, by which is suggested both the speaker's interaction with the listener and the psychological revelation of character on which the poem depends, whether the Bishop ordering his tomb, the Duke negotiating for the hand of a new bride, or St Simeon attempting to con God into conferring on him his sainthood. In Browning, character is normally revealed *through* the fiction; in other words, there is genuine interplay between speaker and listener going on behind the language, which involves action, movement, or development. Between the beginning and end of the monologue something either happens or a transformation or recognition is effected, in which the speaker, the listener, and the reader participate and are changed. In Tennyson, almost without exception, the character is *posited*; the speaker is a talker rather than a doer, and his language is more likely to be reflective, introverted, philosophical, rather than direct and forceful; the action is invariably either static or retrospective. 'Ulysses', it will be urged, surely lies outside this formulation, and it may do, depending on whether his exhortation to his real or imagined mariners is given a conventional or, in Dwight Culler's phrase, a 'revisionist' reading.[6] What is clear, however, is that Tennyson's listeners are formal rather than dramatic foils to the speakers. They are integral to the situation of the poem, but they play no catalytic role because no change transpires; there is no development, no reversal, no recognition, no trans- formation—in effect, no action. Tennyson's monologues more closely resemble interior monologues than dramatic encounters, which may explain why in both 'St Simeon Stylites' and 'Ulysses' the listeners are shifting and indefinite—God and the 'good people' in the first, Ulysses himself, his people, and the mariners in the second; that they are interior may also explain why, in the major monologues, the speakers are at the point of death, that final closure expressly remarked by Ulysses. The persistent effect in Tennyson's monologues, then, is stasis, and they might, with more accuracy, be labelled dramatic soliloquies than dramatic monologues.

It is perhaps worth stressing at this point that Tennyson's adaptation of the monologue form must be presumed to be as intentional as Browning's; and that the two took inherent tendencies in the form in opposite directions provides insights into their respective personalities and artistic methods rather than a critical yardstick to measure one poet against the other. 'St Simeon Stylites', though it is nearer in form to Browning's model of the dramatic monologue than any other Tennyson poem, is not a good poem because of its 'Browningesque' qualities—'Browningesque before Browning' was Jerome Buckley's description[7]—but because it is successful within the limits Tennyson set himself.

In the most recent and most provocative study of the dramatic monologue since Langbaum, Dwight Culler veers dangerously close to this kind of comparative value judgement. Culler examines in detail the twin forms of the monodrama and the dramatic monologue in the nineteenth century, tracing with clarity and precision the evolution of the monodrama from its continental sources and related modes, including *prosopopoeia* (impersonations), 'attitudes', melodramas (in the original, musical sense of the term), and even the lesser art forms of pantomime, shawl dances, and *tableaux vivants*, and offering distinction between monodramas and dramatic monologues that are both interesting and illuminating. Summarising the influences that were to culminate in the verse form that Langbaum identifies as distinctly modern, Culler says:

... there arose in the decades immediately before and after the turn of the century several related art forms that focused on a solitary figure, most frequently a woman, who expressed through speech, music, costume, and gesture the shifting movements of her soul. That the figure was solitary and that virtually the entire text consisted of her utterance was evidence of an attempt to focus on her subjectivity; that she was feminine was a further indication that the drama was one of passion. For this reason a moment of high intensity was normally chosen, and though occasionally there are monodramas, like that of Gretchen at the spinning wheel or Mariana in the moated grange, which insist on the unvarying round of a single emotion, for the most part the character is distracted, divided in will, torn between conflicting emotions, so that he or she can run through a whole series of kaleidoscopic changes.[8]

That in its purest form, derived from Rousseau's *Pygmalion* (1772), the monodrama, combining music with declamation and having marked affinities with the masque and heroic tragedy, was essentially a dead-ended genre on its importation into England—degenerating, on the one hand, into conventional melodrama and dividing, on the other, into both operatic and non-musical modes—does not, unfortunately, lend convincing support to Culler's speculation that 'if one could hear [*Maud*] performed by a virtuoso actor, with intervals of music to interpret the shifting moods, one would have a better idea of the kind of work it was supposed to be'.[9] Culler's investigations were inspired by a serious attempt to get behind the monodramatic label of Tennyson's *Maud* in order to establish the poem's generic lineage and to clarify its consanguinous ties with other forms. His thorough examination of the antecedents of the monodrama and his main observation, that 'after the beginning of the nineteenth century the principal importance of monodrama is not as a separate form but as a stylistic element or technique which enters into other forms',[10] can be usefully applied, as Culler himself does, in analysing the complex variety of shifting moods in the poem, to the formulation of a definition, not only of the form of *Maud*, but of numerous other dramatic poems which partake of the form.

That Culler is less successful on the applied than the theoretical level is a matter of opinion with which not all readers will agree, though his conclusion of a lengthy generic discussion of *Maud* with only the begging assertion that the poem is 'neither a pure monodrama nor a proper dramatic monologue'[11] may strike other readers besides me as less than profound. Like most critics, Culler equates the dramatic monologue with Browning; probably no critic, however, has gone quite so far as he in arguing Browning's exclusive proprietary claim to the form. After summarising the particulars of Langbaum's definition—empiricism, tension, dramatic irony, and the rest—Culler concludes that 'in its special nineteenth century form' the dramatic monologue 'applies *only* to Browning'[12] (my emphasis). Yet, even granting his insistence that his catalogue of lacunae in Tennyson's monologues, based on the identifying characteristics of Browning's models, can ultimately determine definition, it seems presumptuous, without strong supporting evidence, to hypothesise as Culler does that, 'if Tennyson had been asked what kind of poems ['Oenone', 'Ulysses', 'Tithonus', and 'Tiresias'] were, he probably would have replied *prosopopoeiae*'; Culler's own uncertainty is clear enough in the second half of his hypothesis, which is self-cancelling: 'on the other hand, it is possible that he might have called them monodramas'.[13] That Tennyson apparently used the term 'monodramas' to refer to most of his dramatic poems will be evident in a later quotation.

Culler is right to remind readers that the term 'dramatic monologue' was 'not in use . . . when the great Victorian dramatic monologues were being written',[14] and it is most convenient to have tracked with such certainty the chronological emergence of the term, which escaped the scrutiny of the editors of *Oxford English Dictionary* even if it does prove to have been first applied critically by Mrs Grundy's gigolo, Robert Buchanan, two years before his celebrated attack on the fleshly poets. But one might wish that Culler had pressed more closely the finer distinctions of the form as it is used by Browning and Tennyson rather than seeking to prove on the basis of what, after all, is a generic quibble, that, notwithstanding his application of both 'monodrama' and 'dramatic monologue' to his own works, Tennyson did not really understand the meaning of monodrama, and, with the grudgingly admitted exception of 'St Simeon Stylites', he did not really write conventional monologues.

Before turning to Tennyson's major monologues, it is necessary to broach one further subject, the matter of point of view, a twin-edged concern in the dramatic monologue. On the one hand, the nature of the genre itself tends, as Langbaum has suggested, to abolish the 'distinction between subjective and objective poetry and between the lyrical and dramatic or narrative genres'.[15] This condition of the monologue was, as has been said, its principal attraction for both Tennyson and Browning. The other closely related level on which point of view operates in the monologue pertains to the fictional intermediary between the poet and his audience. Both poets depend on the form to preserve their anonymity, yet readers are much more willing to dissociate Browning from his speakers than Tennyson from his, notwithstanding the fact that Browning's monologues, no less than Tennyson's, are dramatisations of his own artistic, social, and moral ideas and ideals, and that his prejudices and sympathies are equally evident in the poetry. Two reasons may be advanced for the tendency to equate Tennyson with his fictional speakers. First, though he is clearly concerned with the particularity of his speakers—and that they all are modelled on mythological or historical figures supports this view— Tennyson lacks Browning's facility for delineating characters who are psychologically unique; even those characters deriving from actual historical prototypes seem not to exist in a temporal setting in which they live and move. Thus, ironically, Tennyson's choice of stasis over action may lead commentators to read him into poems from which, by the very act of consciously choosing to write in the form of the dramatic monologue, he was attempting to extricate himself and to gain aesthetic distance.

At the same time, there is a biographical bias that dominates much even of the best writing on Tennyson, which leads commentators to focus unduly, and sometimes uncritically, on the known crises of Tennyson's life to explain both strengths and weaknesses in the poetry. More crucially, this bias shapes to too great an extent the interpretation of the works themselves by imposing readings that are biographically oriented—to Tennyson's natural morbidity, to his hostility towards his father, to his disappointment in his relationship with Rosa Baring, to his insecurity before 1850 or his complacency after that date, and, especially, to his psychological and spiritual collapse following the death of Hallam. No critic now accepts the stunning impact of Hallam's loss as having generated a 'ten years' silence', but Hallam still hovers heavily over too many poems, from 'The Two Voices' (R 522), which Christopher Ricks has shown was at least half written before Hallam's death, and most of the new titles in the 1842 *Poems*, to *In Memoriam*. Hallam cannot, of course, be readily expunged from *In Memoriam*, but owing to the biographical bias, few critics are willing to take at face value Tennyson's own remarks about that poem. Indeed, so obsessive has the preoccupation with Hallam become that more than one writer has obliquely questioned whether Tennyson might have succeeded at all as a poet without this posthumous muse who nurtured his latent necrophilia. Hallam's seminal role as a shaping influence in Tennyson's imaginative life is incontrovertible, but it does not follow that his presence must lurk behind *every* poem written uner the impress of Tennyson's grief over Hallam's loss.

The preoccupation with Tennyson's biography is, of course, not restricted to superficial one-to-one equations of the poet with his characters. As an aside at this point, it is instructive, if somewhat diversionary, to look at an extreme modern example of biographical loading, in this instance through psychoanalytical criticism. David Shaw's Freudian interpretation of 'St Simeon Stylites' is a strangely and uncharacteristically perverse reading in an otherwise sensitive study of *Tennyson's Style*.[16] Shaw sees Simeon's 'lust for sainthood' as deriving from 'a typically Freudian linkage between anality and power'. In the 'lower voices' that 'saint' Simeon from above, Shaw hears 'voices of flatulence'; and he translates Simeon's catalogue of his physical sufferings—'coughs, aches, stitches, ulcerous throes and cramps' (R 542, 1 13)—as literal catharsis, dismissing the possibility of a 'genuine catharsis of the spirit' with the statement: 'Even if the first alternative is a genetic fallacy, and saintly power transcends its "anal" origins, what assurance has the "saint" that he is not leaving one excremental form for a corruption more subtle?' Shifting his sights, Shaw sees Simeon's whole life's argument as a 'systematic substitution of the fantasies of childhood for theology': Simeon's desire to be 'whole, and clean, and meet for heaven' (R 542, 1 210) is an 'infantile regression'; his 'Sucking the damps for drink' (R 542, 1 76) is equated with 'a child at its mother's breast'. In summary: 'The doors flung open on secret places disclose a prenatal orgy of sensual excess, a fantastic riot of apes and monsters, in the course of which the saint's embryo is presumably conceived'. Fortunately (for the reader) Shaw does not push the implications of this reading as he might to apply them directly to Tennyson, contenting himself with the observation that 'Monologues such as "St Simeon Stylites" that conform too closely to the dramatic model are in danger of so dissolving the poet's ideas in the abnormal psychology of the characters that the author's voice is barely audible'. Candidly, I have to respond that in this reading, which is more grotesque even than Tennyson's self-deluded 'saint', I cannot detect even the 'still small voice' of the poet; and I suspect that Tennyson's reaction to Shaw's reading might approximate that described in Margot Tennant's recollection of the poet's response to a small girl sitting on his knee to whom he recited that passage from *Maud* (R 1037) about the birds in the 'high Hall-garden' 'crying and calling' Maud's name: 'I asked her what bird she thought I meant. She said, "A nightingale". This made me so angry that I nearly flung her to the ground: "No, fool! . . . Rook!" said I.'[17]

I have belaboured this embarrassingly bad piece of psychological criticism, lifting it out of the context of many fine stylistic analyses, not to further embarrass its author, but to underscore dramatically the fact that critics hear the voice in the poem that they want to hear. For it was Shaw who in the quotation cited earlier labelled monologues, like 'Tiresias' (R 568) 'exercises in ventriloquism'; about 'St Simeon Stylites' he appears disappointed that the voice of the poet is 'barely audible'.

Tennyson's injunction[18] about the use of the perpendicular pronoun in *In Memoriam* is apposite to most of his poems; less well known is his comment made expressly on his monodramatic poems (printed in the notes to the *Eversley* edition of 'Locksley Hall'):

In a certain way, no doubt, poets and novelists, however dramatic they are, give themselves in their works. The mistake that people make is that they think the poet's poems are a kind of 'catalogue raisonné' of his very own self, and of all the facts of his life, not seeing that they often only express a poetic instinct, or judgment on character real or imagined, and on the facts of lives real or imagined. Of course some poems, like my *Ode to Memory*, are evidently based on the poet's own nature, and on hints from his own life.[19]

One can only conclude that private exposure is the price that some poets pay for going public.

II

There are dozens of poems in Tennyson's canon that approximate the form of the dramatic monologue, principally because they are narrated in the first person. Among the English Idyls, 'The Miller's Daughter', 'The Flight' (R 657), 'The Spinster's Sweet-Arts' (R 1327), and 'The May Queen' (R 418) are obvious examples; but so are 'Oenone' (R 384), 'Sir Galahad' (R 610), and 'St Agnes' Eve' (R 552), which are more difficult to classify. Other poems—'Rizpah' (R 1245), the two 'Northern Farmers' (R 1189 and 1123), and 'The Northern Cobbler' (R 1256), 'The First Quarrel' (R 1254), 'In the Children's Hospital' (R 1261), and 'The Wreck' (R 1334)—to name only a few—exploit the single-narrator technique of the monologue for tragic or comic effect. 'Despair' (R 1299) and 'Locksley Hall Sixty Years After' (R 1359) Tennyson specifically labelled 'dramatic monologues' and, like 'Rizpah', on which Swinburne said Tennyson's fame would rest if his other works were lost, they do meet all the external and superficial requirements of the form. (On the 'Table of Classifications' of Ina Beth Sessions, they receive a 'Perfect' rating.)[20] These poems also evince most of the characteristics already enumerated as usual in Tennyson's major monologues, with two distinctions: first, all three are written in rhymed couplets; second, they lack any focus on character, which is totally subordinated *not* to action, but to the retrospective narratives of the speakers, whose presence is reduced to the ravings of madness or the enervated despondency of age. Their listeners are, if not incidental like the lady visitor who hears Rizpah's story, passive. The berated minister who saved the speaker from drowning in 'Despair' was, it is true, also responsible for driving him and his wife to their suicide pact, through his 'Bawl[ing] the darkside of [his] faith and a God of Eternal rage' (R 1299, 1 39), so he can be seen as an active agent in two central events of the speaker's life, but that was in the past; in the poem's present he becomes hardly more than a target for the invective of the now maddened, heretical speaker, whose diatribe is one of the most strident attacks on orthodox Christianity in Victorian poetry, which may account for Tennyson's reluctance to publish 'Despair' 'without' its pendant poem of 'Hope' or 'Faith' (R 1455).[21] Young Leonard, the speaker's grandson in 'Locksley Hall Sixty Years After' ought, since he will become the new 'Lord and Master' of Locksley Hall, to be more involved in the poem than he is. But he remains unmaterialised in the background of the poem, on the receiving end of the old man's updating of Amy's story in which the reputation of her 'clownish' husband from the earlier poem is rehabilitated; little more than a passive, though youthful, thematic foil for the old man's indictment of the times. Leonard's time, after all, is in the future. Significantly, however, all three poems share the similarity with the major monologues that in each the speaker is old and approaching death.

On this transitional note we can now move to a brief consideration of the major monologues and attempt to clarify Tennyson's conception of the form. With the single exception of 'Ulysses', it will be all too apparent that I have made no effort in this paper to support my theory about the monologues with detailed explications. However, in weighing the alternatives it has seemed preferable on this occasion to concentrate on the formal and thematic elements common to the monologues and to venture some explanation for their recurring patterns than merely to provide inadequate abbreviated readings of the better known poems.

The nine monologues in Tennyson's canon that can be regarded as major span fifty years in the poet's creative life. Chronologically, by compositional and publication dates, they may be grouped as early, middle, and late: 'Ulysses' and 'St Simeon Stylites' (written 1833, published 1842); 'Tithonus' (R 1112) (written as 'Tithon' [R 566] in 1833, completed 1859, published 1860); 'Lucretius' (R 1206) (written 1865–68, published 1868); 'Columbus' (R 1264) and 'Sir John Old-castle' (R 1285) (published in *Ballads and Other Poems*, 1880); 'Tiresias' (R 568) and 'The Ancient Sage' (R 1349) (published in *Tiresias and Other Poems*, 1885, the title poem begun in 1833, completed 1883); and 'Romney's Remorse' (R 1417) (published in *Demeter and Other Poems*, 1885). To this list only 'Oenone' and its paired late poem (R 1427) and 'Akbar's Dream' (R 1441) from the poet's posthumous volume might be added. Since these poems vary significantly from the discernible recurring pattern in the other monologues—Oenone is female and Akbar's death is unsignalled—they have been excluded from this discussion; however, it should be noted that they do meet two of the criteria to be identified. Conversely, 'Sir John Oldcastle', though properly a soliloquy, whose listener, anticipated throughout the poem, does not appear until the final lines, is included because it does share the basic pattern.

While all these poems are experimental in some distinguishing way, each sounding subtle modifications on any preconceived model of the monologue, the poems share so many common elements that it is difficult not to regard them as a kind of minicorpus within the larger canon, even more difficult to comprehend why their commonality has not before been recognised. All nine of the monologues are composed in blank verse; all save 'The Ancient Sage' take their titles from the proper names of their monologuists; and, most importantly, all are narrated by aged men, at or predictably near the point of death.

Ulysses, an alien in Ithaca, resigns his kingship and embarks metaphorically on that final voyage where 'death closes all'. St Simeon waits out on his pillar the end presaged by the death-sting, hallucinatively convinced, by his own benediction, of sainthood. Tithonus, trapped in his Strulbruggian limbo, longs for mortality, not, significantly, to return to life, but to the human condition, the common denominator of which is final realisation through death. Lucretius, brought to the point of madness by the love-potion administered by his wife Lucilia, and unable to reconcile his own sensuality with his vision of life, commits suicide, the only one of the monologuists whose death is shown. But the poem presents the internal debate leading up to death, and it is interesting that Lucretius dies not in the poem proper but in the frame. 'Tiresias' is mainly concerned with the blind sage's persuasion of Menoeceus to sacrifice himself to insure the salvation of Thebes. The poem ends with Menoeceus' greatness assured and Tiresias' longing to be gathered to his rest. The Ancient Sage, like Simeon, has inklings of his death and is on his way when the poem opens 'To spend my last year among the hills'; his final 'Farewell' to the author of 'the deathsong of the ghouls', to which his monologue is an intercalated response, echoes, albeit more optimistically, Lucretius' final words. In the three late historical monologues, impending death provides the occasion for each poem. Two are death-bed laments—Columbus's for the symbolic 'chains' that overshadow all his triumphs and discoveries; Romney's for his lifelong negligence of his wife, Mary, whom he had deserted for art. Sir John Oldcastle, betrayed by his enemies, envisions at the end of the poem his future martyrdom: 'I am not like to die for lack of bread,/For I must live to testify by fire' (R 1285, ll 195–6).

In my article on 'St Simeon Stylites'[22] I observed that Tennyson's poems tend not to have positive closures, that the focus he consistently maintains is on the 'penultimate moment before the end, which is unrevealed'.[23] Several critics, notably Christopher Ricks and David Shaw, have applied this generalisation beyond the limits that I was able to take it in the article, Ricks to demonstrate through broad exegesis its applicability to a wide spectrum of Tennyson's works, Shaw to examine how the principle operates stylistically in the language and techniques of the poems.[24] Each of the major dramatic monologues, exploring what Ulysses calls 'something ere the end', concludes before any revelation is possible, and the reader is left to draw his own conclusions, in much the same way that suspended anticipation operates in the 'Morte d'Arthur'. At the end of Book 11 of Everard Hall's 'Epic' (R 582), the barge bearing Arthur's corpse disappears over the horizon; Arthur's return, the only possible subject of the destroyed Book 12 is inaccessible precisely because it treats what Hamlet calls 'The undiscover'd country from whose bourn/No traveller returns'. The monologues, then, do not explore death *per se*—in fact, only in Lucretius' final words, 'Fare thee well', and in the precision of Simeon's prophecy that he will die 'tonight,/a quarter before twelve' (R 542, ll 217–8) is death actually heralded—but they depend for their effects on the propinquity of death, a subject which had for Tennyson not only perennial fascination but on which he drew throughout his poetic career as one of the shaping forces of his imagination.

In fictional terms, age and impending death influence and shape each of the monologues, but the narrators themselves, suspended in a variety of situations, have come to their respective passes before the commencement of the poem. We pick them up, as it were, *in extremas res*, poised in a brief hiatus in the *dénouements* of their lives, where, because there is no outlet in action available, talk is the only recourse. This condition provides the perspective for comprehending Tennyson's narrators. The crisis of most of Browning's speakers are not terminal; though one thinks of the obvious exceptions—the Bishop, the Grammarian, Pompilia and Guido—examples do not spring readily to mind. Most are caught in moments where decision, affecting change, is an option, and the characters succeed or fail according to their insights into their own personalities. But even when they are victims of their own delusions, movement is possible for Browning's speakers; they can go backward or forward. Tennyson's, on the other hand, are cornered; they can only, as Ulysses puts it so well (in a different context) 'pause' and 'make an end'. Tennyson's monologues focus on those pauses.

In fact, Ulysses' context may not be all that 'different', for the poem can be read, at least on one level, as just such a pause—a poem whose epicentre, like the eye of a hurricane, is dominated by inaction, suspension, and stasis. That 'Ulysses' has generated such opposing responses testifies to the complex ambiguity that informs the poem as a whole; but even without entering into the question of assessing the relative merit of Ulysses' quest, on which hinge the traditional or 'revisionist' readings of the poem, the essential problem is to discover or decide whether anything actually transpires in the poem, whether, that is, the 'action' is external or internal, real or rhetorical. The commentaries, as anyone familiar with the small library of criticism on the poem well recognises, are contradictory, bifurcating those critics who see the concluding voyage as a recycling of those epical energies that impelled Ulysses during the twenty years spanned by the *Iliad* and the *Odyssey*, and those—to put the case at its most extreme—who interpret the voyage as the senile imaginative meanderings of a vainglorious and impotent old man, long past the prime of discovery. Neither the Homeric or Dantean sources of the poem nor the vagueness of Ulysses' aspirations as he articulates them—'To follow knowledge like a sinking star' (R 560, l 31) and 'To sail beyond the sunset, and the baths/Of all the western stars, until I die' (ll 60–1)—provides much assistance in resolving this essential contradiction between literal and metaphorical statement in the poem. The structure does, however, suggest a reading which has not before been advanced and which is consistent with the theory of Tennyson's dramatic monologues argued in this paper.

'Ulysses' has essentially a quatrapartite structure. Commencing with a five-line proem, the poem contains three verse paragraphs of varying lengths, which, both tonally and temporally, appear to be climactically arranged, culminating in Ulysses' final blast of purple rhetoric (ll 68–70):

> One equal temper of heroic hearts,
> Made weak by time and fate, but strong in will
> To strive, to seek, to find, and not to yield.

The proem posits Ulysses as he is, both in the present of his life and the present of the poem: a kind of Ithacan Gerontion, who, having returned from the glories of his heady adventures, cannot accept a life of ennui and stasis (ll 1–5):

> It little profits that an idle king,
> By this still hearth, among these barren crags,
> Matched with an aged wife, I mete and dole

Unequal laws unto a savage race,
That hoard, and sleep, and feed, and know not me.

Virtually all the diction in Ulysses' opening lines, especially the adjectives and verbs, underscore the impotence, sterility, and blandness of the speaker's present condition, which contrasts so forcefully with the diction he uses to describe his previous existence in the first verse-paragraph, in which he seems to have regained, vicariously, his missing youth. The central fact about Ulysses is, of course, that he is old, and his age is a constant in the poem, as he himself, somewhat reluctantly, admits in the concluding section when he reminds his mariners that, their years notwithstanding, 'Old age hath yet his honour and his toil' (l 50). But as age is a constant in the poem, so, too, is the present established in the proem, and one of the problems is to reconcile what seems to be action or movement in the three verse-paragraphs with the stasis of the opening lines. The resolution lies, in my view, in recognising the temporal qualities of each of the paragraphs as they relate to the past, the present, and the future of Ulysses' own life. If the three verse-paragraphs, which comprise most of the poem, are seen as imaginative projections by Ulysses from the constant vantage of what is patently an unsatisfying present, the poem attains a consistency which is not so readily apparent in either a literal or a metaphorical reading that does not depend on the structure. In this reading of the poem, Ulysses, embittered and discontent, projects imaginatively in the first verse-paragraph his virile salad days when life was pure adventure. That these days are uppermost in his mind is clearly indicated by his casting all his experiences and aspirations in the present tense; yet at the same time that he declares, 'I cannot rest from travel' (l 6), he is, like Tithonus, trapped in an exorable present: 'How dull it is to pause, to make an end/to rust unburnished, not to shine in use' (ll 22–3). Recognising that of this life 'little remains' (l 26) and that all he can look forward to is a continuance of the 'three suns' he has spent storing and hoarding himself, and that he is only a 'gray spirit yearning in desire' (l 30), Ulysses seizes on the only course of action open to him. He sublimates his past into a projected future that involves abdicating his throne and responsibilities to Telemachus in the second verse-paragraph and embarking on a life of renewed experience in the third, both of which clearly run counter to the facts in the story of the Homeric Odysseus.

'Ulysses', then, is a poem in which, within a constant present, there is seeming movement and action; and yet, if this reading has validity, the poem actually does not move beyond the stasis posited in the opening lines. That Tennyson himself signalled such a reading is partially endorsed by his separation of the first five lines from the first verse-paragraph in the 1875 edition of his collected works. Until that point, they had always been printed together. Since Ulysses is old and moving towards death, the poem may reasonably be seen—and the deathward trend of the metaphorical voyage in the conclusion supports this view—as consistent with patterns reiterated in Tennyson's other dramatic monologues.

A comparison with Eliot's 'Gerontion' was suggested earlier in passing. While one might not wish to push too hard analogies between the two characters, they do clearly have affinities. Both are old men in dry months waiting for rain; both subsume in a sterile present the fertilities of a frustrated past; both are given to 'Thoughts of a dry brain in a dry season'. Ulysses might well ask, with Gerontion, 'I have lost my passion: why should I need to keep it/Since what is kept must be adulterated?' But Ulysses, for all his cravings, lacks the insight of Gerontion, who, for all his questioning, seems aware of processes that Ulysses appears not to understand:

> These with a thousand small deliberations
> Protract the profit of their chilled delirium,
> Excite the membrane, when the sense has cooled,
> With pungent sauces, multiply variety
> In a wilderness of mirrors.[25]

Eliot's epigraph, from *Measure for Measure*—'Thou hast nor youth nor age/But as it were an after dinner sleep/Dreaming of both' (III, i, 32–4)—is equally apt for Ulysses. Gerontion is 'as old man driven by the trades/To a sleepy corner', a description which also perfectly fits Ulysses.

III

A sustained reading of any of the poetic groupings in Tennyson's works—whether of the lady poems, the voyages, the early seed poems for the *Idylls*, the laureate poems, even of the English Idyls, as I attempted to demonstrate in my monograph on Tennyson's domestic vision—'The Sphere of Common Duties'[26]—invariably underscores the extraordinary diversity of his talent. This diversity is especially prominent in the monologues, in which Tennyson introduces so many formal variations—in language, structure, and situation—not to mention the shifts in the thematic burdens of several of the poems.

As concerned as Tennyson is with the role of the monologues, it would be fanciful to suggest, given the number of years separating their composition and the fact that Tennyson himself never linked them, beyond his remarks concerning the *pendancy* between 'Ulysses' and 'Tithonus', that he consciously or intentionally set out to create a gallery of old men to make a collective statement transcending the possible scope of any single monologue. Nor do the poems themselves suggest the viability of any such sequential meaning. However, the formal and thematic resemblances between them are too striking to be accidental, and it is clear that both in his choice of the form and in the special way he adapted it, Tennyson was as conscious in his artistry as Browning was in his. Throughout his career, Tennyson wrote lyrics and narratives which may be described (in his sense of the term) as monodramas; yet he clearly reserved the formal dramatic monologues for his more serious experiments with point of view and characterisation. That he composed so few distinguishes, on one level at least, his own from Browning's use of the form. For Browning, the genre is organic to his poetic preoccupations, a uniquely suitable form for his indepth analyses of character, and compatible with the narrowness of his dramatic vision.

Tennyson's plays more than convincingly demonstrate that his dramatic talents were not great; neither did he have the technical interest in point of view which motivated Browning. Tennyson was as incapable of creating fifty 'Men and Women' for a volume of dramatic monologues as Browning was of composing, or even of imagining, the *Idylls*. Yet many of Tennyson's best shorter poems are dramatic monologues, and, as we have seen, he was experimenting with the form while Browning was still writing confessional poems. Tennyson may initially have been attracted by the dignity of the form, by its controlled use of language, by the economy of its single speaker, or by its dramatic forcefulness, even its masculinity. Or, there may have been another reason; and with this hypothesis I shall end the discussion.

'Death,' says Ulysses, projecting one final spurt of discovery, 'closes all', and it is partially because that absolute statement seems at such variance with Tennyson's total poetic and personal commitment to a belief in immortality that one school of modern critics (myself among them) has refused to credit Ulysses as a spokesman for Tennysonian values. But that poem may, as David Shaw posits in his fine study of the 'Problem of Mortality' in 'Ulysses' and 'Tithonus', 'record Tennyson's discovery that death is what confers on life its individuality and uniqueness'.[27] Since death is the only avenue for the completion of personality and total individuation in a temporal world of change,

Tennyson's location of each of his monologuists just at the verge of human fulfilment, through death, may have been for him an artistic device for utilising the dramatic monologue's potential for realising characters objectively, in psychological terms, without exposing the nerve-ends of his own subjectivity.

7 Tennyson and the Idea of Decadence

John Bayley

The art that might be called decadent always makes, it seems to me, a conscious claim to impersonality. Some say it is unwise to compare pictures with poems or stories, but at least until our own day the relationship of the two was so close and obvious that a comparison often serves to bring out the conscious intention of poets and artist in contrast with the less conscious factors involved, if any. Gustave Moreau's picture of Salome dancing before Herod is perhaps as good an example of decadent art as one could hope to find. It has a technical fascination, and it is also quite impersonal, but the same could be said of many pictures—and some very great ones, by Masaccio or Piero della Francesca for instance—which have nothing in the least decadent about them. What is decadent about this 'Salome Dancing' is the very evident ambition to exclude any suggestion of personal feeling from the treatment of the subject; decadence involves a policy of conscious exclusion in order to produce an artificial state in the beholder of what Vladimir Nabokov called 'aesthetic bliss', the sense of a job well done, a kick well administered. 'Salome Dancing' is a choice and memorable picture, and it is of course a subject traditionally associated with *La Décadence*, as a late nineteenth-century historical and cultural phenomenon.

As we look at the picture we notice and enjoy details, peculiarities of styling, seemingly just as we might in any other picture, or, if it comes to that, in any comparable poem. Herod's peevishly hunched position, an old man in a dressing gown, bemused with senile nostalgia for lust now extinguished, dimly seeking to get his old grip on the situation and grasp what is going on. Salome's remarkable biceps as her white arms wave before his face; they look as if they might have strayed in from another favourite subject of the Decadence—Judith cutting off the head of Holofernes—and indeed they probably have. The bare sinewy foot of the executioner, which occupies an ample and commanding space in the centre foreground of the picture. These physical details do not, we notice, have the virtuosity and extravagance of mannerism, in which strained and eccentric physical pose was sought for and valued for its own sake; and yet they share with the older mannerists, such as Manetti something of the same impersonal grossness: in neither case is the artist scrupulously involved, as a speculating sympathising individual, a being involuntarily revealing itself *as* an individual in every characteristic and peculiarity of the work.

There are many things in Tennyson's poetry which might seem to partake of this aspect of decadence. Take the concept of the single line, mouthed and pondered in the study, or in nocturnal walks round the Lincolshire lanes, until it wholly satisfied in the sure perfection of its syllables. Does not this resemble that impersonal ideal of 'aesthetic bliss', of a job well done? An essay by H. A. Mason takes Tennyson to task for such lines as those describing how the Lady of the Lake wrought the sword of Arthur: 'Nine years she wrought it, sitting in the deeps/Upon the hidden bases of the hills' (R 1742, ll 272–3). Tennyson is said to have declaimed them when out with his friend FitzGerald in a boat on Windermere, and enquired if they were not pretty good.[1] Mason suggests that they only sound pretty good, and indeed are only intended to sound pretty good, suggesting as they do a stylised picture—rather like the mermaid of Copenhagen seated on her rock—beyond which our imaginations are not expected to query or explore. If they *do* so explore, he implies, we shall begin to ask ourselves whether the picture is so satisfactory after all. What facilities did she have down there for making that sword? Why did she sit down to it, as if she were weaving a tapestry?—Perhaps it is not surprising it took such a long time.

To this I would reply that it is precisely such thoughts that the lines invite us to have and with which they harmonise in a sort of subterranean, or perhaps subaqueous, deliberation. Tennyson actually wants us to realise what the situation and specification of lines like these are, or might be; and more obscurely he inviteɔ us to appreciate how they relate to his own self, his ideas in poetry, his ideas on life, and the more instinctual ground of personal and peculiar talent where the two come together. They clearly relate to his doubts about the style and subject of such a poem, and an audience's possible reactions to it— reactions which are anticipated and placed in a chased and scrolled frame of almost burlesque elaboration at the beginning of the poem, the 'Morte d'Arthur'. For the point about such lines is that they are not really so confident as they sound; their confidence is really the weight of diffidence, of a peculiarly Tennysonian kind, which asks from the reader an equally peculiar kind of fellowship and reassurance. Diffidence is not only the most human and most personalised of qualities, but the one that most surely if stealthily reaches out for the enlargement of human contact.

And nothing could be less decadent than this: in fact it is the opposite of what decadent art is trying to do. Take the Moreau picture again. It might be said that, as we study it, we are making just the same kind of 'human' observation as we make about Tennyson's lines—I spoke for instance of Salome's biceps and King Herod's look of peevish incomprehension. But it seems to me absolutely clear that in making such advances—whose irreverence is really friendly, offering admiration—we are knocking on a door which has been carefully locked on the inside. Our speculations receive no response; indeed the poise and look of the picture (which is far from diffident) gives us to understand that we have shown rather poor taste in making them, whereas a Titian or a Tintoretto would not, one feels, have minded such speculations at all.

Hence I feel that H. A. Mason's style of impeachment does not really find its mark on Tennyson, though it has the valuable function of making us think more and harder about the ways in which we do respond to the poetry. Where it would get home is on a certain kind of unsuccessful decadent poem, a poem which has not, so to speak, succeeded in locking the door firmly enough between us and itself. One such poem—apparently an early effort by W. B. Yeats, which never reached the stage of being published—is mentioned by Gerard Manley Hopkins in a letter from Dublin.[2] The poem was about a sphinx and a man on a rock in the ocean, engaged in some activity as implausible as that of the Lady of the Lake manufacturing her sword. How did they get there and what did they live on? This Hopkins wanted to know, and added that though some readers thought such questions uncouth they are really very important to poetry. So they are, not necessarily as an indicator of what has gone wrong, but of what will tell us what sort of poetry we are dealing with. Decadent poetry has its own sort of charms, and the early Yeats, conscientiously hardening into the art of decadence the lambent and fluid allegorical plots of Shelley, was indeed producing a product that did not wish to be asked questions of this kind. (His early poetry is of course very different in this respect from his later and latest, which does invite questions, and of a tough recondite kind, about its literal and symbolic meaning.)

The Lady in the Lake and the sphinx on the rock are thus two quite different sorts of being, poetically speaking. Not only is Tennysonian finish, its sumptuousness, and formality, really very much more cosy and domestic than it seems at first; it is also much more collusive. This combination is at the root of Tennyson's great popular appeal in his own time, and it seems to me also an important aspect of the enduring fascination of his poetry. In taking a subject he adopts towards it attitudes of a complicated sort, transmitted to the reader through machinery whose operation is all the more effective for being so unusually designed. Decadent art appears by contrast not only very simple in the way it goes to work (the kick, as I said, which it administers), but works deliberately on the surface in order to make the boldest immediate impression upon us. Humour, in the sense of something incongruous working beneath the surface, can never be allowed in that early poetry of Yeats for instance, nor in Swinburne and the poets of the 1890s, least of all, oddly enough, in the poetry of such a naturally humorous personality as Oscar Wilde.

Decadence, then, shows us a picture, usually exotic, and requires us to attend to it and to nothing else. Almost the whole point of Tennyson's pictures on the other hand is to lead us through delight to curiosity— curiosity about why these have been chosen, about the often deprecating manoeuvres that attends their choice, most of all about the nature and creative process of the poet himself. Consider the haunting landscape of 'Mariana' (R 187). It transmits its powerful charm to us because it is so detestable to the heroine of the poem. It repels her and attracts us to the extent that it both repelled and attracted Tennyson himself, as a landscape fraught with the boredom and melancholy, the deep rich depression of adolescence and early manhood. The poem identifies consciousness and landscape more graphically and compulsively than any other I know, making a perhaps deliberately incongruous use of Shakespeare to link at a deeper level with some of the most imaginative and original of nineteenth-century novels. It is typical of these collusive and intimate methods of Tennyson that its apparent subject is not its real one. Mariana's forlornness is not because her lover has abandoned her and she is pining for his return; it is in the nature of her being itself, a nature from which she cannot escape or be delivered, whatever change of fortune may take place, and this of course brings us into the presence of Tennyson's own sense of himself. One of the most remarkable things about the new realisations of landscape in nineteenth-century literature is how they can teach the viewer things about his own nature and its limitations. Tennyson can remind us of

Dickens's use of Italian scenery in *Little Dorrit*. Confronted with that overpowering picturesqueness, Little Dorrit—and Dickens with her—is faced with a knowledge of the scene that is *really* herself, the courts of the Marshalsea prison, the bleak skies and streets of London. 'Beauty' depresses and diminishes her with an impersonal glory and glitter to which she cannot respond. The role of intimacy in our response to the aesthetic is singularly well understood by the Tennysonian imagination, which is very close here to the most subtle imagination of the novel in its greatest period, and as far as could be from the achievements and intentions of decadence.

Thanks to that imagination every novelist has come to know that it is no use describing things and scenes with impersonal virtuosity and expecting the reader to admire them. The attempt to do so, or something very like it seems to me make *The Waves* the most decadent—in my sense—of Virginia Woolf's works. Virginia Woolf is often spoken of as a particularly personal sort of creative imagination; her real weakness seems to me, on the contrary, her tendency to take refuge in the impersonal, her fear of an undercover intimacy with the reader, with its awkwardnesses, its incongruities, and above all its buried humour. I suspect that in her imaginative conceptions she feared the odd incalculability of humour as much as she relied on the impersonal powers of fantasy. It is curious that Jane Austen, the most reserved of novelists, comes much closer to us in these undercover ways than Virginia Woolf ever does. And there are moments when her use of landscape is distinctly Tennysonian, distinctly, as it were, Mariana-like. The hollow hedge, or rather two hedges with a hollow or vestigial path between them, is a feature of Hampshire upland; and it is a feature as much suited to Anne Elliot, the heroine of *Persuasion*, as the favourite spot of Leopardi—the hedged summit that cut off a too extended further prospect—was to the poet. In the very suitability of the place there lives for these authors a kind of unspoken comedy, of a wry or wistful kind.

What I am trying to work round to is an idea of the implicit nature of Tennysonian humour, which I hope these parallels and contrasts may help in revealing; the initial premise being that humour of such a sort is for me the great anti-Decadence factor, the inconspicuous door which opens between writer and reader, and which the reader is always tacitly encouraged to find his way through. Humour is one way of sharing depression, its 'secret source' as Mark Twain called it. I must try to be more effective in a moment in defining what I mean by the implicit humour of Tennyson, and why I want to call it that, why indeed it seems the only word one can use, but I want first to attempt yet another illustration by way of both parallel and contrast. In Gogol's *Dead Souls* the richest, densest, most scintillating passage in the novel is the account of the garden of the old miser, Plyushkin, on whom the hero calls on the chance of picking up a few more of those insubstantial but valuable and mortgage-worthy individuals of whom he is in search. The description, of which I give some passages below, is highly Tennysonian:

The united summits of trees that had once grown wide in liberty spread above the skyline in a mass of green clouds and irregular domes of tremulous leafage. The colossal white trunk of a birchtree shorn of its top, broken off by gale or thunderbolt, rose out of those dense green masses and disclosed its rotund smoothness in mid-air, like a well-proportioned column of sparkling marble; instead of a capital it terminated high up in an oblique, sharply-pointed fracture, which showed black against its snowy whiteness like a kind of head-piece or a dark bird. After smothering the bushes of elder and rowan and hazel below, strands of hop had meandered all over the top of the fence, from which they had given a final leap to encircle the truncated birch halfway up. Reaching its middle they hung down from there, and were already beginning to catch at the tops of other trees, or had to leave hanging in the air, and gently oscillated by it, their intertwined loops and thin clinging hooks. In some places the green mass broke asunder in a blaze of sunshine and revealed a deep unlighted recess, gaping like dark jaws. All that could be made out in the black depth were the course of a narrow footpath, a crumbling balustrade, a toppling summerhouse, the hollow trunk of a decrepit willow, dense grey sedge bristling out from behind it, a tangled maze of twigs and dead leaves, dry and stiff in an impenetrable wilderness; and, lastly, a young branch of maple, thrusting the green paws of its leaves sideways, under one of which a gleam of sunlight had somehow managed to creep in after all, making of the one leaf a translucent marvel burning in the dense darkness.

It is evident that Gogol, who was writing in Italy, feels a nostalgia for this monumental Russian dishevelment, which bursts out in his prose, grafted on to concepts and vistas nearer at hand, columns and picturesque ruins sunk in greenery. In the arbitrariness of the description and its wholly contingent association with the hero's interview with a miserly landowner, there is a feeling of intimacy, an incongruous and beautiful joke proffered to the reader obliquely and to the side of the story. However different Tennyson's tone, his descriptions do seem to me to have, at their best, the same kind of bizarre relation to their setting and story. Gogol's leaf 'burning in the dense darkness' is a highly personal leaf. Such descriptions seem to be a way of getting in touch with us, and indulging their marvellous skills with a huge wink, a deep reverberant chuckle of enjoyment. It is true that I am thinking of the story of Fitz in the boat, and the whole massively and equanimously dirty and shabby image of the bard with his deep eyes looking through tobacco smoke as he 'Read, mouthing out his hollow oes and aes,/Deep-chested music, and to this result . . .' (R 582, ll 50–1), as he imagines Everard Hall doing in the prologue to the 'Morte d'Arthur'. But it seems to me that Tennyson is a poet whose physical image in his poems is well worth keeping before us, because it is so much a part of that large collusive amusement on which even apparently his most 'serious' poetry depends for its full effect, and without it can sound pompous and disembodied. Gogol, too, in his different way, is both shy and forthcoming, furtive and yet suddenly whooping with gaiety in our faces. However different the personality, in both cases richness of description depends on our sharing in it.

Neither Gogol nor Tennyson are in the least ironical. Sooner or later criticism tends to find irony in every great writer, even the most unlikely ones, and Tennyson is no exception. But though of course a critic is entitled to use such a *Catch 22* word as irony in any way he wants—and J. R. Kincaid has used it persuasively in his study of Tennyson's 'Comic and Ironic Patterns'[3]—it seems to me that the word is fundamentally unsuited to any of the effects and impressions that the poet gives us, various and subtle as these undoubtedly are. In order that his technique should work an ironist must take us directly into his confidence, as Browning does for instance, in 'My Last Duchess' or 'Soliloquy in A Spanish Cloister'. The ironist watches us react to the unexpectedness of the situation—the monstrous sangfroid of the Renaissance noble, the lack of congruity between the monk's vocation and his stream of consciousness—and then by implication explains to us how it was done. Although irony used thus by a nineteenth-century poet brings us close to its manipulator, it is in one important respect not so different from the effect that decadence obtains, for it firmly closes the door on the reader after the effect is secured—bidding him goodbye as it were—while the impersonal ideal of decadent art never admits a relationship at all.

Browning is not reticent but elusive, as Swift is at the end of that classic of the ironist's art, 'The Modest Proposal'. Having made sure we have got the point he wants to terminate the relationship and be off elsewhere. Tennyson lingers; indeed it is his genius to linger in a situation in which nothing appears to be done—nothing else, it appears, can be done—but to hang around. Such a situation is involuntarily, almost inevitably, full of subdued tremors of comedy. Yet it is not comic, certainly not funny, in the usual sense in which that is the author's intention, as it is also in the case of the ironist. When Tennyson sets himself to be comic, as he not infrequently does, the results can be happy enough (R 667, ll 1–8):

> O plump head waiter at the Cock
>> To which I most resort
> How goes the time? 'Tis five o'clock.
>> Go fetch a pint of port:
> But let it be not such as that
>> You set before chance-comers
> But such whose father-grape grew fat
>> On Lusitanian summers

Well and good, but a little deliberate, as is the charnel-house humour of 'The Vision of Sin' (R 718, ll 67–70):

> Bitter barmaid, waning fast!
>> See that sheets are on my bed;
> What! the flower of life is past:
>> It is long before you wed.'

Deliberateness, although of a beautifully accomplished kind, seems to me also too much in evidence in what is admittedly a most attractive poem of a later time, the stanzas 'To the Rev. F. D. Maurice' (R 1022). Maurice, the enlightened Anglican whose doubts about the truth or suitability of the dogma of perpetual hellfire for the wicked had resulted in his resignation from an academic post, is invited to visit the poet in his new home in the Isle of Wight, and get to know better the child Hallam, his godson. It is a deliberately Horatian poem, whose light tone is well grounded in domestic and social realities. Like Horace, or Cowley following, it advocates taking a humorous and civilised view of things, letting the mad world of superstition and bloodshed—the Crimean War was then in progress—continue while we have our 'honest talk and wholesome wine'. A reviewer at the time, anticipating a typically modern response, called it complacent. Not so I would think, but there is certainly too neat a finish to it, a finish which in Tennysonian terms is somehow inappropriate, and which is not found in its metrical congener, 'The Daisy' (R 1019), most enchanting and open of all poems. 'To the Rev. F. D. Maurice' presents its picture in too full and humorous a light for the bard to muse and loiter with us in its composition, 'resolving towards fulfilment'—'To walk, to sit, to sleep, to wake, to breathe'—the kind of fulfilment which art working with temperament achieves in Tennyson. The Oblomov Tennyson is the true humorist, and then he may make us remember, too, that other Russian whom I mentioned, the self that lingers at the end of a humorous story by Gogol, and observes unexpectedly through the narrator: '*Skuchno v etom svetom, Gospoda*'—'it's boring in this world, gentlemen'. Old friend FitzGerald, whom Tennyson gloomily implored not 'to bore me about my book', was perhaps only half right when he wrote that 'Alfred cannot trifle—many are the disputes we have had about his powers of badinage . . . his smile is rather a grim one'.

But Tennyson *could* trifle, almost too well, and in a sense he is most trifling when he is going through the motions of being grim. The truest as well as the most moving humour is when he shares with us his awareness that he is writing 'beautiful' poetry as a means of making his life supportable: *that* speaks to us, and the bosom of the reader who intuits it returns an echo. The more lingeringly tranquil the lines, and their suspension rather than ending, the more transparently does their tranquillity seem his art's way of sustaining the vexation of spirit, of life. His humour is indistinguishable from this kind of transparency, and the honesty that goes with it. Not many poets, after all, would tell us as Tennyson does, in the course of that sustained treatment of grief and recovery that is *In Memoriam*, that the best anodyne for insupportable loss is 'sad mechanick exercise', and this is what and why he is writing. A sad mechanick exercise sounds wonderfully plangent and mellow, as Tennyson always does when he is really telling home truths about himself, but the more we read him the more we feel he is always well aware of the necessary and healing gap between the words of poetry and the sort of state you are in when it is a comfort to write it; and this muffled but shared awareness seems to me to constitute his real humour, a humour in its way as down-to-earth and commonsensical as that of Sydney Smith about the *skuchno* conditions under which life must be carried on, and the consequent necessity of 'taking short views, never further than dinner or tea'.

It is a speechless communion between the lines of the most exquisite speech, an awkward humour of the unspoken in relation to lines that are spoken with such sonorous beauty. It is this beauty that H. A. Mason objects to in relation to the Lady of the Lake and her underwater manufacturing process—'the impossibility of attaching any meaning to these lines'. But meaning in relation to poetry can have many meanings, and never more so than with Tennyson. Walt Whitman understood this very well, for in him too a kind of slyness and sending-up of his own processes is essential to their originality and personal vigour. 'To me', he writes, 'Tennyson shows more than any poet I know (perhaps has been a warning to me) how much there is in finest verbalism. There is such a latent charm in mere words, cunning collocutions, and in the voice ringing them.'[4] The voice is the point, for it is the giveaway inflections and formalities of Tennysonian utterance that remove it so completely from the decadent or Parnassian utterance which it so often seems almost to mimic. The word Parnassian in this context is that of Gerard Manley Hopkins, who of course knew in his own being and practice what the note of personality in poetry could mean. *A propos* 'Enoch Arden' he wrote that it was the hallmark of Parnassian style that 'one could conceive oneself writing as if one were the poet'.[5] This is a good way of putting the fact that Parnassian poetic is impersonal: everyone can imagine writing in this high-falutin' way; imitating the 'Tennysonian', because the 'Tennysonian' itself can become a de-personalised and 'beautiful' official style.

Of course Tennyson can be easily imitated, but when he really *inspires* another poet, then we can see something important about what he is like himself. The present Poet Laureate has been inspired by his love for Tennyson and the Victorian age to exaggerate and make positive the humour and also the down-to-earthness which lurks in Tennysonian fine writing. Betjeman's Victorianism has the curious effect of making his poetry wholly up to date; Tennyson's treatment of his mediaevalism, his romance and costume pieces, had exactly the same effect: 'Far far beneath me roll the Coulsdon woodlands/White down the valley curves the living rail . . .'.[6] Though the metre is taken from Meredith the tone of the description is unmistakably Tennysonian. The electric railway is absorbed into the style without the slightest ripple of facetiousness, and yet of course the humour of it is there, indistinguishable from the success of the verbal melody. The end of Betjeman's 'A Subaltern's Love Song' has a similar seriousness about it, which Dylan Thomas brought out in his recording of it by reading in a vibrant, wholly deadpan voice: 'We sat in the car-park till quarter to one,/And now I'm engaged to Miss Joan Hunter-Dunne.'[7] Both poets show that a conventional verbal melody, a seemingly decorous and decorated

Parnassian style, can in fact be a wholly flexible and personal instrument, returning to the reader, in transformed and exotic trappings, his own sense of the up-to-dateness and incongruities of the age he lives in. It is no wonder that both poets are national institutions of their own time.

Tennyson's popularity was closely connected with how modern he seemed in his own time, a modernity the paradox of which puzzled and sometimes irritated the critics and reviewers. But there was no doubt about it. William Roscoe, man of letters and minor poet, unexpectedly observed of *Poems Chiefly Lyrical*, that their author 'is a mind in exact harmony with the times in which he lives'. There may be a slight sneer in that, but there is perception and admiration too. Tennyson could not have been in exact harmony if he had not been acutely conscious of the problems for a poet of being so—perhaps too conscious—and his audience had their own anxieties about the *Zeitgeist*, which elements in his poetry prismatically focused. Tennyson was able to turn his own and their anxieties into various and subtle kinds of reassurance, most notably in *In Memoriam*. And in a simpler and cruder way his readers were reassured by a poem that simply began 'I waited for the train at Coventry', and then went on to tell in beautiful language the charming old tale of Lady Godiva. The modern age seems taken for granted by such a device, not evaded, and this quite unemphatic acceptance has something of the diffidence of humour in it, even though by Tennyson's standards the poem is not much good. *The Idylls of the King* are equally modern in that their spacious official grandeur mirrors a culture which in its official self-representation had settled down into being spacious and grand. And the tone of their tale of adultery in high places is realistic in that it is just the tone which later Victorian society liked to hear in the poetic discussion of such things.

There still remains the very marked gap between the pseudo-humour and the true implicit humour. The pseudo-humour seeks for reassurance—the poet making it for himself and seeking it from the reaction of his audience—as in the prologues to 'Lady Godiva' and 'Morte d'Arthur'. 'I waited for the train at Coventry' (R 732) is excellent—as uncompromising an opening as Philip Larkin's 'I work all day and get half drunk at night'—but Leigh Hunt was right to find something not quite right in the tone of the lines that follow, the poet telling us how he hung around with the porters, contemplating the city's spires and 'shaping' his poem. Indulgent to his own weaknesses and those of others, Hunt had nonetheless a sharp eye for them, though it is significant that he misunderstands the note that Tennyson was trying to catch in these passages, and says there is 'a drawl of Bond Street in it'.[8] Surely not: the trouble is the almost embarrassingly tentative way in which Tennyson loads weighty and genial measures with a tentative, deprecatory undertone. He is overdoing the humorousness to protect himself a little, even from his friends. In the 'Morte d'Arthur' prologue (R 582), as in 'Audley Court' (R 704), and 'Edwin Morris' (R 708), an imagined poet protects Tennyson and gives him licence to laugh at himself for his friends' benefit; and the best part of the process is the suggestion of a more private humour underlying the public performance of it (R 582, ll 24–32):

> . . . we knew your gift that way
> At college: but another which you had,
> I mean of verse (for so we held it then),
> What came of that?' 'You know,' said Frank, 'he burnt
> His epic, his King Arthur, some twelve books'—
> And then to me demanding why? 'Oh, sir,
> He thought that nothing new was said, or else
> Something so said 'twas nothing—that a truth
> Looks freshest in the fashion of the day' . . .

The mock modesty ('for so we held it then') merges into something less defensive. Tennyson did in fact have a deep instinct for what 'looks freshest in the fashion of the day', as he was to show, and behind the overdone charade of horseplay one can detect an altogether more private kind of awareness.

In all this there is almost too much of Tennysonian consciousness, laborious contriver of camped-up personal situations, of which *The Princess* is the most elaborate of all. It brings us face to face with a truth which Tennyson was perhaps as much aware of in his own secret way as his friends and critics more openly were. It is the fact that 'Alfred can't write anything *serious*', that, like Edwin Morris, he can only read them 'rhymes elaborately good' about Arthur or the Lady of Shalott and sleeping princesses and Greek legends. The most striking thing about all these poems is the quality and nature of the poet's awareness of their apparent triviality. He needs it desperately, but he is also aware that there is something rather humorous about such a need. Hence the even more elaborate gambits of evasion and deprecation. The point about Tennyson's 'beauties' is the exceptionally complicated relation between these

> jewels five-words-long
> That on the stretched forefinger of all Time
> Sparkle for ever (R 741, ii, 355-7)

and the psychological needs and drives of their maker. The decorated surface of decadent art, and its choice of subject, inform us fully of their specification, and with complete confidence that this is the way things ought be—art for art's sake. Tennyson's awareness of all this is expressed, sometimes almost obsessionally, in various undercover ways, in the bland and lucent dialogues and discussions about the epic and poems like 'Edwin Morris'; in contrived yet searching pieties of the heroic strain, 'And God fulfils Himself in many ways,/Lest one good custom should corrupt the world' (R 585, ll 241-2).

The odd comedy of Tennysonian appearance and withdrawal is most evident in 'The Palace of Art', his temperamental sub-humour highly marked there. The poet's soul lives in her palace until she can bear it no more (R 400, ll 291-6).

> 'Make me a cottage in the vale', she said,
>   Where I may mourn and pray.
>
> Yet pull not down my palace towers, that are
>   So lightly, beautifully built:
> Perchance I may return with others there
>   When I have purged my guilt'.

The resolution of the first two lines has its dirge suddenly checked by the wilfully fragile rising tone. Guilt, surely, does not really come into the picture. Tennyson's highly positive endings are always a little suspect, like the end of 'The Vision of Sin', where sin is as much a mere concept as guilt is in 'The Palace of Art'. Both are full of nightmare visions which have nothing to do with either sin or guilt, but everything to do with solutionless—as it must have seemed to him—interior stagnation. It is typical of Tennyson not only to turn these blank broodings into pictures as finished and in a sense as self-complacent as those of decadent art, but to transform images, the workmanship on which had saved him, into something that is psychologically closely related but at the same time quite different: beauties among which the soul lives in a state of doomed and self-deceiving contentment. Psychologically the relation of complacence to misery is a jest of which Tennyson is fully aware as an original verbal artist.

The end of 'A Vision of Sin' parodies the acceptance world of Homer and the rosy-fingered dawn which can be relied upon to recur with a monotony as comforting as Sydney Smith's dinners and teas. The oxymoron in the 'big' line—'God made himself an awful rose of dawn'—becomes doubly ambiguous in its context, because the adjective seems to incline to its trivial measuring by drawing attention to its more grandiose. A rose is not awe-inspiring, but the notion of another awful old day brings its own kind of reassurance, and the renewed ability to find solace in writing about it. If his words are taken at their face value Tennyson is indeed talking 'in a tongue no man could understand', and yet they have their own kind of literalness. His is the sort of 'finest verbalism', in Whitman's phrase, which encourages our awareness of his creative process and its human needs. There lurks in his verbalism a kind of forceful simplicity, in terms of what it means to him and can do for him.

Like 'Mariana', 'The Palace of Art' succeeds—though not on the same poetic level—by dissembling its real subject and putting us in a picture more interesting than the one formally framed and decorated; and the reader seems tacitly invited to a private view. The lady of the palace contemplates 'mosaic choicely planned/With cycles of the human tale' (R 400, ll 145–6), until

> God, before whom ever lie bare
> The abysmal deeps of Personality,
> Plagued her with sore despair. (R 400, ll 222–4).

The unusual movement produced by putting 'ever' before 'lie' announces a change immanent in the oddly undecorative word 'Personality', with its capital P. And personality—Tennyson's own highly idiosyncratic one—is present in all the beautiful objects the poetry creates in the same love–hate, even serio–comic, sense in which the objects are created around Mariana. 'Tennyson, we cannot live in art', R. C. Trench had announced to him at Trinity, and Tennyson had agreed. Yet he lived *by* art, and he knew it, as the poem does. In those depths of personality there is the knowledge that so far from being a glittering vision that turns to sterility and nightmare, art was his sole means of salvation: and it is this knowledge which emerges openly and movingly in the long convalescence by art and nature of *In Memoriam*. In 'The Palace of Art' humour remains disembodied in the gravity of the moral message—'this poem is the embodiment of my own belief that the Godlike life is with man and for man'. Maybe so, but what is actually

going to happen in that cottage in the vale? Is the soul going to undergo
a course of penitential therapy there—by writing poems in praise of the
deplorable palace? That would be the best that could happen, and that
was what did happen. The word guilt, on whose light rising note the
poem deftly, almost cheerfully, closes, carries nothing of its proper and
weighty meaning. Indeed it would not be too fanciful to say that the last
word of the poem carries a suggestion of that other sense of guilt, on
which Lady Macbeth punned; the 'slim gilt soul' to which Oscar Wilde
referred; the gilt that glitteringly encrusts the pictures of Gustav Klimt
and Gustave Moreau.

The poem is slotted through with oddities that beckon us not into the
impersonal world of aesthetic delight, 'holding no form of creed,/But
contemplating all', but into the very personal situation which required
the poet to keep sane by fashioning those delights, even by putting
himself as a figure among them. Again there is a tacit humour in the
relation of those other poets in the poem, whose pictures adorn the
palace (R 400, ll 133–6):

> For there was Milton like a seraph strong,
>   Beside him Shakespeare bland and mild;
> And there the world-worn Dante rasp'd his song,
>   And somewhat grimly smiled . . .

with the unmistakable images of the poet himself, seen as a figure in a
tapestry (R 400, ll 65–8):

> One seem'd all dark and red—a tract of sand,
>   And someone pacing there alone,
> Who paced for ever in a glimmering land,
>   Lit with a low large moon.

or as the dead calm beside a moving seascape (R 400, ll 245–52):

> A spot of dull stagnation, without light
>   Or power of movement seem'd my soul,
> 'Mid onward-sloping motions infinite
>   Making for one sure goal.
>
> A still salt pool, lock'd in with bars of sand,
>   Left on the shore; that hears all night
> The plunging seas draw backward from the land
>   Their moon-led waters white.

The Lady of the Palace—Tennyson's soul—is a decidedly ambivalent figure—natural enough in view of the close relationship. When 'loathing of her solitude' falls on her it breeds 'Scorn of herself; again, from out that mood/Laughter at her self-scorn' (R 400, ll 231–2). And it is odd to hear of the mistress of the palace of art that 'of the moral instinct would she prate'. It contradicts the theme that what Cambridge calls the Moral Sciences have no place in the fatal palace; 'prate' trembles with a dangerous levity that makes audible in the poem the high-minded discussions of the Apostles and the equally high-minded prologue that Tennyson addressed with the poem to R. C. Trench. That prologue begins 'I send you here a sort of allegory', but by the end of the poem it is clear that the Lady has become too unmanageable, too compromised with 'Personality', of the floating, weightless Tennysonian kind, to fit neatly into an allegorical pattern. Identified with the Tennysonian consciousness she becomes as robust a figure as her sisters, Mariana and The Lady of Shalott. In all three cases it is the uncontrolled singularity of key words that brings in the irrepressibly personal element. Many critics have noted the effective realism of the lines in 'Mariana' (R 187, ll 77–80):

> but most she loathed the hour
> When the thick-moted sunbeams lay
> Athwart the chambers, and the day
> Was sloping towards his western bower.

'Thick-moted' is certainly a compound adjective that catches the eye, but 'loathed' is the operative word. It joins the heroine's predicament not only to Tennyson's but to Everyman's experience of the mere grossness of boredom and mental stagnation. 'Most suicides', observed Dwight Culler in *The Poetry of Tennyson*, 'occur not on a gloomy Monday morning but on a pleasant Friday afternoon', and the black joke in this statistic is as native to the poem as its pathos, is indeed an aspect of that pathos.

An unexpectedness in the word joins it to Shakespeare's Mariana, and her 'brawling discontents', the discontents of a comedy, even if a dark one. As one might expect, Tennyson's subliminal humour, in these and other poems, is of the trench humour variety. A reviewer of *Maud* wrote: 'If our author pipe of adultery, fornication, murder and suicide, put him down as a practiser of those crimes'. 'Adulterer I may be', Tennyson commented, 'fornicator I may be, murderer I may be, suicide

I am not yet.'[9] His art is instinct with incongruities all the more compelling for not being overt. The Lady of Shalott is 'like some bold seer in a trance,/Seeing all his own mischance'. She knows how absurd she is being and she cannot help it. The absurdity of her act makes its own wholly naturalistic comment on the fairytale preposterousness of the poem's properties—the web, the song, the boat, her death. The incongruity was sharper, too evidently so, in the original 1832 ending, where 'the well-fed wits of Camelot' are puzzled by the phenomenon, naturally enough; and the poem concludes with a simple statement of her identity, as if her odd conduct were predestined by her being the self she was.

There is thus an important sense in which such poems achieve their particular sort of individuality and truth by sending up their own subject-matter, a process invisibly perfected in *Maud* and *In Memoriam*. The 'wild Poet' of section XXXIV, who 'works without a conscience or an aim', and to whom Tennyson compares the appearance of Nature, is indeed in complete harmony with the way Nature works, with its unending season of birth and death, wounding and healing, suffering and calm. The deepest comfort that 'lurks'—suggestive word—in the wild Poet, as in the developed life of the poem, and which has secretly rewarded all its readers, is the way in which it accepts and transforms the meaninglessness of things. The universe, like the poet, is indeed without a conscience or an aim, but that is precisely why life flourishes as well as dies, why the poet is inspired to create and briefly to realise himself by creating.

But the things that lurk, particularly in the early poems, can easily give rise to misunderstanding. Victorian readers probably took them in their stride, as naturally as they did in the very different case of Dickens, abandoning themselves to his alternation of wholehearted sentimentality and wholehearted derision—the two being sides of the same coin. We can see in 'The Two Voices' (R 522, ll 412–20) the young Tennyson following through his argument with a concentration that is quite happy to 'darken sanctities with song', as *In Memoriam* puts it, and to present those sanctities with a correspondingly fervent pleasure in the comfort they bring.

> One walk'd between his wife and child,
> With measured footfall firm and mild,
> And now and then he gravely smiled.
>
> The prudent partner of his blood

Lean'd on him, faithful, gentle, good,
Wearing the rose of womanhood.

And in their double love secure,
The little maiden walk'd demure,
Pacing with downward eyelids pure.

For all his admiration and fellow-feeling, T. S. Eliot had to shake his head sadly over this notorious 'Sabbath morn' passage at the end of 'The Two Voices'. To the post-Victorian sensibility it seemed impossible to take: the very apotheosis of Victorian smugness. In fact the stanzas have the exultation that often goes with parody, but is here the result of Tennyson's capacity to identify, in the saving art of his poetry, with a state of being so wholly unlike his own. Unlike most poets, he was not only a good man but a man by whom the sensations of a settled goodness were physically craved, as much as other kinds of genius have needed drugs or debauchery. Is this not why the stanzas have their own version of the devout intensity with which Baudelaire, for instance, writes of the idea of lying with his 'affreuse Juive', as if one corpse were lying clasped by another? Tennyson projects himself—his poetic powers allow it within their own dimension of fulfilment—into the 'unity so sweet' represented by paterfamilias, madonna and little maiden: the unity blends into one image of authority, safety and submission which the poet's need makes intensely, even if rather gruesomely, memorable. Like Baudelaire, or Byron in his lines about his estranged wife, Tennyson conveys a predicament and an emotional need very powerfully; but the peculiarity of his poetic art is the way in which reticence, and the verbal gorgeousness embodying it, seems itself the medium of disclosure, one of whose functions is to produce misunderstanding. Perhaps this is bound to happen when the need for human warmth and love, and the need to work through elaborate verbalism, are in the incongruous relation evident in 'The Palace of Art' and 'The Two Voices'. It is certainly a source of buried humour.

And key words touch that off. What I called their 'uncontrolled singularity' promotes the floating or weightless quality of Tennysonian suggestion. At its most straightforward this can give us the unexpected picture of the guard eating a sandwich in 'Geraint and Enid' (R 1551, ll 629–30) '. . . the brawny spearman let his cheek/Bulge with the unswallowed piece, and turning stared'. That cheeks can bulge in the world of Camelot is distinctly reassuring, and Mr Gladstone was especially struck by the felicity of the sketch. There is something rather similar in a much earlier poem, 'The Day-Dream' (R 628, ll 8–9), when there comes to awaken the Sleeping Beauty 'A fairy Prince, with joyful eyes,/And lighter-footed than the fox'. The last word turns the reader's mind into a channel of association as unexpected in the context as it is in fact wholly suitable: the explorer is likely to be as sharpwitted and predatory as he is romantic and handsome. A much more far-reaching and disturbing tremor of meaning is touched off by a casual epithet towards the end of the *Idylls*, where Arthur is referred to as 'the guileless king'. The word itself seems guileless, but its effect is devastating, for it transposes the context in which we see the legendary figure. In the world of the nineteenth-century novel, the world of Trollope or Henry James, a hero cannot afford to be guileless, and the placing term is a tacit admission of anachronism, not one that makes the telling of the tale less real, but by suggesting the difference between the qualities desirable in a new narrative and an old, summons up both before us. It is a moving way of saying: 'They don't make them like that anymore'; and yet the way the adjective seems to float in the space of the poem implies no hint of patronage.

In 1888 Tennyson wrote a poem to the Viceroy of India, the Marquis of Dufferin and Ava, in gratitude for the kindness shown to his son Lionel, who died on passage home from India of a fever contracted there. It incorporates words from a letter of Lionel's (R 1406, ll 35–6): 'Dying, "Unspeakable", he wrote/"Their kindness", and he wrote no more'. Like 'abysmal' in 'The Palace of Art' ('The abysmal deeps of personality'), 'unspeakable' hovers between the colloquial exaggeration of social use (where it is more likely to be used about a stupid than a kindly act) and a word that can mean exactly what it says. The surprise effect on the reader is of an expression usually debased by overdoing things which here does the thing with appalling adequacy. Its social sense, applied to the Viceroy's kindness, is also the literal sense applicable to the grief of the bereaved; and it is touchingly right that the father should find how to fit into his poetry the word his son used. The same silent dimension of meaning comes in a monosyllable when Tennyson thinks of his son's burial at sea 'Beneath a hard Arabian moon' (R 1406, l 45)—the word 'hard' conveying everything that the feeling in the poem is not. For Tennyson's diction too is hard, in the sense of being perfectly chiselled and precise. The poem revives the metre of *In Memoriam*, and gives the same feel of a close relation—the clasping contrast—between workmanship and feeling. In *In Memoriam* art confronts a sense of the futility of human existence more completely and more successfully than in any other work of imagination of the nineteenth century, perhaps of any work of the specifically modern sensibility. And this short poem on his son's death—even that single line in it—gives us the sense in microcosm of how it was done.

It was, above all, a triumph for the personal factor in an art where the polished surface and an impersonal profile are usually assumed to go together. In decadent art they certainly do. And Tennyson sometimes makes us feel that decadence has an unacknowledged existence in art today, at least in the sensibility of certain kinds of writing, where an impression of impersonality triumphs through mere excess of the personal, of the artists's not troubling to conceal himself in any sense. The self too openly revealed may cease to appear as an individual self at all, whereas Tennysonian contrivance lends his a very special sort of individuality, even when his eloquence appears most lofty, most insidiously formal. Let me illustrate that to end with a quotation from one of my own favourites—the poem called 'Will' (R 1017, ll 15–20). Tennyson contrasts the fate of 'him whose will is strong' with the weak man incapable of moral progress or achievement.

> He seems as one whose footsteps halt,
> Toiling in immeasurable sand,
> And o'er a weary sultry land,
> Far beneath a blazing vault,
> Sown in a wrinkle of the monstrous hill,
> The city sparkles like a grain of salt.

Led up to with such deliberate and unswerving artifice, the final effect comes none the less as a shock of surprise. That grain of salt sparkles like the sudden wink of an elephantine eye. So the goal the will should be striving towards, the just city founded upon a rock, is also perhaps sterile, not worth the arduous journey? Does the attempted exercise of will travail towards a barren advent? The idea of the poem appears very simple, its moral prejudged; its diction seems to confirm that massive confidence; and yet, in the exercise of verbal art, Tennyson has contrived to show us not only how complex such questions really are, but something masterfully unexpected in his own relationship to them.

Notes

PART I—CHAPTER 1

Hallam Tennyson, born 10 December 1920, is Sir Charles Tennyson's youngest and only surviving son. Educated at Eton and Balliol, he spent the war in Egypt and Italy with the Friends' Ambulance Unit and later, with his wife, started a rural reconstruction programme in West Bengal for the American Quakers. Six years as a freelance writer and journalist followed; he published a book of short stories, *The Wall of Dust* (1948), a biography, books of history, travel and biography and a novel about India, *The Dark Goddess* (1958). From 1956 until 1979 he worked for the BBC, retiring as Assistant Head of Radio Drama. He broadcasts frequently and has written many plays and documentaries for radio and television.

This lecture was delivered on 9 May 1979, under the auspices of the Lincoln County Council.

1. Wordsworth's *Prelude* (de Selincourt edition, Oxford University Press, 1933).
2. Ibid., Book II, 1, 69–71; Book VIII, 1, 404–9.
3. *Across the Gaps*, first broadcast 26 December 1974; text and recording in BBC Radio Archives.
4. Wordsworth's *Prelude*, op. cit., Book II, 1, 447.
5. Ibid., Book II, 1, 282–3.
6. Ibid., Book II, 1, 272–6.
7. Margot Asquith, *Autobiography*, vol. 1 (1962 edition: Eyre & Spottiswoode), p. 137.
8. *Lionel Tennyson* (Macmillan, 1891; privately printed), Tennyson Research Centre, Lincoln, p. 1.
9. This tradition comes from the family of Annie Thackeray Ritchie. It is known that Annie's husband, Richmond, was in love with Eleanor during her four years of widowhood.
10. *Lionel Tennyson*, op. cit., p. 49.
11. Charles Tennyson, *Stars and Markets* (Chatto & Windus, 1957), p. 56.
12. David Garnett, *The Flowers of the Forest* (Chatto & Windus, 1955).
13. Lionel, later the third Lord Tennyson, was to become Captain of Hampshire, and later England, at cricket. He was the father of Harold, the present Lord Tennyson.
14. Charles Tennyson, *Stars and Markets*, op. cit., p. 260.
15. Ibid., p. 65.
16. Michael Holroyd, *Lytton Strachey*, vol. 1 (Heinemann, 1967), pp. 407 and 419.
17. Charles Tennyson, *Stars and Markets*, op. cit., pp. 103–4.
18. Ronald W. Clark, *The Life of Bertrand Russell* (Jonathan Cape and

Weidenfeld & Nicolson, 1975), p. 126.
19. Cf. V. Sackville-West, *Pepita* (Hogarth Press, 1937).
20. *Spectator*, review of *The Psychology of Prestige* (3 January 1914), pp. 24–5.
21. Ibid. (21 June 1953), p. 1004.
22. Ibid. (23 November 1912), p. 861.
23. Ibid. (29 November 1913), p. 915.
24. Ibid. (13 July 1912), pp. 60–1.
25. Charles Tennyson, *Cambridge from Within* (Chatto & Windus, 1913).
26. Cf. Charles Tennyson, *Stars and Markets*, op. cit., pp. 147–51.
27. Charles Tennyson, *Life's All a Fragment* (Cassell, 1953), p. 188. Julian Tennyson went on to write *Suffolk Scene* (1939), perhaps the first 'County Book' to achieve high status as literature. His adolescent poetry freely quoted in *Life's All a Fragment* shows astonishing facility as well as feeling.
28. Cf. *Alfred Tennyson*, especially Part I, chapters 2, 4 and 6, and Part II, chapter 2.
29. Cf. *Across the Gaps*, op. cit.
30. Wordsworth's *Prelude*, op. cit.
31. Gerard Manley Hopkins, *Selected Poems* (Heinemann, 1953), p. 64.

PART I—CHAPTER 2

Robert Bernard Martin was born on 11 September 1918. He taught at Princeton University from 1951 until 1975; since then he has been Professor Emeritus of English, Princeton University. He is a BA, University of Iowa; MA, Harvard University; BLitt, Oxford University, and now lives and works in Oxford.

His principal publications are *A Companion to Victorian Literature* (1955); *Charles Kingsley's American Notes: Letters from a Lecture Tour* (1958); *The Dust of Combat: A Life of Charles Kingsley* (1959); *Enter Rumour: Four Early Victorian Scandals* (1962); *Victorian Poetry: Ten Major Poets* (1964); *The Accents of Persuasion: Charlotte Brontë's Novels* (1966); *The Triumph of Wit: A Study of Victorian Comic Theory* (1974).

His full-length biography of Alfred Tennyson was published in 1980. He has also written four thrillers under the pseudonym of 'Robert Bernard'.

This lecture was delivered on 9 March 1979 to the Tennyson Society in Lincoln.

1. Charles Tennyson, *Stars and Markets* (Chatto & Windus, 1957), p. 11.
2. Ibid., p. 257.
3. Ibid., p. 260.
4. *Sir Charles Tennyson: An Annotated Bibliography of his Published Writings* (1973); *A Supplement to the Bibliography of Sir Charles Tennyson*, Tennyson Research Bulletin, vol. 3 (November 1977), pp. 6–9.
5. *Spectator* (4 October 1913 and 2 December 1911).
6. 'The Future of the Classics', *Contemporary Review*, vol. XCVI (December 1909), Literary Supplement, p. 1.
7. *Spectator* (6 July 1912), p. 22.

8. 'Tennyson and his Brothers, Frederick and Charles', in *Tennyson and his Friends*, (ed.) Hallam Lord Tennyson (1911), p. 68.
9. *Spectator* (22 February 1913), pp. 317–18.
10. Ibid. 'New Lives of the Poets' (16 May 1914), p. 836.
11. Charles Tennyson, *Cambridge from Within* (Chatto & Windus, 1913), p. 40.
12. Charles Tennyson, *Stars and Markets* (Chatto & Windus, 1957), p. 124.
13. Charles Tennyson, *Six Tennyson Essays* (Cassell, 1954), p. 162.

PART II—CHAPTER 1

W. W. Robson was born on 20 June 1923 and was a scholar of New College, Oxford, 1941–4 (BA, 1944; MA, 1948). He has been Masson Professor of English Literature at the University of Edinburgh since 1972. He was a Fellow of Lincoln College, Oxford, 1948–70, and Professor of English, University of Sussex, 1970–2. His publications include *English as a University Subject* (Cambridge University Press, 1965); *Critical Essays* (Routledge, 1966); *The Signs Among Us* (Routledge, 1968); *Modern English Literature* (Oxford University Press, 1978). He is the author of many uncollected articles and essays.

1. Christopher Ricks, *Tennyson* (Macmillan, 1972).
2. Blake, *Songs of Experience*.
3. Keats, 'Ode to a Nightingale'.
4. R. W. Rader, *Tennyson's 'Maud': the Biographical Genesis* (University of California Press, 1966), pp. 1–2.
5. Quoted by Rader, ibid., p. 98.
6. C. S. Lewis, *Of Other Worlds* (Harcourt, Brace & World, 1966), p. 67.
7. T. S. Eliot, *On Poetry and Poets* (Faber & Faber, 1957), p. 244.

PART II—CHAPTER 2

Christopher Ricks was born on 18 September 1933 and educated at King Alfred's School, Wantage, and Balliol College, Oxford: BA, 1956; BLitt, 1958; MA, 1960; Junior Research Fellow, Balliol College, 1957; Fellow of Worcester College, Oxford, 1958–68; Professor of English, Bristol University, 1968–75; Visiting Professor, Berkeley and Stanford, 1965; Harvard, 1971; Wesleyan, 1974; Brandeis, 1977. Christopher Ricks was appointed Professor of English at the University of Cambridge in 1975. A Vice-President of the Tennyson Society, Professor Ricks' publications include *Milton's Grand Style* (1963); *The Poems of Tennyson* (1969) (editor); *Tennyson* (1972); *Keats and Embarrassment* (1974).

This lecture was delivered on 23 February 1979 at King's College, Cambridge.

1. Eversley edition (1907–8).
2. The author adapts here, as elsewhere, some paragraphs from his *Tennyson* (Macmillan, 1972). Full references for parallel passages from other poets are only given when these do not appear in *Tennyson*.

3. Ibid., pp. 298–312.
4. Wordsworth, 'Descriptive Sketches'.
5. Richard Holt Hutton, *Literary Essays* (1888); reprinted in *Tennyson: The Critical Heritage*, ed. John D. Jump (Routledge, 1967), p. 364.
6. Humphry House, *All in Due Time* (Hart-Davis, 1955), p. 125.
7. Coleridge, *The Ancient Mariner*, ll, 585–7.
8. Alexander Pope, *Eloisa to Abelard*.
9. Ricks, *Tennyson*, op. cit., p. 65.
10. Shelley, 'Alastor'.
11. T. S. Eliot, *Selected Essays* (Faber & Faber, 3rd edition, 1951), p. 336.
12. Keats, 'Hyperion'.
13. James Thomson, 'Autumn'.
14. Shakespeare, Sonnet 86.
15. Milton, *Paradise Lost*, Book 1, ll 312–15.
16. The author discusses this in 'Allusion: the Poet as Heir' in *Studies in the Eighteenth Century*, ed. R. F. Brissenden and J. C. Eade (1976), pp. 209–10.
17. Wordsworth, 'Ode on the Intimations of Immortality'.
18. Shelley, *Prometheus Unbound*, III, iv, 204.
19. For a discussion of Pope's 'reflected grace' within an allusion to Milton, see 'Allusion: the Poet as Heir', op. cit., p. 210.
20. J. B. Broadbent, *Paradise Lost: An Introduction* (Cambridge University Press, 1972), pp. 100, 102.
21. Pope, *The Dunciad* (1728–9), i, ll 5–6.
22. Wordsworth, 'Tintern Abbey', ll 102–7.
23. G. G. Loane, *Echoes in Tennyson* (Arthur H. Stockwell, 1928).
24. Churton Collins, *Illustrations of Tennyson* (Chatto & Windus, 1891), pp. vii, 23.
25. For a discussion of this, see 'Allusion: the Poet as Heir', op. cit., pp. 210–11.
26. Shelley, *Prometheus Unbound*, I, v.
27. From 'Ford Madox Ford' by Robert Lowell in *Life Studies* (Faber & Faber, 1959).
28. Geoffrey Hill, 'Lachrimae: Pavana Dolorosa' from *Tenebrae* (André Deutsch, 1978).
29. Wordsworth, *Prelude*, VI, 624–5. This section of the *Prelude* was published in 1845, well before Tennyson's revision of his early poem, 'Tithon'.
30. William Empson, 'Missing Dates' from *Collected Poems* (Chatto & Windus, 1955).
31. From 'Wherefore in these dark ages of the Press' quoted from an unpublished manuscript in the author's *Tennyson*, op. cit., p. 161.
32. Wordsworth said of his decision to do without poetic diction: 'it has necessarily *cut me off* from *a large portion* of phrases and figures of speech which *from father to son* have long been regarded as the common *inheritance* of Poets' (from the Preface to the *Lyrical Ballads*, Ricks' italics).
33. Robert Lowell's To Delmore Schwartz' has the poet Schwartz say: 'We poets in our youth begin in sadness;/therefore in the end comes despondency and madness'.
34. Ricks, *Tennyson*, op. cit., pp. 65–6.
35. *Mem.*, i, 318.
36. Milton, *Paradise Lost*, Book I, ll 500–2.

37. Dryden, *Absalom and Achitophel*, ll 597–8.
38. 'Allusion: the Poet as Heir', op. cit., p. 234.
39. Sir Walter Scott, *Lord of the Isles*, VI, xxiii.
40. T. S. Eliot, *The Nation and Athenaeum* (18 December 1926).
41. Edward FitzGerald, *Some New Letters of Edward FitzGerald*, ed. F. R. Barton (Williams and Norgate, 1923), pp. 55–6.
42. Pope, 'Elegy to the Memory of an Unfortunate Lady', ll 9–10.
43. Byron, *Don Juan*, Dedication 9.
44. Sir John Denham, 'On Mr John Fletcher's Works'.
45. This poem was published in 1830.
46. *Inferni raptoris equis adflataque curru/sidera Taenario caligantesque profundae/Iunonis thalamos . . . .*
47. William Mason, *Caractacus* (1759), pp. 26–7.
48. Erasmus Darwin, *The Economy of Vegetation*, IV (1792).
49. Pope, *The Dunciad*, iii, ll 31–4.
50. Dryden: *The Aeneis*, vi, ll 1194–5. See also 'Allusion: the Poet as Heir', op. cit., p. 239.
51. Wordsworth, 'Vernal Ode', ll 40–7.
52. Spenser, 'Epithalamion'. The author owes this parallel to Dorothy Mermin.
53. Marvell, 'An Horatian Ode'.
54. Wordsworth, 'Lines Suggested by a Portrait', ll 76–8.
55. House, *All in Due Time*, op. cit., p. 134.
56. Wordsworth, 'The White Doe'.

PART II—CHAPTER 3

Theodore Redpath was born on 17 August 1913. He was educated at The Leys School, Cambridge; St Catharine's College, Cambridge (Scholar in english), 1931–6; St John's College, Cambridge (Strathcona Research Student for philosophy), 1937–9; PhD (in metaphysics), Cambridge, 1940. He was called to the Bar in 1948. He is Fellow, Senior Lecturer, and Director of English Studies at Trinity College, Cambridge, and University Lecturer in English. He was Tutor at Trinity College from 1960 to 1970.

His publications include: editor of Donne's *Songs and Sonnets* (1956, many times reprinted); *Tolstoy* (1960, 2nd edition 1969); (with P. Hodgart) *Romantic Perspectives* (1964); editor (with W. G. Ingram) *Shakespeare's Sonnets* (1964, 3rd impression 1978); *The Young Romantics and Critical Opinion 1807–24* (1974). He has also published articles in various literary and philosophical periodicals and collections, and in the proceedings of international congresses.

This lecture was given on 20 January 1979 at Trinity College, Cambridge.

1. For further information on this extraordinary man see especially Sir Charles Tennyson, *Alfred Tennyson* (London, 1949), and Sir Charles Tennyson and Hope Dyson, *The Tennysons: Background to Genius* (London, 1974).
2. This is at the Tennyson Research Centre at Lincoln, and is numbered 2281 in Nancie Campbell's Catalogue of the Collections in the Centre, *Tennyson in Lincoln*, 2 vols (Lincoln, 1971–3). A specimen page is reproduced by Susan Shatto, 'Tennyson's Library', *The Book Collector* (Winter 1978), p. 499.

3. Written on an endpaper of his copiously annotated Oxford 1821 edition of the *Iliad* (Lincoln 1167) in an interesting passage quoted by Susan Shatto which states that it was George Tennyson who told the boys to write out in the margins of their Classical texts 'the criticisms of their several commentators'.

4. Sir Charles Tennyson and Hope Dyson, op. cit., p. 36.

5. The only exception among poems published before Tennyson's death are the dozen or so couplets at the start and end of 'The Vision of Sin' (R 718–19; 724–5). Recently, however, Christopher Ricks has published 'The Ganges' (R 162), an early poem of twenty-three heroic couplets (written 1826–7), and 'Napoleon's Retreat from Moscow' (*Times Literary Supplement*, 21 August 1969, p. 919), probably started in 1825, and consisting of between forty and fifty couplets.

6. Christopher Ricks has printed some of this material in his edition (R 1159; ll 779–80). Hallam Tennyson also quotes in *Eversley* a prose translation by the poet of the passage from Book VI. This is more satisfactory than the verse rendering.

7. R 1156–7.

8. For a good collection of some of the results (arranged under Classical authors) see W. P. Mustard, *Classical Echoes in Tennyson* (New York, 1904).

9. *Lavacrum Palladis*, 72.

10. In Gosse's account as given in Evan Charteris's *Life and Letters of Sir Edmund Gosse* (London, 1931), Gosse reports Tennyson as saying of Collins 'I think—he's a Louse on the Locks of Literature', and adds 'The phrase from such a source was infinitely restoring'. Gosse had also suffered at the hands of Churton Collins. On the other hand, in a letter from Sir Edmund to Lady Gosse dated 6 August 1888, and printed in the *Catalogue of the Ashley Library*, ed. T. J. Wise, 11 vols (London, 1930), X, 209, Gosse writes that Tennyson asked him 'How's Churton Collins?', and then continued 'Would you like to know what I think of him?' Gosse goes on: 'Of course, I, with a coy smile, said I should. "Well! He's a jackass. That's what he is. But don't say I said so."' It was Christopher Ricks who first pointed out the discrepancy in these two accounts.

11. Alcman, fr. 26 in vol. I of *Lyra Graeca*, ed. J. M. Edmonds (London, 1958).

12. See Sir Charles Tennyson's Introduction to his edition of *Unpublished Early Poems by Alfred Tennyson* (London, 1931), p. x; and Christopher Ricks's Chatterton Lecture for the British Academy, *Tennyson's Methods of Composition* (Oxford University Press, 1966).

13. It would be interesting to look for cases where Tennyson uses Classical 'borrowings' on more than one occasion in different contexts; but the 'similarity' I have mentioned does not demand that the 'reminiscence' of the Classical word, phrase, or passage be analogous to the 'reminiscence' of the English word, phrase, or passage to which Tennyson imparts a new context.

14. Pindar, Fragments 129 and 130 (Bergk), 95 (Boeckh).

15. *Mem.*, ii, 318.

16. 14 August 1883. The letter (quoted R 568) is at Lincoln.

17. At all events, virtually at the end, though it is hard to see what could come after the end of the 'Morte d'Arthur', or its later form, 'The Passing of

Arthur'; and the reference to the 'Morte d'Arthur' in the introductory part of 'The Epic' (R 582) as 'the eleventh' book is mystifying, as, indeed, it may have been meant to be.

18. *Mem.*, i, 194.

19. For example, by John Forster in the *Examiner* (28 May 1842), pp. 340–1; and by *Morning Post* (9 August 1842), p. 6. For a scholarly treatment of the reviews of Tennyson's poetry from 1827 to 1851 see E. F. Shannon, Jr, *Tennyson and the Reviewers* (Harvard University Press, 1952).

20. Sterling in *Quarterly Review*, LXX (September 1842), pp. 385–416; reprinted in *Tennyson: The Critical Heritage*, ed. J. D. Jump (London, 1967), pp. 103–25; Hunt in *Church of England Quarterly Review*, XII (October 1842), pp. 361–76; reprinted *Critical Heritage*, pp. 126–36.

21. *William Allingham: A Diary*, ed. Helen Allingham and D. Radford (London, 1907), p. 150 (see also pp. 314–5). James Knowles corroborated this in 'Aspects of Tennyson, II', *Nineteenth Century*, XXXIII, January 1893, pp. 181–2; and so did Hallam Tennyson in *Eversley, Idylls*, vol. 2, p. 436.

22. *Mem.*, ii, 130.

23. Paul Turner, one of the modern writers on Tennyson who shows most awareness of the poet's Classical heritage, rightly draws attention to the Theocritan elements in this poem of Tennyson's, and to a certain 'epic dignity' added to it by allusions to Homer and Virgil [*Tennyson* (London, 1976), 60–1].

24. *Mem.*, i, 196, and I quote the passage in the form there given. *Eversley* reads 'gives the feeling' for 'gave my feeling'.

25. Recorded in *Nineteenth Century*, XXXIII (1893), p. 182. Both passages are quoted on R 560.

26. The poet's son Hallam in his notes on the poem in *Eversley*, writes that the 'mysterious voyage' which Tiresias prophesies that Odysseus will take after killing the suitors 'is elaborated by the author of the *Telegoneia*'. 'My father,' Hallam continues, 'like Eugammon, takes up the story of further wanderings at the end of the *Odyssey*.' That is true enough; but the resemblance ends there. Eugammon's version of the story (sixth century BC) was utterly different from Tennyson's. Eugammon's yarn (according to Proclus) was that after the death and burial of the suitors, Odysseus sacrificed to the nymphs, and then went to visit the oxherds in Elis. He then returned to Ithaca and carried out the sacrifices Tiresias had prescribed. After that he journeyed to the Thesprotians, and married their Queen Callidice, who bore him a son, Polypoites. The queen eventually died, and Odysseus then returned home to Ithaca, leaving Polypoites to rule Thesprotis. Meanwhile, Circe had sent out Telegonus, her son by Odysseus, to fetch Odysseus to her island. Telegonus was blown on to Ithaca by a storm, wandered about fruitlessly, evidently became hungry, and started to plunder for food. Odysseus and Telemachus went out to stop him, and Telegonus killed Odysseus with a spear, not knowing it was his father. When he came to know what he had done he took his father's body, together with Telemachus and Penelope, to Circe's island, and there he married Penelope and Telemachus married Circe (see, for example, Roscher's *Lexikon der Griechischen und Römischen Mythologie* (Leipzig, 1897–1909), III, 627b). As will readily be seen, there is mighty little in

common either in fact or in motivation between this bizarre story and either Dante's or Tennyson's version. There are many other post-Homeric Greek versions of Odysseus's life after his first return home. On the whole history of the Ulysses theme from pre-Homeric times till the present day see W. B. Stanford, *The Ulysses Theme* (Blackwell, 1954, 2nd edition, 1963).

27. For example, P. F. Baum, *Tennyson Sixty Years After* (Chapel Hill, 1948), p. 303, in the course of a thoughtful analysis.
28. See, for instance, W. H. Auden, *Tennyson: An Introduction and Selection* (London, 1946), p. xix.
29. For example, E. J. Chiasson (see note 32 below).
30. In his *Télémaque* (1699).
31. P. F. Baum, op. cit., p. 301.
32. E. J. Chiasson in his interesting article 'Tennyson's Ulysses—A Reinterpretation', *University of Toronto Quarterly*, XXIII (1954), pp. 402–9; reprinted in *Critical Essays on the Poetry of Tennyson*, ed. J. Killham (London, 1960).
33. Miss M. J. Donahue first printed 'Tithon' from *Heath MS* in *PMLA*, 64 (1949), pp. 401–2, and she discusses the revisions.
34. Christoper Ricks, *Tennyson* (Macmillan, 1972), p. 131.
35. Campbell, *Tennyson in Lincoln*, no. 208.
36. Ibid., no. 209.
37. Ibid., no. 1437.
38. Ibid., no. 1438.
39. Ibid., no. 1439.
40. Ibid., no. 1440.
41. *Euphues*, ed. M. W. Croll and H. Clemons (London, 1916), p. 334.
42. Though I must confess myself much attracted by L. P. Wilkinson's suggestion that the name of Lucretius may well have been confused with that of Lucullus (possibly by mistaking the significance of an abbreviation Luc.). Lucullus is known to have died in 56 BC, reputedly after taking a love-philtre [see L. P. Wilkinson, 'Lucretius and the Love-Philtre', *Classical Review*, 63 (1949), pp. 47–8].
43. *Macmillan's Magazine*, XVIII (1868), pp. 97–103.
44. *Mem.*, ii, 13; and *Eversley, Demeter and Other Poems*, 361.
45. *Mem.*, i, 166, well quoted by A. Dwight Culler, *The Poetry of Tennyson* (Yale University Press, 1977), p. 90.
46. See, for example, Owen Chadwick, 'Tennyson and Virgil', an address to the Tennyson Society in Bag Enderby Church (4 August 1968).

PART II—CHAPTER 4

Philip Collins was born on 28 May 1923. He was educated at Brentwood School and Emmanuel College, Cambridge, where he was Senior Scholar. He was Staff Tutor in Adult Education at the University of Leicester, 1947; Warden of Vaughan College in 1954; Senior Lecturer in English, 1962–4; Professor, 1964, and Head of the Department of English, University of Leicester, 1971–6. He has been Visiting Professor at the Universities of California and Columbia, and

Victoria University, New Zealand. He is a member of the National Theatre Board and has written many scripts and given many performances for the stage and for BBC Radio and Television. His numerous publications include *Dickens and Crime* (1962); *Dickens and Education* (1963); *The Impress of the Moving Age* (1965); *Thomas Cooper the Chartist* (1969); *Dickens: the Critical Heritage* (1971) (editor); *Reading Aloud: A Victorian Métier* (1972) etc.

This lecture was delivered on 14 November 1978 at the University of Leicester.

1. See A. Walton Litz, ' "That strange abstraction, Nature" ': T. S. Eliot's Victorian Inheritance' (which refers to earlier studies), in *Nature and the Victorian Imagination*, ed. U. C. Knoepflmacher and G. B. Tennyson (California University Press, 1977).

2. James Knowles, 'Aspects of Tennyson: a Personal Reminiscence', *Nineteenth Century*, XXXIII (1893), p. 169; 'Armageddon', and Sir Charles Tennyson thereon, quoted in *The Poems of Tennyson*, ed. Christopher Ricks (1969), pp. 64, 72.

3. 'Tennyson and the Spirit of the Age', in House's *All in Due Time* (1955), p. 125. House's 'The Mood of Doubt', in the BBC's *Ideas and Beliefs of the Victorians* (1950), is full—as the whole book is—of references to Tennyson on this theme. The best short treatment is in Christopher Ricks, *Tennyson* (1972), pp. 298–315. See also James Kissane, 'Tennyson: the Passion of the Past and the Curse of Time', *ELH*, XXXII (1965), pp. 85–109; David F. Goslee, 'Spatial and Temporal Vision in Early Tennyson', *Victorian Poetry*, XI (1973), pp. 323–9; John D. Rosenberg, *The Fall of Camelot: a Study of Tennyson's 'Idylls'* (1973), chapter 3, 'Timescape'; Catherine Barnes Stevenson, 'Tennyson's "Mutability Canto": Time, Memory and Art in *The Princess*', *Victorian Poetry*, XIII (1975), pp. 21–33.

4. See Alan Sinfield, ' "That Which Is": the Platonic Indicative in *In Memoriam* XCV', *Victorian Poetry*, XIV (1976), pp. 247–52.

5. 'The Science of History', in his *Short Studies on Great Subjects* (1893 edn.), I, 18n.

6. G. Poulett Scrope, *The Geology and Extinct Volcanoes of Central France* (2nd edition, 1858), pp. 208–9; Charles Lyell, *Principles of Geology* (1830), pp. 1, 2, 73. On these matters, and on much to do with this chapter, I have found useful Stephen Toulmin and June Goodfield, *The Discovery of Time* (1965) and Jerome Hamilton Buckley, *The Triumph of Time: A Study of Victorian Concepts of Time, History, Progress, and Decadence* (1966).

7. Cited by F. Sherwood Taylor, 'Geology Changes the Outlook', *Ideas and Beliefs of the Victorians* (1950), p. 189.

8. Basil Willey, *More Nineteenth Century Studies* (1956), p. 62; Sir Charles Tennyson, *Alfred Tennyson* (1950), p. 73.

9. Reprinted in *Critical Essays on the Poetry of Tennyson*, ed. John Killham (1960), p. 37. Maurice Mandelbaum, drawing on Super's edition of Arnold's prose, confirms this allegation: *History, Man and Reason: A Study in Nineteenth Century Thought* (1971), p. 454.

10. 'The Voice of His Time: Tennyson's *In Memoriam*', *The Listener* (12 February 1942), p. 212. On the 'greatness' of astronomy and geology, see Agnes Grace Weld (note 44 below), p. 395.

11. Helen Gardner, *The Composition of Four Quartets* (1978), p. 28.
12. See Ricks, *Tennyson*, p. 51.
13. *Bleak House* (1852–3), chapter 1; Susan Shatto, 'Byron, Dickens, Tennyson and the Monstrous Efts', *Yearbook of English Studies*, VI (1976), pp. 144–55.
14. William E. Fredeman makes some pertinent remarks on Dickens in his '"The Sphere of Common Duties": the Domestic Solution in Tennyson's Poetry', *Bulletin of the John Rylands Library*, LIV (1972), pp. 357–83.
15. *A Christmas Carol* (1843), Stave V. See on this aspect of Dickens, George Ford, 'Dickens and the Voices of Time', *Nineteenth Century Fiction*, XXIV (1970), pp. 428–48; Robert L. Patten, 'Dickens Time and Again', *Dickens Studies Annual*, II (1972), pp. 163–96; Stephen L. Franklin, 'Dickens and Time', ibid., IV (1975), pp. 1–35; N. N. Feltes, 'To Saunter, to Hurry: Dickens, Time, and Industrial Capitalism', *Victorian Studies*, XX (1977), pp. 245–67.
16. 'The Oxford Counter-Reformation', *Short Studies*, IV, 231.
17. 'Tennyson's Methods of Composition', *Proceedings of the British Academy*, LII (1967), pp. 209–30.
18. R 493 and note: a frequent theme in Tennyson: cf. 'Love thou thy Land' (R 616), 'An Idle Rhyme' (R 663), 'Godiva' (R 732), *Maud* (R 1042).
19. *The Victorian City: Images and Realities*, ed. H. J. Dyos and Michael Wolff (1973), II, pp. 477–8.
20. House, op. cit., p. 125.
21. *Three Essays on Religion* (1885), p. 127. The 'Introductory' chapter of John Morley's *On Compromise* (1874) is a classic statement of this 'Historic Method' of discussing earlier 'ideas, usages, or beliefs'. Among the many relevant modern studies are *Nineteenth-Century Thought: The Discovery of Change*, ed. Richard L. Schoenwald (1965); J. W. Burrow, *Evolution and Society: A Study in Victorian Social Theory* (1966); Buckley (note 6 above); Mandelbaum (note 9 above). One aspect of this notion was sufficiently unfamiliar for Tennyson's friend Jowett to be able to say: 'to most persons the very notion that ideas have a history is a new one' (quoted by Willey, note 8 above, p. 151).
22. *The Writings of Arthur Hallam*, ed. T. H. Vail Motter (1942), p. 233.
23. A. P. Stanley, *Sermons on Special Occasions*, reprinted in *Religious Controversies of the Nineteenth Century: Selected Documents*, ed. A. O. J. Cockshut (1966), p. 249.
24. Reprinted in *Tennyson: the Critical Heritage*, ed. John D. Jump (1967), pp. 325–9. For other studies, see Charles Tennyson, *Six Tennyson Essays* (1954), chapter 2, 'Tennyson's Politics'; Robert Preyer, 'Alfred Tennyson: The Poetry and Politics of Conservative Vision', *Victorian Studies*, IX (1966), pp. 325–52; and Stevenson (note 3 above).
25. But I read 'brain' for 'body' (which Hallam Tennyson mistakenly wrote), following John Killham, *Tennyson and 'The Princess': Reflections of an Age* (1958), p. 234. Killham's chapter on '*The Princess* and Evolution', and indeed much else in his book, is highly germane to this chapter.
26. Spencer, *An Autobiography* (1904), II, pp. 8, 486, 488.
27. T. H. Huxley, *Evolution and Ethics and Other Essays* (1894), pp. 51–3.
28. Quoted by G. B. Shaw, Preface to *Great Expectations* (1947 reprint), p. xi.

'The grandest and most fully representative figure in all Victorian literature is of course Alfred Tennyson', Inge argues in his Rede Lecture for 1922, 'The Victorian Age' (*Outspoken Essays, Second Series*, 1922, p. 199). His Romanes Lecture (ibid., pp. 158–83) on 'The Idea of Progress' contains much that is relevant to Tennyson.

29. Austin, *The Poetry of the Period* (1870), reprinted in *Tennyson: The Critical Heritage*, pp. 310, 308. For other remarks on Tennyson as 'the poet of the age', or on 'the Age of Tennyson', see *Critical Heritage*, pp. 10–11, 113, 180, 272–3, 349–50; Saintsbury, quoted by Young (note 9 above), p. 27. W. H. Roscoe's survey of Tennyson in *National Review*, I (1855), pp. 377–410, is a notable discussion of how his mind is 'in exact harmony with the times in which he lives'.

30. Gertrude Himmelfarb, *Darwin and the Darwinians* (1968 edn.), p. 228.

31. Buckley (note 6 above), pp. 1–2.

32. Froude, *Thomas Carlyle: A History of His Life in London 1834–1881* (1884), I, pp. 289–91.

33. Letter to W. B. Donne (1 June 1835), in Frances Brookfield, *The Cambridge 'Apostles'* (1906), pp. 267–8.

34. *Letters and Private Papers of W. M. Thackeray*, ed. Gordon N. Ray (1945), II, p. 26.

35. House, op. cit., p. 99; *Mem.*, ii, 35; Charles Tennyson, *Alfred Tennyson*, p. 264; *In Memoriam*, XXXIV, 15–16; Brookfield, op. cit., p. 329.

36. *William Allingham: a Diary*, ed. H. Allingham and D. Radford (1907), p. 137.

37. Rowell, *Hell and the Victorians: a Study of the Nineteenth Century Theological Controversies Concerning Eternal Punishment and the Future Life* (1974), pp. 5–6, 31. See also John Morley, *Death, Heaven and the Victorians* (1971) and R. H. Hutton, 'The Late Lord Tennyson on the Future Life', *Aspects of Religious and Scientific Thought* (1899), pp. 409–15.

38. Eleanor Bustin Mattes, *In Memoriam: The Way of a Soul* (1951), chapter 4; A. Dwight Culler, *The Poetry of Tennyson* (1977), pp. 169–75.

39. Quoted by A. C. Benson, *Tennyson* (4th edition, 1913), p. 151 (italics mine); cf. Derek Patmore, *The Life and Times of Coventry Patmore* (1949), pp. 94, 98.

40. *Mem.*, i, 322 (and cf. i. 15): a point he often made in conversation, according to Julia Cameron (MS letter, 1877, quoted by Rowell, op. cit., p. 150). On the controversy, see Rowell, pp. 73, 110, 130, 140.

41. Frederick Maurice, *Life and Times of F. D. Maurice* (4th edition, 1885), p. 162 n; dedication reprinted in *Mem.*, i, 430. Another such revisionist book about the future life, dedicated to Tennyson as the poet of 'the larger hope', was Dean Farrar's *Mercy and Judgment* (1881), see Rowell, p. 145.

42. Charles Tennyson, *Alfred Tennyson*, pp. 330–1, 343.

43. Rowell, op. cit., pp. 9, 15.

44. Agnes Grace Weld, 'Talks with Tennyson', *Contemporary Review* (March 1893), p. 397.

45. Ricks, *Tennyson*, p. 239. Having mentioned the Cabinet, I should perhaps remark that in 'great offices' Tennyson does not, of course, have Whitehall in mind.

46. Rowell, op. cit., pp. 14–15.
47. Blood's pamphlets are quoted in William James's *Varieties of Religious Experience* (1902), pp. 383–4 nn, 389–91 nn—'this farrago', he calls them.
48. Harold Nicolson, *Tennyson* (2nd edition, 1949 reprint), p. 46.

The author of this paper (revised from its original lecture form) wishes to thank, for their answers to his enquiries, Professor R. B. Martin, Dr R. K. Biswas, Dr John Dixon Hunt, Dr Susan Shatto, Canon Eric Devenport and Mr Aidan Day.

PART II—CHAPTER 5

Michael Mason was born in 1943 and graduated from Oxford University in 1962; BLitt, 1964. He then taught at Edinburgh University and in the United States. He is now Lecturer in English, University College, London. He has published *Ulysses*, a critical study (1972), as well as several periodical contributions and essays in published collections on Victorian literature, especially on Browning and George Eliot.

This lecture was delivered on 23 November 1978 at University College, London.

1. First published by Browning in *Men and Women* (1855).
2. 'Of the Pathetic Fallacy' is chapter XII of vol. III of *Modern Painters* (1856).
3. Charles Kingsley, *Alton Locke* (first published 1850).
4. See *Val d'Arno* (1874), paragraph 170.
5. See the tables in Josephine Miles, *Pathetic Fallacy in the Nineteenth Century* (1942).
6. See *Sesame and Lilies* (1865), para. 94.
7. The failure of the relationship with Maud is, of course, sympathetically regarded in the poem, and Ruskin (in the obscure context of what seems to be a plea for fallen women) treats the 'fancy' of this and stanzas 1 and 10 of *Maud* (L, xxii) (the latter already being praised as exquisite in 1856) as a noble thing. Tennyson seems to have taken Ruskin's remark in too critical a spirit.

PART II—CHAPTER 6

William E. Fredeman was born on 19 July 1928, and is Professor of English at the University of British Columbia. He obtained his BA at Hendrix College, Conway, Arkansas, in 1948, and his MA and PhD, at the University of Oklahoma in 1950 and 1956. He is a Fellow of the Royal Society of Canada (FRSC) and of the Royal Society of Literature (FRSL). His publications include *Pre-Raphaelitism: A Bibliocritical Study* (Harvard, 1965); *Prelude to the Last Decade: Rossetti in the Summer of 1872* (Rylands Library, 1971). He edited *The P.R.B. Journal*, and the special double number of *Victorian Poetry* on William Morris. Representative articles of his work include ' "A Sign Betwixt the Meadow and the Cloud": The Ironic Apotheosis of Tennyson's *St Simeon*

Stylites', University of Toronto Quarterly, 38 (1968); ' "The Sphere of Common Duties": The Domestic Solution in Tennyson's Poetry', *Bulletin of John Rylands Library*, 54 (1972).

This essay was given as a paper at the Plenary Session of the Australian Universities Language and Literature Association on 21 August 1978.

1. Robert Langbaum, *The Poetry of Experience* (Random House, 1957), p. 28.
2. *Patterns of Morbidity: Repetition in Tennyson's Poetry*, in *The Major Victorian Poets: Reconsiderations*, ed. Isobel Armstrong (University of Nebraska Press, 1969), pp. 7–34.
3. Although the use of this term is admittedly arbitrary, as it is used in this paper it refers to the nine blank verse monologues discussed in the second part of this chapter.
4. *Tennyson's Style* (Cornell University Press, 1976), p. 102.
5. Browning, *Strafford* (Longmans, 1837). 'I had for some time been engaged in a Poem of a very different nature, when induced to make the present attempt; and am not without apprehension that my eagerness to freshen a jaded mind by diverting it to the healthy natures of a grand epoch, may have operated unfavourably on the represented play, which is one of Action in Character rather than Character in Action.'
6. 'Monodrama and the Dramatic Monologue', *PMLA*, 90 (May 1975), p. 368.
7. *Tennyson: The Growth of a Poet* (Houghton Mifflin, 1965), p. 26.
8. 'Monodrama and the Dramatic Monologue', op. cit., p. 375.
9. Ibid., p. 380.
10. Ibid., p. 372.
11. Ibid., p. 380.
12. Ibid., p. 367.
13. Ibid., p. 369.
14. Ibid., p. 366.
15. *The Poetry of Experience*, op. cit., p. 54.
16. *Tennyson's Style*, op. cit., pp. 102–6.
17. Quoted in *The Oxford Book of Literary Anecdotes*, ed. James Sutherland (Pocket Books, 1976), p. 295.
18. *Mem.*, ii, 75.
19. *Poems II* (Macmillan, 1908), p. 341. 'My father' Hallam says, 'spoke and wrote of this and *Maud* and other dramatic monologues thus.'
20. 'The Dramatic Monologue', *PMLA*, 62 (1947), pp. 503–16.
21. Ricks, p. 1299. 'Hope' was never composed; 'Faith' was published in *The Death of Oenone and Other Poems* (1892).
22. '"A Sign Betwixt the Meadow and the Cloud": The Ironic Apotheosis of Tennyson's *St Simeon Stylites*', *University of Toronto Quarterly*, 38 (October 1968), pp. 69–83.
23. Ibid., p. 72.
24. Ricks, *Tennyson* (Macmillan, 1972); Shaw, *Tennyson's Style*, op. cit.
25. T. S. Eliot, *The Complete Poems and Plays* (Faber & Faber, 1969), pp. 37–9.
26. *Bulletin of John Rylands Library*, 54 (Spring, 1972), pp. 357–83.
27. *Philological Quarterly*, 52 (April 1973), p. 275.

PART II—CHAPTER 7

John Bayley was born on 27 March 1925 and has been Professor of English Literature and Fellow of St Catherine's College, Oxford, since 1974. He was educated at Eton and New College, Oxford. He was a member of St Antony's College and Magdalen College, Oxford, 1951–5, then Fellow and Tutor in English, New College, Oxford, 1955–74. His publications include *In Another Country*, a novel (1954); *The Romantic Survival: A Study in Poetic Evolution* (1956); *The Characters of Love* (1961); *Tolstoy and the Novel* (1966); *Pushkin: A Comparative Commentary* (1971); *The Uses of Division: Unity and Disharmony in Literature* (1976). He is married to the novelist Iris Murdoch.

This lecture was delivered at the University of Oxford on 8 February 1979.

1. H. A. Mason, 'The First Setting of Tennyson's "Morte d'Arthur"', *Essays and Studies* (1978).
2. *Further Letters of G. M. Hopkins*, ed. C. C. Abbott (1938).
3. J. R. Kincaid, *Tennyson's Major Poems: The Comic and Ironic Patterns* (Yale University Press, 1975).
4. Quoted by Christopher Ricks in *Tennyson* (Macmillan, 1972). Ricks calls it the 'best criticism of Tennyson' [His own book is certainly the best critical study. *J.B.*]
5. G. M. Hopkins, op. cit.
6. From John Betjeman, 'Love in a Valley', *Collected Poems* (Murray, 1958).
7. Ibid., from 'A Subaltern's Love Song'.
8. Leigh Hunt, *Church of England Quarterly Review* (1842), quoted in *Tennyson: The Critical Heritage*, ed. John D. Jump (Routledge, 1967).
9. Quoted by Philip Henderson in *Tennyson: Poet and Prophet* (Routledge, 1978).

Index